John Whitaker

Gibbon's History of the Decline and Fall of the Roman Empire

In vols. iv, v, and vi, Quarto, Reviewed

John Whitaker

Gibbon's History of the Decline and Fall of the Roman Empire
In vols. iv, v, and vi, Quarto, Reviewed

ISBN/EAN: 9783744773850

Printed in Europe, USA, Canada, Australia, Japan

Cover: Foto ©ninafisch / pixelio.de

More available books at **www.hansebooks.com**

GIBBON's HISTORY

OF THE

DECLINE AND FALL

OF THE

ROMAN EMPIRE,

IN VOLS. IV, V, AND VI, QUARTO,

REVIEWED.

By the Rev. JOHN WHITAKER, B.D.

RECTOR OF RUAN-LANYHORNE, CORNWALL.

LONDON:

PRINTED FOR J. MURRAY, N° 32, FLEET STREET.

M.DCC.XCI.

ADVERTISEMENT.

THE following remarks were drawn up by me, for insertion in the ENGLISH REVIEW. *I am no reviewer by profession. I became one in this instance, from a desire of serving the cause of religion. And the remarks were published in that review, through a course of ten months. In a little time afterwards, I was advised by a nobleman of the first rank in respectability, and nearly the first in reality, to republish them in the present form. I proposed the plan to my bookseller the proprietor of the Review, and he demurred upon it. He found however afterwards, that the remarks were called for when the Reviews were no longer to be had. He now urged me himself, therefore, to an immediate republication of them. I resolved to revise them for the purpose, and waited for an hour of leisure to do so. That hour was long in coming. The republication has thus been delayed to the present moment. And I now prefix my name to the whole, in order to serve the same cause for which the whole was originally written. Religion (to use the allusion, which I once heard from a witty man of genius) I hope, I shall always consider as the* 'Sanctum Punctum,' *and learning only as the* 'Glory' *surrounding it.*

J. W.

March 3d, 1791.

ERRATA.

l. 14. *for* cæli *read* Cæli.
l. 14. *for* quidam *read* quidem.
l. 24. *for* in adfueto *read* in-adfueto.
l. 21. *for* lives *read* loves.
l. 21. *for* free *read* fresh.
l. 27. *for* known *read* had.
l. 25. *for* and is about *read* and about.
l. 2. *for* Tacob *read* Jacob.
l. 18. *for* its *read* his.
l. 11. *for* vinea *read* vineas.
Note, l. 2. *for* ad *read* and.
l. 22. *for* upon *read* up in.
l. 23. *for* of *read* to.
l. last. *for* strange digression *read* strange system of digression.

TO THE BINDER.

bis at the back of the Advertisement, to face page 1.

REVIEW

OF

Mr. GIBBON'S HISTORY, &c.

Gibbon's History of the Decline and Fall of the Roman Empire, in Volumes IVth, Vth, and VIth, Quarto.

CHAPTER FIRST.

IN the first rude state of historical composition, it is a mere *intimation* of the *greater* facts. It notes the *battles* of contending nations; but it goes no farther. It points out no political causes, that led to this decision by the sword. It indicates no political consequences, that resulted from the victory or the defeat. And it even gives no other circumstances of facts, than to tell which of the parties won the day. This is the very *skeleton* of history; appearing at present in the *Saxon Chronicle* among ourselves, and once appearing probably in those first chroniclers of Rome, Fabius Pictor and others, who have since sunk away in the meagerness of their own wretched annals, and in the plenitude of the succeeding histories.

The next grand stage of improvement, is to *dwell* upon all the principal events of history; to draw out the train of causes preceding; and to link together the chain of consequences following. It particularly loves to rest upon those splendid incidents of history, *battles*. It describes them with a fulness and a circumstantiality, that fasten upon the mind, and give it a kind of sanguinary satisfaction. Such was the work of Cœlius among the Romans, we suppose; a writer, to whom Livy occasionally refers, and one of the later chroniclers, from whom he compiled his history. And such is *Baker's Chronicle* among ourselves; that standing mirror of history to our fathers, and now remembered with fondness by us as the delight of our childhood. This is the skeleton clothed with muscles, supported by sinews, and exhibiting the form and figure of history to the eye.

But this species of writing, by a regular gradation of improvement, afterwards assumes a higher port. It takes the incidents of the first stage, and the circumstances of the second. It combines causes, facts, and consequences, in one regular order of succession. It throws an illumination over the whole, by the clearness of its narration, the judiciousness of its arrangement, and the elegance of its language. And it gives the reader an interest in the scenes before him, by the liveliness with which it presents them to his mind, and by the reflections with which it points them to his heart. Such is the history of Livy among the Romans, and such are some of our *best* histories written

by

by the *laſt* generation. This is the ſkeleton not merely clothed with fleſh, but actuated with nerves, animated with blood, and bearing the bloom of health upon its cheek.

Here had hiſtorical compoſition reſted, it would have anſwered all the uſeful, and all the elegant, purpoſes of life. But the activity of the human mind, is always on the wing. The ſpirit of improvement is ever puſhing forward. And there is a degree of improvement beyond this, which may ſhed a greater warmth of colouring over the piece, give it a deeper intereſt with the affections of the ſurveyor, and ſo reach the full point of hiſtorical perfection. But alas! man can eaſily imagine, what he can never execute. The fancy can ſee a perfection, and the judgment can recommend it; but the hand cannot attain to it. Whether this be the caſe with the preſent idea of hiſtorical perfection, I know not; but it is certain, I think, that it has never been attained hitherto. Hiſtory, indeed, having once advanced to the third ſtage of improvement, cannot but ſtrain to reach the fourth and laſt. Then it lays itſelf out in a ſplendour of imagery, a frequency of reflections, and a refinement of language; and thus makes the narrative more ſtriking, by its additional vivacity and vigour. But it is melancholy to obſerve, that in proportion as we thus advance in the *ornamental* parts of hiſtorical writing, we are receding from the *ſolid* and the *neceſſary*; we loſe in *veracity* what we gain in *embelliſhments*; and the *authenticity* of the narration fades and ſinks away, in the luſtre of the *philoſophy* ſur-

rounding

rounding it. The mind of the writer, bent upon the beautiful and sublime in history, does not condescend to perform the task of accuracy, and to stoop to the drudgery of faithfulness. The mirror is finely polished and elegantly decorated; but it no longer reflects the real features of the times. The sun shines out, indeed, with a striking effulgence; but it is an effulgence of glare, and not a radiation of usefulness. Such historians as these, we may venture to pronounce, are Tacitus among the ancients, most of our best historians in the *present* generation, and Mr. Gibbon at the head of them. And these present us with the skeleton of history, not merely clothed with muscles, animated with life, and bearing the bloom of health upon its cheek; but, instead of carrying a higher flush of health upon its cheek, and shewing a brighter beam of life in its eyes, rubbed with Spanish wool, painted with French *fard*, and exhibiting the fire of falsehood and wantonness in its eyes.

That we should thus rank Tacitus, may surprise those who have *lately* been so much in the habit, of admiring and applauding him as the first of all human historians; and who may suppose he stands, like the other historians of the ancients, invested with oracular consequence for facts, and incapable of being convicted of unfaithfulness from any cotemporary records. That he has been *lately* rated beyond his merit, taken out of the real line in which he ought to stand, and transferred from the rank of *affected* and *fantastical* historians to that of the judicious and manly, has been long my persuasion.

suasion. But I have lately met with an evidence, that shews him to us in a new light, as an historian *careless* and *unfaithful* in his representations. This evidence has never yet been given to the world; but it is a very decisive one. In 1528 were found within the earth at Lyons in France, two brass plates, that had a speech of the Emperor Claudius engraven upon them, and are now set up against the wall, in the vestibule of the *Hotel de Ville* of Lyons. These form a very singular object of curiosity, for the antiquary. But they are still more curious to the historian. For this very speech is pretended to be given by Tacitus; yet the speech in the history is very different, from that upon the plates. And, as such an opportunity of collating an ancient historian with a cotemporary monument, can seldom occur at all, and perhaps occurs only in this single instance; as this opportunity has never yet been used by any writer; and as it shews the inaccuracy and unfaithfulness of Tacitus, in a strong point of view; I doubt not but my readers will be pleased, to see the collation here.

"ORIGINAL.

'..... mae rerum nostr..... sii........ equidem primam omnium, illam cogitationem hominum quám maximé primam occursuram mihi provideo. Deprecor ne quasi novam istam rem introduci exhorrescatis; sed illa potiùs cogitetis, quám multa in hâc civitate novata sint; et quidem statim ab origine urbis nostræ, in quot formas statusque respublica nostra diducta sit.

' Quondam

' Quondam reges hanc tenuêre urbem. Ne tamen domesticis successoribus eam tradere contigit. Supervenêre alieni, et quidam externi: ut Numa Romulo successerit, ex Sabinis veniens; vicinus quidem, sed tunc externus: ut Anco Martio Priscus Tarquinius, propter temeratum sanguinem quód patre Demarato, Corinthio, natus erat, et Tarquiniensi matre, generosâ sed inopi, ut quæ tali marito necesse habuerit succumbere, cúm domi repelleretur a gerendis honoribus. Postquam Romam migravit, regnum adeptus est. Huic quoque, et filio nepotive ejus (nam et hoc inter auctores discrepat), insertus Servius Tullius; si nostros sequimur, captivâ natus Ocresiâ, si Tuscos, cæli quondam Vivennæ sodalis fidelissimus, omnisque ejus casûs comes, postquam variâ fortunâ exactus, cum omnibus reliquiis Cæliani exercitûs Etruriâ excessit, montem Cælium occupavit, et a duce suo Cælio ita appellitatus, mutatoque nomine (nam Tuscé Mastarna ei nomen erat) ita appellatus est ut dixi, et regnum summâ cum reipublicæ utilitate optinuit. Deinde, postquam Tarquini Superbi mores invisi civitati nostræ esse cœperunt, quá ipsius quá filiorum ejus; nempe pertæsum est mentes regni, et ad consules, annuos magistratus, administratio reipublicæ translata est.

' Quid nunc commemorem dictaturæ, hôci pso consulari, imperium valentius repertum apud majores nostros, quo in asperioribus bellis, aut in civili motu difficiliore, uterentur; aut in auxilium plebis creatos, tribunos plebeios? Quid a consulibus ad decemviros translatum imperium; solutoque

postea

postea decemvirali regno, ad consules rursus reditum? Quid imp..... Quinqueviris distributum consulare imperium; tribunosque militum consulari imperio appellatos, qui seni, et saepe octoni, crearentur? Quid communicatos postremò cum plebe honores, non imperii solùm, sed sacerdotiorum quoque? Jam, si narrem bella a quibus coeperint majores nostri, et quò processerimus; vereor ne nimio insolentior esse videar, et quaesisse jactationem gloriae prolati imperii ultra oceanum. Sed illoc potiûs revertar. Civitatem ...... sane ...... novo .... Divus Augustus ...... no ..... lus et patruus, Ti. Caesar, omnem florem ubique coloniarum ac municipiorum, bonorum scilicet virorum et locupletium, in hâc curiâ esse voluit. *Quid ergo non Italicus senator provinciali potior est?* Jam vobis cúm hanc partem Censurae meae approbare coepero, quid de eâ re sentiam rebus ostendam. Sed ne provinciales quidem, si modò ornare curiam poterint, rejiciendos puto.

' Ornatissima ecce colonia valentissimaque Viennensium! Quàm longo jam tempore, senatores huic curiae confert! Ex quâ coloniâ, inter paucos equestris ordinis ornamentum, L. Vestinum familiarissimé diligo, et hodieque in rebus meis detineo; cujus liberi fruantur, quaeso, primó sacerdotiorum gradu, postmodó cum annis promoturi dignitatis suae incrementa. Ut dirum nomen Latronis taceam, et odi illud palestricum prodigium, quod antè in domum consulatum intulit, quàm colonia sua solidum civitatis Romanae beneficium consecuta est. Idem de fratre ejus possum dicere, miserabili

bili quidem indigniſſimoque hôc caſu, ut vobis utilis ſenator eſſe non poſſit.

' Tempus eſt jam, Tiberi Cæſar Germanice, detegere te patribus conſcriptis, quo tendat oratio tua. Jam enim ad extremos fines Galliæ Narbonenſis veniſti.

' Tot ecce inſignes juvenes! Quot intueor! Non magis ſunt pænitendi ſenatores, quàm pænitet Perſicum, nobiliſſimum virum, amicum meum, inter imagines majorum ſuorum Allobrogici nomen legere. Quód ſi hæc ita eſſe conſentitis, quid ultra deſideratis, quàm ut vobis digito demonſtrem, ſolum ipſum ultra fines provinciæ Narbonenſis jam vobis ſenatores mittere; quando *ex Lugduno habere nos noſtri ordinis viros non pænitet.* Timidé quidam, patres conſcripti, egreſſus adſuetos familiareſque vobis provinciarum terminos ſum; ſed deſtrictè jam Comatæ Galliæ cauſa agenda eſt. In quâ ſiquis hoc intuetur, quód bello per decem annos exercuerunt divom Julium, idem opponat centum annorum immobilem fidem obſequiumque, multis trepidis rebus noſtris pluſquam expertum. Illi patri meo Druſo, Germaniam ſubigenti, tutam quiete ſuâ ſecuramque a tergo pacem præſtiterunt; et quidem, cúm ad cenſus, novo tum opere et in adſueto Gallis, ad bellum avocatus eſſet. Quod opus quàm arduum ſit, nobis nunc cúm maximé, quamvis nihil ultra quàm ut publicé notæ ſint facultates noſtræ exquiratur, nimis magno experimento cognoſcimus.'

We have thus publiſhed a ſpeech, which has been preſerved by a fate peculiar to itſelf, in its own original paragraphs; and, for the firſt time, with modern

dern punctuation, and with modern discrimination of *objections* from the rest. But let us now turn to the

COPY IN TACITUS.

' Majores mei (quorum antiquissimus Clausus, origine Sabinâ, simul in civitatem Romanam et in familias patriciorum ascitus est) hortantur, uti paribus consiliis rempublicam capessam, transferendo huc quod usquam egregium fuerit. Neque enim ignoro Julios Albâ, Coruncanios Camerio, Porcios Tusculo; et, ne vetera scrutemur, Etruriâ Lucaniâque et omni Italiâ, in senatum accitos. Postremó ipsam ad Alpes promotam, ut non modó singuli viritim, sed terræ gentesque, in nomen nostrum coalescerent. Tunc solida domi quies, et adversus externa floruimus, cúm Transpadani in civitatem recepti; cúm, specie deductarum per orbem terræ legionum, additis provincialium validissimis, fesso imperio subventum est. Non pænitet Balbos ex Hispaniâ, nec minús insignes viros e Galliâ Narbonensi transivisse. Manent posteri eorum, nec amore in hanc patriam nobis concedunt. Quid aliud exitio Lacedæmoniis et Atheniensibus fuit, quanquam armis pollerent; nisi quód victos pro alienigenis arcebant? At conditor noster Romulus tantum sapientiâ valuit, ut plerosque populos eodem die hostes, dein cives, habuerit. *Advenæ in nos regnaverunt.* Libertinorum filiis magistratus mandari, non (ut plerique falluntur) repens, sed priori populo, factitatum est. *At cum Senonibus pugnavimus.* Scilicet Volsci et Æqui nunquam adversam nobis aciem
struxere.

ftruxere. *Capti a Gallis fumus.* Sed et Tufcis obfides dedimus, et Samnitium jugum fubivimus. Attamen, fi cuncta bella recenfeas, nullum breviore fpatio quám adverfus Gallos confectum. *Continua deinde ac fida pax.* Jam moribus, artibus, affinitatibus, noftris mixti, aurum et opes fuas inferant potiús, quam feparati habeant. Omnia, patres confcripti, quæ nunc vetuftiffima creduntur, nova fuere. *Plebei magiftratus poft patricios,* Latini poft plebeios, ceterarum Italiæ gentium poft Latinos. Inveterafcet hoc quoque, et quod hodie exemplis tuemur inter exempla erit [1].'

The copy here is apparently very different from the original. We have noted in Italics the only points, in which it is at all fimilar. The mockfun, we fee, has caught only *three* rays of the real one. And Tacitus feems, like our own Dr. Johnfon, to have had fome report of the real fpeech made to him, and then to have fabricated another from the intimations. But the report made to Tacitus, was evidently a much flighter one than that to Dr. Johnfon. The doctor, we believe, always comprehended fome of the leading topics of the reality, in his reprefentation; while Tacitus has merely *glanced* at what Claudius faid. And, whatever excufe may be made for the Englifhman, then, to the difgrace of the reign of George the Second, refiding ' in a garret behind Exeter-'Change;' compelled to procure himfelf a fubfiftence, by the exertion of his great powers; and naturally ftudying to

[1] Ann. xi. 24.

gratify

gratify that rage for reading parliamentary speeches, which was then beginning to rise in the nation, and has shot out to such a wonderful extent since; yet, not a shadow of an excuse can be made for Tacitus. The bastard offspring in him, has scarcely any the faintest resemblance of the legitimate. The speeches of Johnson, too, were evanescent in their nature, and would have evaporated and been lost in air; had not the essence of them, a little rectified and heightened, been caught in his alembic. But the speech of Claudius was actually recorded, was engraven upon plates of brass, and hung up in the town-hall of Lyons, &c. Yet Tacitus did not give himself the trouble to procure a copy, when a copy was so easy to be had. He chose rather to display his abilities, in framing a new one for the emperor. He thus, in the unfaithfulness of his temper and in the vanity of his spirit, imposed a fictitious speech for a genuine one, upon the credulity of his reader. But he could not, like Johnson, assimilate himself to the character of the speaker, whom he personated. The speech of Claudius is all in the style of Tacitus, brisk, brief, and compacted. And as this single instance shews us in the plainest manner, from what source of information Tacitus derived all his set speeches, those numerous decorations of his history and annals, that all reflect strongly the features of their common parent; so, in this particular instance, Tacitus appears to have given the lie to history and to himself, and to have furnished a man, whom he himself describes to have been of a feeble
understanding,

understanding, 'imminuta mens¹,' with a speech pointed, informed, and vigorous. Indeed, the suggested speech is so nearly, in all its parts, different from the pronounced one, that some have supposed the one to have been never meant for the other; especially as Tacitus directs *his* speech in favour of all the extra-provincial Gauls in general, and of the Ædui in particular. But there is just similarity enough, to evince the intended sameness; even while the difference is great and striking enough, to prove it an actual forgery. And his mention of the Ædui, is no evidence to the contrary at all; as these appear from Ptolemy, to have been the superior lords of the Segusiani, and so to have been the head-sovereigns of their capital city—Lyons².

This forms a very extraordinary proof of the licentious hand, with which this 'philosophical historian of antiquity,' as Mr. Gibbon calls him, has abused the honest confidence of history. He is apparently Mr. Gibbon's model in writing. Mr. Gibbon has *his* strain of irreligion; *his* resplendence of passages; *his* 'philosophy of history;' and *his* unfaithfulness to the truth. And the last point, that 'crimen læsæ majestatis' in history has been proved so plainly upon him by the Rev. Mr. (now Archdeacon) Travis; and much more by that extraordinary young man, that early victim to studiousness, the late Mr. Davis of Baliol college in Oxford; as nothing should ever efface from the mind of the public. Indeed the tone of opinion concern-

¹ Ann. vi. 46.   ² Bertius, Lib. ii. c. 8. p. 52.

ing Mr. Gibbon, has been decisively settled among the discerning few; ever since Mr Davis wrote.

Mr. Gibbon has ever since been considered, as a writer who, whatever else he may have to recommend him to notice, wants that first grand quality of an historian, *veracity*. This defect, indeed, with the generality is of little moment. They read, but never examine; rely with an indecent kind of implicitness, on these dictators in history; and are delighted at once with the sight and with the music, of these fairy scenes before them. But with others, with all who read to know truths, and with all whose good opinions are worth the having; this mere 'semblance of truth,' and this actual hollowness of falsehood, must hang upon the thought, must damp the ardour of praise, and poison admiration with suspicion.

Nor has my own experience of Mr. Gibbon's preceding volumes, been different. I too have examined some of his authorities; and I too have found him, like Tacitus, taking great freedoms with them. I will produce an instance of this, that has not been noticed by any other writer, and has even no excuse from the disingenuity of prejudice. It is founded only, on the too natural carelessness of a *philosophical* historian; and occurs in his first volume. There, in p. xvii. of his notes on chapter the fifth, and in note 5, he places the Prætorian camp of Rome, ' close to the walls of the city, and on the broad ' summit of the Quirinal and Viminal hills;' upon the authority of Nardini Roma Antica, p. 174, and Donatus de Româ Antiquâ, p. 46. I dwell not
upon

upon the grofs abfurdity, of placing one camp upon the fummit of *two* hills; or on the grand error of fixing it upon the 'broad fummit' of hills, one of which (the Quirinal) abuts fo clofe upon the capitol, and both had for ages been occupied with buildings. Our prefent bufinefs is not with miftakes, but mifquotations. Nor does either of the authors here referred to, pitch the Prætorian camp upon 'the broad fummit of the Quirinal and Vimi-'nal hills.' They both unite, inplacing it *beyond* 'the broad fummit' of either, *beyond* the bank of Tarquin, on a *projecting point* of the Viminal hill, and in the ftill remaining fquare of walls *at the north-eaftern angle of the city*. Donatus refers to fome infcriptions in Panvinius, dug up at the ground, and mentioning the camp exprefsly. And Nardini declares Panvinius, to have proved the point by the cleareft arguments; and appeals to thofe infcriptions and that fquarenefs, as a decifive evidence concerning it[1]. So greatly inattentive has Mr. Gibbon here been, to the very teftimony that he cites! So little can we depend upon his accuracy, even in fubjects where he had *no bias of prejudice* to lead him aftray! And fo ftrongly does this unite with all, which Mr. Davis, Mr. Travis, and others, have expofed, of the fame nature in his work!

This fundamental defect, that has been found in

---

[1] Grævius's Thefaurus, iii. 510 and 512—513, for Donatus; iv. 1065, 925, and 1082, for Nardini; and iii. 225—226, for Panvinius.

the preceding parts of his history, must act like a cancer in the human body, gradually be seen to spread its taint over all the vital parts, and eat away the substance of it in time. Where that grand principle of probity is wanting, *veracity*; the *man* or the *work* sinks of course into contempt. And I have dwelt the more upon this necessary qualification for the historian, because I think the public is running wild after the pomp and pageantry of history, and forgetting the only circumstances that can support them, accuracy of knowledge and integrity of representation. But, before I close these preliminary observations, I wish to subjoin two remarks, upon the *style* and the *arrangment* of Mr. Gibbon, in the antecedent volumes of his history.

The style of Mr. Gibbon has been much applauded; nor would we wish to detract greatly from its merit. But it has been applauded beyond its desert. It is often just, elegant, and manly; but is often also stiff, affected, and latinised, carrying the poor air of a translation, and forming harsh and unclassical combinations of words. Thus no shield, we are told, could sustain ' the impetuosity ' of the weight' of the Roman pilum, when it was launched at the enemy [1]. It is not easy, we are also told, to ' appretiate the numbers in the Ro- ' man armies [2].' The savage independence of certain tribes, is said to ' *describe* the doubtful li- ' mits of the Christian and Mahometan power [3].' The Roman senators think it it an honour, and al-

[1] V. i. p, 13.   [2] p. 16.   [3] p. 23.

moſt an obligation, to 'adorn the ſplendour' of their age and country¹. We have perſons 'dri-ven by the *impulſion* of the preſent power²;' the command of the Prætorian guards, 'becoming 'into' the firſt office of the empire³; ſoldiers too little acquainted with certain virtues, 'to appre-tiate' them in others⁴; and the Germans aban-doning 'the vaſt ſilence' of their woods⁵, an ex-preſſion borrowed from Tacitus, who with his uſual harſhneſs of language, more than once ex-preſſes a deep ſilence by *vaſtum ſilentium,* and in Engliſh carrying an aſpect of boyiſh vulgarity. And as, in one place, we have even 'more infe-'rior⁶;' ſo we ſee that pert antitheſis every where affected by Mr. Gibbon, which is ſo unbecoming the dignified vivacity of hiſtory.

But we have much more to cenſure, in Mr. Gibbon's arrangement of his materials. In page 1 of Vol. I. he ſets out with declaring, that 'it is the 'deſign of *this and the ſucceeding chapters,* to de-'ſcribe the *proſperous* condition of the empire; 'and *afterwards,* from the death of Marcus An-'toninus, to adduce the *moſt important circumſtances* 'of its *decline* and *fall.*' Let us therefore exa-mine the chapters of this very volume, and ſee how the execution comports with the deſign.

Chapters fourth and fifth give us the hiſtory of the empire, under the reigns of Commodus, Perti-nax, and Severus. The account is pleaſing and ſenſible, and the train of hiſtory judiciouſly dwelt

¹ p. 45. ² p. 122. ³ p. 127. ⁴ p. 172. ⁵ p. 227. ⁶ p. 272.

upon. But how are the principles of the decline and fall of the empire, at all unfolded in this account? How are they, in chapters sixth and seventh? These pursue the history through the elevation of Maximus, Balbinus, and the third Gordian, the deaths of the three Gordians, and the accession of Philip. And where is the *decline* and *fall* of the empire, in all this? *Nowhere*. We are reading the full history of the empire. We see nothing of its beginning to decline; we think nothing of its approaching fall; and this fall and decline are in reality not one degree more advanced, at the end of the seventh chapter, than they were at the beginning of the fourth. The chapters since, have only served to shew what the elevation of Galba, Otho, Vitellius, and Vespasian, had shewn strongly before, the arrogated superiority of the military over the civil power; and what the putting up of the throne to *auction* evinced more strikingly afterwards, the peculiar insolence of the Prætorian guards. All these chapters, therefore, should have been omitted; as, if proper in themselves, not giving us ' the important circumstances' of the empire's decline and fall, but *all* the circumstances of *all* the history; and as not very proper in themselves, as foreign to the design, and superfluous in the execution, of such a history. And we can only travel on in the work, sensible that so far we have been wandering out of our way; and hoping immediately to recover the right path, and pursue it steadily to the end of the volume.

Accordingly

C

Accordingly we enter upon the eighth chapter; but find ourselves diverted into an account of the rise, the principles, and the spirit, of the new Persian empire erected upon the Parthian. But how does this link connect itself, with the chain of declining empire at Rome? Only thus; a new enemy appears against the Romans, under the revived title of Persians. This is all the connexion, which it has with the history of the decline and fall of the empire. And, holding by this slender thread, does the author divert from the whole course of his history here; and wander away to describe an empire, that was only the old one under a new name. And his additional digression into a delineation of the Persian *religion*, is a striking proof of the injudiciousness of his management. This religion has not the smallest influence upon the history; it ought not therefore to have been dwelt upon by the historian. But such just laws of writing history, do not suit with the excentric genius of Mr. Gibbon. He lives to make excursions into geography, into metaphysics, into religion; and is always aiming a side-blow at Christianity. He has thus introduced into his history, a dissertation upon the Persian religion; which is all a mass of impertinence in itself, as a part of his history; and, as containing strokes of indirect attack upon Christianity, is much worse than impertinence, the impotent exertions of an infant against a giant.

In the same strain of excentricity Mr. Gibbon, in chapter ninth, again bursts from the orbit of his history,

history, and ranges into the interiors of Germany. He delineates the state of Germany before the reign of Decius; but his delineation is principally taken from Tacitus, *who wrote one hundred and fifty years before.* Nor can his account, so large as it is, be considered in any other light, than as an ill-judged excrescence upon the body of his work. Mr. Gibbon, either in a great want of judgment, or in a bravery of spirit that loves not to be controled by it, leaps over all the fences and bounds of legitimate history, and gives himself a free range in the wilds adjoining. And, in this mode of writing the history of the decline and fall of the empire, the author may leave his history perpetually, and *make the circuit of the globe,* in describing, delineating, and moralising upon, all the nations that form the frontier of the empire. Common-sense shews us, that such a conduct as Mr. Gibbon pursues is infinitely absurd; that a very different one should have been adopted by him; and that, as any new nations emerged to view in the current of the history, a short pause should have been made in the narration, the power, the skill, and the spirit of the strangers, should have been briefly and generally explained, and any qualities besides, that were necessary to the better understanding of the subsequent facts. All the other parts of their character, should have been left to display themselves by degrees, in the train of the military operations. Thus the stream of the history would have been suspended, only for a short period, for an obvious purpose, and for necessary information; and would then

C 2 have

have resumed its course, with the more force for the interruption. And these long and rambling dissertations of Mr. Gibbon, in which we lose sight of the decline and fall of the empire, and behind which even the whole empire itself disappears from our view; would have been totally precluded.

In chapter tenth, Mr. Gibbon returns from his philosophical and geographical excursions, to his history. He now gives us an account of the attacks made upon the empire, by the Goths, the Franks, and the Persians, in the reigns of Decius and others, to the reign of Gallienus; of the Goths and Franks; and of the rise of what are called the thirty tyrants. The history becomes tiresome, from its minuteness. And we still find ourselves grasping the whole vast bulk of the Roman history, instead of the mere history of its decline and fall.

In chapter the eleventh, we find ourselves more deluded than ever concerning the expected decline of the empire. This describes to us *the restoration* of the empire, made by Claudius and Aurelian. In all the preceding chapters indeed, we have not seen ourselves one foot nearer to the great causes and principles, that begun the decline, and terminated in the fall, of the empire. The civil wars of the first century, were to the full as destructive as those of the second and third. And *now* the bad effects of the reigns preceding, appear to be *cured* by the present reigns. So grossly injudicious is the *progress* of the history!

But chapter twelfth continues the detail, to the elevation of Dioclesian. Then we see ourselves
still

still farther off, from the decline and fall of the empire. The restoration of it by Claudius and Aurelian, is improved by Probus, and is pursued by Carinus. And the history is going most absurdly *retrograde in its motions*;

Downwards to climb, and backwards to advance.

Chapter thirteenth carries on the detail, to the abdication of Dioclesian. But we have the same complaint to make here, which we have repeated so often before. Except in some *reflections* at the end of the chapter, we see no symptons in the history, of that decline and fall for which we have been preparing our minds so long. We see, indeed, the very contrary. The vigour of the preceding emperors is kept up by Dioclesian, and the empire is *considerably enlarged* to the *east*. Thus, as far as the facts which Mr. Gibbon lays before us, can give us an insight into the present state of the empire; we, who were called to the sickness, the death, and the burial of it, find ourselves employed by our inviter, in tracing the *grandeur*, and in following up the *enlargement*, of it. If these facts are not decisive evidences of its present state, what facts can be? And, if they are, why in the name of common-sense are they related by Mr. Gibbon?

Chapter fourteenth prosecutes the history, to the elevation of Constantine. Nor can we yet forbear the same complaint. We are not yet one inch nearer to the decline and fall of the empire, from any of the facts so particularly recited here. We have

have only a tax impofed upon Italy, a country that had long been exempt from taxes, which could have no influence upon the duration or ftability of the whole ftate; and a repetition of thofe civil wars, which had fubfifted as frequently and as deftructively before, and of which if the mere repetition could give them a place in his hiftory, as weakening more and more the internal refources of the country, he ought to have equally taken in thofe of Vefpafian, Vitellius, Otho, and Galba, and fo begun with the beginnings of the empire. And, by a fingular addition to the continued injudicioufnefs before, at the clofe of this chapter we fee the decline and fall of the empire, farther removed from us than it was at the end of the laft. The plan of government begun by Dioclefian, and purfued to the prefent period, that of creating two emperors, and appointing two delegates under them; is now all overthrown. And the many dangers that threatened to refult from it, are now all precluded by the exaltation of Conftantine to the whole undivided empire.

Chapter fifteenth forms another digreffion. For the laft five chapters, Mr. Gibbon has kept with fome regularity to the clue of hiftory; though it is a hiftory of facts, all alien from the purpofe of his work, and indeed fhewing the very reverfe of what he means to fhew. But he here refumes his *exorbitant* love of digreffion, differtation, and philofophifing. He here rambles away from his hiftory, to trace through a length of labyrinths the progrefs of Chriftianity in the empire, before the Converfion of of Constantine. In the general history of the empire, this departure of the emperor from the old faith to a new religion, is undoubtedly a very memorable incident, that ought to be explained at full length, because of its consequences to the state. But, in a history of "the decline and fall" only of the empire, it is of little or no consequence. The secret or open diffusion of this new religion, had not the slightest influence upon the general fabric; so as to bring on a decline, or to hasten a fall. It sapped none of its political foundations. It tore down none of its political pillars. It even must have had a very contrary effect; a tendency to support the superstructure, by strengthening the foundations. It introduced a stricter and severer morality, among the great body of its subjects. And it thus tended greatly, to recall the best manners of the republic; to heighten them infinitely, in their comprehension and efficacy; so to renew with an addition of energy, the vital spirit of the whole empire; and to give it a free and supernatural principle of seminal vigour. So progressively injudicious and absurd, is the conduct of this history! So much does one chapter rise superior to another, in contrariety to its design, and in preposterousness from its own execution!

We thus reach chapter the sixteenth and last. This shews us the conduct of the emperors towards the rising religion of Christianity, from Nero down to Constantine; and is merely an account of the Ten Persecutions, as they are generally called. But let us ask once more, What concern has all this

this with the decline and fall of the empire? The subject, with which we set out, is all gone from our view. It is whirled away as by the force of magic. And we have been wandering into a mixed wilderness of facts and speculations, that relate only to the change of its religion. Instead of a regular history of facts, that point out the principles of dissolution in the empire, and explain the progress of their operation on the body politic of Rome; we are treated with a *dissertation on ecclesiastical history*, and a dissertation calculated only by a misrepresentation of facts, and a falsification of sentiments, by sly touches of sarcasm at one time, and by bolder strokes of effrontery at another, to restore the sottishness of Paganism upon the ruins of Christianity; to tear down this *sun of the human system* from its sphere in the universe, and so reduce the moral world into its ancient chaos again.

From this useful analysis of the first volume, we see the general folly of it in a glaring light. The whole is evidently in one gross contradiction to its prefixed title, and in one continued violation of its professed design. And having thus laid before my readers my ideas, with regard to the matter and the manner of Mr. Gibbon in the previous volumes of his history, by a pretty full dissection of the first of them; I shall now proceed, to a consideration of the present volumes.

CHAPTER

CHAPTER THE SECOND.

IN the general preface to thefe three volumes, I meet with the following paffage; which claims a particular notice from me.

'Were I ambitious of any other patron than the public,' fays Mr. Gibbon, 'I would infcribe this work to a ftatefman, who, in a long, a ftormy, and at length an unfortunate adminiftration, had many political opponents, almoft without a perfonal enemy; who has retained, in his fall from power, many faithful and difinterefted friends; and who, under the preffure of fevere infirmity, enjoys the lively vigour of his mind, and the felicity of his incomparable temper. LORD NORTH will permit me to exprefs the feelings of friendfhip, in the language of truth; but even truth and friendfhip fhould be filent, if he ftill difpenfed the favours of the crown.'

This is feemingly well faid. In appearance it does honour to Lord North, and honour to Mr. Gibbon. And it ftrongly reminds us of that honeft burft of generofity in Mr. Pope, amidft all the cunning and meannefs of his artificial character; when, in 1721, he addreffed the Earl of Oxford in the following lines:

In

In vain to deserts thy retreat is made,
The muse attends thee to the silent shade:
'Tis hers the brave man's latest steps to trace,
Rejudge his acts, and dignify disgrace.
When int'rest calls off all her sneaking train,
And all th' oblig'd desert, and all the vain;
She waits or to the scaffold or the cell,
When the last ling'ring friend has bid farewell.
Ev'n now she shades thy ev'ning walk with bays,
(No hireling she, no prostitute to praise);
Ev'n now, observant of the parting ray,
Eyes the calm sun-set of thy various day;
Thro' fortune's cloud one truly great can see,
Nor fears to tell that MORTIMER is he.

Here we see the poet and the historian seemingly contending with each other, in delicacy of attention to their own honour, and in dignity of sentiment towards an ejected minister. But Mr. Gibbon's apparent generosity of conduct, loses all its force with those; who know the original enmity of his spirit to Lord North, and the sudden conversion of that enmity into friendship. And I therefore lay the following anecdote before my readers, assuring them that I firmly believe it to be all true. In June 1781 Mr. Fox's library came to be sold. Amongst his other books, the first volume of Mr. Gibbon's history was brought to the hammer. In the blank leaf of this was a note, in the handwriting of Mr. Fox; stating a remarkable declaration of our historian at a well-known tavern in Pall-Mall, and contrasting it with Mr. Gibbon's political conduct afterwards. ' The author,' it observed, ' at Brookes's said, That *there was no*
' *salvation for this country,* until SIX HEADS of the
' PRINCIPAL

'PRINCIPAL persons in administration,' LORD
NORTH being then prime minister, ' WERE LAID
' UPON THE TABLE. Yet,' as the observation
added, ' *eleven* days afterwards, this same gentle-
' man *accepted a place of a lord of trade* under those
' very ministers, and *has acted with them ever*
' *since*.' This extraordinary anecdote, thus recorded, very naturally excited the attention of the
purchasers. Numbers wished to have in their own
possession, such an *honourable* testimony from Mr.
Fox, in *favour* of Mr. Gibbon. The contention
for it rose to a considerable height. And the
volume, by the aid of this manuscript addition to
it, was sold for three guineas. From such a state
of savage hostility in Mr. Gibbon, did the rod of
this ministerial Hermes charm him down, in *eleven
days* only; and change the man who stood, as it
were, with his axe in his hand, ready to behead
him and five of his associates, into a sure friend; a
friend *in* power; and—now the spirit of ambition is
forced to sleep in the breast of Mr. Gibbon, and he
himself is to obliged to retire into Switzerland, a
friend *out* of it.

The FIRST
chapter of this volume [chap. thirty-ninth in the series
of the volumes] contains the history of Theodoric, the
Gothic sovereign of Italy. But the history *at first* is
so broken, short, and uninteresting; that the reader
becomes tired at the very outset. This arises principally, we believe, from the imperfectness of the original notices. Yet, from whatever it arises, it has a
very unpropitious influence upon the present chapter.

We

We see a set of barbarians moving before us, of whom we know little, and for whom we care less; doing nothing, either to attract our attention or to provoke our regard. This disgust, however, goes off by degrees. Theodoric, reigning peaceably in Italy, becomes in some measure a favourite with us; and the deaths of Boethius and Symmachus interest us in their favour.

In one place Nardini is cited for saying, what he does not say. 'These horses of Monte Cavallo' 'at Rome,' Mr. Gibbon tell us in a note, 'had 'been transported from Alexandria to the baths of 'Constantine (Nardini, p. 188)[1].' Yet, what are the very words of Nardini? I have not the original Italian by me; but in Grævius's translation of the work into Latin, they are these: '*Pan-* '*vinius*, parte primâ de Rep. Romanâ, a Constan- 'tino Alexandriâ deportatos *asserit*, et in Thermis 'ejus positos; quod *vero proximum videtur*[2].' Nardini, we see, does not assert the point himself; he only cites Panvinius for asserting it. And this assertion, he adds, 'seems to be *nearest to the* '*truth*.' We mention not this instance, as any striking deviation in Mr. Gibbon from his cited authorities. We notice it only as a small one; as a slight evidence of that want of accuracy in him, which we marked in the first volume. And a trifling one of this nature, where no prejudice could interpose, and no unfaithfulness take place, is the best evidence of the general inaccuracy of his references.

[1] p. 26.   [2] Grævius, iv. 1098.

In another place Mr. Gibbon speaks of Ennodius, as 'the bishop of Pavia; I mean the ec-
'clesiastic who wished to be a bishop[1].' This is
so darkly worded, that it leaves the reader without a
meaning. Nor can he understand it, till he comes
to a subsequent page. There he finds that, 'two
'or three years afterwards, the orator [Ennodius]
'was rewarded with the bishopric of Pavia[2].'
And then, for the first time, he observes that
Mr. Gibbon intended to tell us before, Ennodius
was *then* seeking the bishopric which he *now* obtained.—— 'Theodoric's march' is said to be
'*supplied* and illustrated by Ennodius[3];' where
the author means, that the *account* of it is 'sup-
'plied,' and the *course* of it 'illustrated,' by
Ennodius.——The wife or concubine of Theodoric is said, to have met his flying troops at the entrance of their camp, and to have turned them back
by her reproaches. 'She presented, and almost
'displayed,' adds a note, 'the original recess[4].'
Here the obscurity may be pardoned perhaps, for
the sake of the modesty. But the modesty might
have been retained, and the obscurity avoided. It is
in that page, where we note 'the indecency of the
'women on the ramparts, who had revealed their
'most secret charms to the eyes of the assailants[5].'
——He mentions 'the volume of public epistles,
'composed by Cassiodorus in the royal name,'
as 'having obtained *more implicit credit* than they
'seem to *deserve*[6].' Yet, throughout the whole

[1] p. 3. [2] p. 13. [3] p. 10. [4] p. 12.
[5] p. 108—109. [6] p. 13—14.

chapter

chapter afterwards[1], he builds his history upon the groundwork of these very epistles; without *one* hint of doubt concerning the author's knowledge, and without *one* shadow of derogation from his veracity.——We have also this *petty* stroke of arrogance: ' I will neither *hear* nor reconcile the ' arguments,' &c.[2]——Theodoric is said to have ' loved, the virtues *which he possessed*, and the ' talents of which he was destitute[3].' The meaning is obscured by the defect in the language. The sentence should have said, that he ' loved' *in others* ' the virtues which he possessed' *himself*, &c.——Theodoric is likewise said very harshly, to have ' *imprinted the footsteps* of a conqueror on the Capitoline hill[4];' when he should have been declared only, to have *set the foot* of a conqueror upon it. In the same page Mr. Gibbon speaks thus, concerning the cloacæ or common-sewers at Rome: ' How such works could be executed by ' a king of Rome, is yet a problem.' This is not ill said; but the observation ought to have been carried much farther. Historical scepticism is the natural exertion, of a mind vigorous and thinking; while the scepticism of religion, is the mark generally of a head enslaved to the tyranny of the passions, and reduced by it into a religious debility. In reading the *earlier* annals of the Romans, we meet with incidents that no *sober* credulity can admit.

---

[1] In pages 16, 17, 19, 20, 22, 23, 24, 25, 27, 29, 30, 31, 34, 37, 40, and 41.
[2] p. 21.   [3] p. 23.   [4] p. 23.

mit. We see a city, that was reared only by a few fugitives, in the space only of *five* reigns become so exceedingly populous, according to the *best* and *oldest* accounts of the Romans themselves; as to contain within it *eighty thousand men capable of bearing arms*[1]; and consequently, of all ages, not less than *four or five hundred thousand persons*. And, in the reign immediately *preceding*, we see those sewers constructed, which existed in the days of Pliny the admiration of the *imperial* Romans; which continue the wonder of all the curious world, to this day; and the cleansing and repairing of which, when they had been once neglected and choaked, cost the Romans no less than *a thousand talents*[2], or about *two hundred thousand pounds* of our money. These historical *miracles*, having no *supernatural* authority to attest them, carry such a monstrous incredibility with them; as must overset every common measure of faith, and shock even credulity itself.

The SECOND chapter, or chapter fortieth, is an account of Justinian and his queen, his court, his fortresses, his introduction of silk-worms, his suppression of the schools at Athens, his ending the succession of consuls at Rome, &c. &c. &c. But, in all this accumulation of miscellaneous matter, how do we trace the decline and fall of the empire? Except in some incidental points concerning his fortresses, we see nothing in the whole, that marks with the slightest

---

[1] Livy, i. 44. from Fabius Pictor.   [2] Grævius, iii. 777.

line

line of fact the falling, or even the declining, frame of the empire. And, in the second page of the first volume, we were assured that we should have only ' the most important circumstances of its de-' cline and fall.' So different from the promise is the performance! And so forgetful is the author of his own purpose and plan!

The manner too is full of short, quick turns, that give us the pointed brevity, and frequent obscurity of Tacitus. These repeatedly stop the advance of the reader. He is obliged to pause and examine, before he can proceed. And these frequent *rubs* in the course of the reading, give a disagreeableness to the movements of the history. The author also adds to this disagreeableness, by another circumstance in his conduct. He writes frequently to *his own ideas* only; and reflects not on the ideas of his reader. He therefore throws out allusions, that are not understood as they arise, that perplex the memory, and that embarrass the judgment. And the narration, if narration it can be called, is still uninteresting. It has, indeed, too much of *dissertation* in it. The whole is little more, than *a dissertation upon the history*. And it is this, which gives a languor and a feebleness to the pages, that the incidents of history would not have given.

In one page, Mr. Gibbon lays open the lascivious character of Theodora, the queen of Justinian. He gives us indeed the most notorious acts of her profligacy, as he says himself, ' veiled in the obscu-' rity of a learned language¹.' But he produces

¹ P. 53.

the passages at full length, when he needed only to have hinted at them; and when a modest man would have done so. He even gives us a repetition of passages. This shews his heart to have been delighted with the subject. And he even subjoins a note in English to one of them, in order to point it out more fully to the notice of his reader.

The language has the same faults as before. Proclus is ' the friend of Justinian, and the enemy of every other adoption¹;' that is, an enemy to the adoption of any other person as heir to the empire. ——We have also these words: ' their religion, an ' honourable problem, betrays occasional confor-' mity, with a secret attachment to paganism².' What is an honourable problem? Their ' occa-' sional conformity to Christianity,' with their ' secret attachment' to paganism? But how is this ' honourable?' And if so, how is it a ' problem?' ——He speaks of the priests and their relics, which had been interposed between two parties of combatants, in order to separate *them*; as ' interposed to ' *separate* the bloody *conflict*' itself³.——He calls the web of the silkworm, its ' *golden* tomb⁴.' He repeatedly speaks of ' the *education*' of *silkworms*⁵; and calls the straits of Bosphorus and the Hellespont, without any qualifying expression, ' the gates of the ' city' Constantinople⁶.——He says, ' a whole ' people, the manufacturers of Tyre and Berytus, ' *was* reduced to extreme misery⁷.'——He mentions a man, whose ' *style* was scarcely *legible*⁸.'

[1] P. 45. [2] p. 48. [3] p. 67. [4] p. 71. [5] p. 78. [6] ibid.
[7] p. 84. [8] p. 86.

A plan is said to be 'described[1],' when the author means *drawn*.——Xenophon, we are told, '*suppose* in his romance the same barbarians, 'against whom he had fought in his retreat[2].'——
We are informed, that the Athenians, 'about thirty 'thousand males, *condensed* within the period of a 'single life the genius of ages and millions[3].'
——And finally, says Mr. Gibbon, 'I *regret this* '*chronology*, so far preferable,' &c[4]. when he ought to have said, 'I regret the *disuse* of this chrono-'logy,' &c.

'I regret [the disuse of] this chronology,' of computing from the creation of the world, 'so far 'preferable to our double and perplexed method, 'of counting backwards and forwards the years 'before and after the Christian æra.' Mr. Gibbon then adds, as many authors have added before him, that ' in the West, the Christian æra was first in-'vented in the sixth century;' and that ' it was 'propagated in the eighth by the authority and 'writings of venerable Bede[5].' The assertion concerning Bede, as if he was the first who used the Christian æra, is surely as false as it is common. Bede only used the æra, *as others had used it before him*. His ' authority,' therefore, did not recommend it to the world. A Saxon of Northumbria was not likely, to have known such an 'authority.' He found it already 'propagated.' It came recommended to him, by the 'authority' of the preceding users. And he accordingly uses it in his

[1] P. 93. [2] p. 105. [3] p. 112. [4] p. 121. [5] ibid.

Chronicon,

Chronicon, *without the least notice previously concerning it*, as what was *common to the writers*, and *familiar to the readers*, of his age and country; coupling it as it had been used to be coupled, with the antecedent æra of the creation of the world. In this manner he enters upon what he calls his

'Anno   'SEXTA ÆTAS;
'Mundi Christi   Anno Cæsaris Augusti—, Jesus
' 3952.   1.   Christus, filius Dei, sextam
                            ' mundi ætatem suo conse-
                            ' cravit adventu [1].'

First invented by Dionysius Exiguus in 525, it was soon adopted, no doubt, as an useful *hinge* of chronology, upon which it could conveniently turn, to look either backward or forward; became *general* upon the *continent*, in conjunction with the old one; and *therefore* was used by Bede in this island, with all that apparent ease, with which our modern writers use it at present.

Mr. Gibbon speaks of that asserted repetition of Archimedes's burning-glasses by Proclus, in these terms: ' A machine was fixed on the walls of ' the city, consisting of an HEXAGON mirror of po-' lished brass,' &c. And the note annexed tells us, that ' Tzetzes describes the artifice of these ' burning-glasses [2].' Mr. Gibbon therefore refers to Tzetzes, for his account of them. Yet an unlucky blunder in his *real* author, detects his delusive

[1] Smith's Opera Bedæ, p. 16.   [2] p. 89.

reference to the *nominal* one. The words of Tzetzes are thefe:

Ὡς Μαρκελλες δ' απιoῖησι ζολην εκεινα; τοξυ,
Εξαγων οτι κατοπτρον ἑξηγωνον ο γερων.

which, tranflated, run thus;

When Marcellus removed the fhips a bow-fhot off,
Old Archimedes actually brought out a mirror and fixed it.

But where is this mirror faid to be, as Mr. Gibbon denominates it, an ' hexagon ?' In thefe very lines, *as Mr. Gibbon renders them.* The word εξαγων in the fecond line, he confiders as εξαγωνος ; and the *production* of the mirror he interprets into the *fexangular* nature of it. Nor is this all. The blunder is not *his own*; he derives it from the hand of another. M. de Buffon, fays Mr. Dutens, ' relat-
' ing this paffage in his Memoirs of the Academy
' for the year 1747, p. 99, fpeaks of a hexagon
' mirror, though Tzetzes mentions no fuch thing;
' that celebrated academician, or the perfon who
' communicated to him this paffage, certainly
' miftook the word εξαγων, which fignifies *educens*,
' for εξαγωνος, a hexagon '.' And, as this produces a moft ridiculous proof of the ignorance of M. Buffon and of Mr. Gibbon in that very language of Greek which they pretend to tranflate; fo it fhews Mr. Gibbon in a ftill more ridiculous light to us, citing Buffon though he refers to Tzetzes, conftruing Tzetzes only by the tranflation of Buffon, ' and expofing his mode of managing his quotations in general, by this detected inftance of his conduct.

' Dutens's Inquiries into the Difcoveries attributed to the Moderns. London, 1769, p. 325—326.

The THIRD,

or forty-firſt chapter.—Mr. Gibbon having, in the three firſt volumes, deduced the hiſtory of the empire to its fall in the *Weſt*, was now to purſue it to its equal fall in the *Eaſt*. But does he do ſo? No. The very firſt chapter of this volume, carries us directly back into the Weſt again. It takes us even into Italy. It there gives us the *ſubſequent* hiſtory, of the late capital of the Weſt; its hiſtory, *after* it has *ceaſed* to be the capital, when it is no longer the metropolis even of Italy itſelf, and when it only ranks as ſecond to Ravenna. This *poſt-obit* kind of hiſtory is exceedingly ſtrange. It ſhews the hiſtorian, to have either fixed no limits to his excurſions, or to have ſlighted them. But he had firſt fixed and then ſlighted. In the preface to this very volume he ſays, that he ' now diſcharges his *promiſe*, and completes his *deſign*, of writing the hiſtory of the *decline* and *fall* of the Roman empire, both in the ' *Weſt* and the *Eaſt*.' Yet, in his very firſt chapter afterwards, he gives us a long account of what happened in the Weſt, in Italy, and at Rome; when the empire had already declined and fallen there. His whole chapter is a detail of events, in which the Roman empire had not the ſlighteſt concern; as they are merely the hiſtory of thoſe, who had previouſly pulled down the weſtern empire, and merely the victories of thoſe, who now conquered the conquerors of the empire. But this third chapter at once partakes in the fault of the firſt, and varies it conſiderably. It relates the tranſactions of Beliſarius, in reducing thoſe who

D 3 had

had rent Carthage and Italy from the weſtern empire, and in annexing both again to the eaſtern. We thus ſee the *decline* and *fall* of the empire all in an *inverted* poſition. We behold that very empire of the Weſt, which we had piouſly buried in the grave, and over which we had ſung a melancholy *requiem*; raiſed by the hand of miraculous violence from the earth, and brought upon the ſtage again. And nothing ſurely can equal the abſurdity of this conduct in the hiſtorian, except that dramatical ſtroke of Dryden's, in which one of the *ſtage-dead* cries out to the man who would have carried him off;

—————— Hold, you damn'd confounded dog,
I am to *riſe* and *ſpeak the epilogue.*

We are told, that the Goths and Vandals had obtained ' a legal eſtabliſhment' in Italy and Africa; and that ' the *titles* which Roman victory had *in-*
' *ſcribed*, were eraſed with equal juſtice by the ſword
' of the barbarians[1].' Here we have a remarkable equivocation, in the uſe of a ſingle word. *Title* is uſed by the author for an *inſcription*, when he actually means a *right*.——We hear of ' a deep
' trench, which was *prolonged* at firſt in *perpendicu-*
' *lar*, and afterwards in parallel, lines, to cover the
' wings of an army[2].' What is the *prolongation* of a trench in *perpendicular*, as oppoſed to *parallel*, lines?——The Roman infantry ' yielded to the
' more prevailing uſe and reputation of the ca-
' valry[3],' that is, we *believe*, were not in ſuch frequent uſe and high reputation as the cavalry.——
Pharas ' *expected*, during a winter ſiege, the ope-

[1] p. 122. [2] p. 128. [3] p. 130.

' ration

'ration of distress on the mind of the Vandal
'king¹;' that is, he waited for it.——We have
this *elegant* jest: 'Labat reckoned at Rome one
'hundred and thirty eight thousand five hundred
'and sixty-eight Christian souls, besides eight or
'ten thousand Jews—*without souls*²?'—*O lepidum
caput!*

There is a quick, glancing turn of reflection in
the author, that very frequently throws the reader
out in the pursuit, and leaves him behind. This is
one of the many touches of Tacitus, in Mr. Gibbon. And it is marked, as in Tacitus, by a hasty
abruptness of ideas, and an involving darkness of
words.——Thus 'the martial train, which attended
'Belisarius's footsteps' in the streets of Constantinople, is said to have '*left his person more accessible
'than in a day of battle*³.' What does this mean?
——Thus also 'Theodosius had been educated in
'the Eunomian heresy; the African voyage was
'consecrated by the baptism and auspicious name
'of the first follower who embarked; and the pro-
'selyte was adopted into the family of his spiritual
'parents, Belisarius and Antonina⁴'. This is a
sentence *Thebano ænigmate digna.*

The author is also involved himself at times, in
the cloud which he spreads over his readers.—We
are told that Belisarius, discovering his wife and an
almost naked youth by themselves in a subterranean chamber, '*consented* to disbelieve the evidence
'of his own senses⁵.' But this *positive* consent is

¹ p. 149.   ² p. 179.   ³ p. 202—203.
⁴ p. 205.   ⁵ p. 205.

imme-

immediately afterwards stated, as a *doubtful* one. 'From this pleasing, and *perhaps* voluntary delu- 'sion,' adds Mr. Gibbon, 'Belisarius was awaken- 'ed,' &c. And, to complete the contradiction, we afterwards return to the positive again, and are told that his ' credulity appears to have been 'singular¹.'——' In the country between the Elbe 'and the Oder,' says the text, ' several populous 'villages of Lusatia *are inhabited by the Vandals*; 'they *still preserve* their language, their customs, 'and the purity of their blood ; support, with some 'impatience, the Saxon or Prussian yoke; and 'serve, with secret and voluntary allegiance, the 'descendant of their ancient kings, who, in his garb 'and present fortune, is confounded with the meanest 'of his vassals².' This is a most extraordinary relation indeed. It is evidently of the same fabric, with a community of *Greeks* still talking their native language in the south of Italy; a race of *Cimbri*, equally talking theirs in the north of Italy; both noticed by men who *have never seen either*, but both unknown to their very neighbours; and, what is a proper accompaniment to both, with the invisible army at Knightsbridge. And Mr. Gibbon here shews us that weakness of historical credulity, which often attends the most vigorous exertors of religious infidelity. We are gravely told by him also, in a note subjoined; that, ' from the mouth of the great 'elector (in 1687), Tollius describes *the secret roy-* '*alty*, and *the rebellious spirit*, of the Vandals of

---

¹ p. 207.   ² p. 155.

'Brandenburgh,

'Brandenburgh, who could muster five or six
'thousand men,' &c. Thus this unknown race of
Vandals, with their unknown sovereign at the head
and at the tail of them, which was revealed to the
eyes of Europe for the first time, by 'the great
'elector in the year 1687;' has strangely sunk behind the veil again, and has been ever since as invisible as they were before. The mountains of India, that have so long concealed the pigmies in
their secret vales, stretch their long arms into Lusatia, and hide a pigmy race of Vandals in their
deserts. Lusatia, indeed, might be removed half
the circumference of the globe from us; by the
turn and tenour of such a wild discovery, as this.
But, after all, the understanding of Mr. Gibbon
seems to awake a little, from its antiquarian dream.
And to the contradiction of all, that he has said in
the text above, and in the note before, he adds immediately afterwards; that 'the *veracity*, not of the
'Elector, but of Tollius, *may justly be suspected*.'
He thus comes at last to *suspect* the *truth*, of what
he himself *has asserted for truth*. The whole is a
mere fiction, no doubt; fabricated either by Tollius himself, or, what is much more probable, in
some jocular moment imposed upon Tollius by
'the great elector[1].'

The

---

[1] *To the* EDITOR *of the* ENGLISH REVIEW.

SIR,

In your continuation of the Strictures on Mr. Gibbon's
History, I find that you attack the account this writer gives, of
a small tribe of Vandals who inhabit part of Lusatia, and
chiefly

The FOURTH,

or forty-second chapter, contains some intimations concerning the Lombards, some concerning the Bulgarians

chiefly that part which is subject to the Elector of Saxony. Whatever may be Mr. Gibbon's mistakes in other respects, in this he is right enough. I will not answer for the truth, 'of 'their serving still the descendant of their ancient kings;' at least the circumstance is unknown to me; and I have never heard it mentioned by any one of that little nation, of which I once knew many individuals. The people certainly exist, and are called in Saxony *Wenden*, i. e. Wendts, or Vandals, or Wendish. They are chiefly peasants; uncouth and uncivilised, and extremely tenacious of their language, their ancient customs, and manners. Their language is equally different from the German, and from any language derived from the Latin; in short, it is a branch of the Sclavonian. Many of them are entirely ignorant of the German, and consequently debarred from all sources of information. They have, in their own language, some books of devotion, and a New Testament; but I do not recollect, whether they have the Old Testament. They send constantly a certain number of young men to the university of Leipsic, many of whom I have known. These, when among themselves, always spoke their native language; and every Saturday one of them preaches, in Wendish, a sermon in the university church, by way of practising his future destination.

The existence of these Vandals is by no means unknown in this country. Some years ago I was asked about them, by a gentleman in the neighbourhood of Eton, who is known for his researches into various languages. I procured him a certain number of radical verbs, some passages of the New Testament, and the Lord's Prayer; and he instantly declared (what I knew very well) the language to be a branch of the Sclavonian.

If you should think it worth your while, Sir, to insert this into your Review; I will add here part of the Lord's Prayer,

which

Bulgarians and Sclavonians, some concerning the Turks, the Abyssinians, &c.; and an account of a war which is very different indeed from that of the Germans, by whom they are surrounded on every side:

'Neisch wotze kizszy ty we ne bessach szweczene bycz broje me no isschindz knam fwoje kralen stwo: twoja wola szo sfain kesiz na nebiu tak seisch na semo.'

Pardon me, Sir, for troubling you with this letter, which, as it tends to information, I thought would not be disagreeable to you from

Dec. 3*d*, 1788.   A Reader of the English Review.

To the EDITORS *of the* ENGLISH REVIEW.

GENTLEMEN,

A correspondent, in your last Review, having doubted whether the Bible has been translated into that dialect of the Sclavonian, which is spoken in Upper Lusatia; I can inform him, that such an one was printed at Budissen or Bautzew, in quarto, in 1728, and in a smaller form in 1742. This translation was made from Luther's, by four clergymen, natives of that country, who appear to have executed their task with very great ability and zeal. Having determined on this laudable undertaking, they met at Budissen, and agreed what part of the work each of them should respectively take. They entered upon it April 14, 1716, and brought it to a conclusion September 27, 1727. During this period they held forty-five meetings, each of which generally lasted three days; for the purpose of mutually discussing the sense of difficult texts, collating their translation with the Sclavonian, Polish, Bohemian, and other versions, and revising every part with the utmost care and attention.

The Wenden, or, as they were anciently called, Sorabi, and more properly, in their own language, Sferbi, became, it is probable, early converts to Christianity. Bishop Otho, who, in the reign of the emperor Lotharius II. at the beginning of the twelfth century, travelled from Bamberg into Pomerania to propagate

war between the Romans and the Persians. But it is made up generally of such petty parts, intimations

so propagate the Christian faith in those parts; is said, in passing through Lusatia, to have completed the conversion of the inhabitants of that country from paganism. It is certain, that they renounced the errors of the Church of Rome, soon after Luther opposed them with so much success; and embraced the doctrines of that great reformer. Little, however, was done to furnish them with religious instruction, by the publication of books in their own proper dialect, till the year 1703; when the pious munificence of a noble female, procured them a translation of the Psalms of David, and, three years after, that of the New Testament. The inhabitants of Lower Lusatia speak a dialect, different in some respects from that abovementioned. The New Testament has been translated into it. I forbear to add more on this subject. If you think the above worthy a place in your Journal, you are welcome to it from

Your constant reader,

Jan 19, 1789.   OXONIENSIS.

To the EDITOR of the ENGLISH REVIEW.

SIR,

Having just read a letter in your postscript to the last Review, calculated to correct a slight notice in your Reviewer's animadversions upon Mr. Gibbon; I beg leave to enter my protest, against the correction.

Your Reviewer observed a strange sort of credulity in Mr. Gibbon, who said 'several populous villages of Lusatia were ' inhabited by *Vandals*,' even now. This assertion however, adds your letter-writer, is true. 'Whatever may be Mr. Gib- ' bon's mistakes in other respects,' he says, ' in this he is right ' enough.' Let us therefore see how he proves his point.

These VANDALS, Mr. Gibbon tells us, '*serve* with *secret* or ' *voluntary* allegiance *the descendant of their ancient kings*, who, in ' his *garb* and *present fortunes*, is *confounded* with the *meanest* of ' his *vassals.*' Who then is there, that must not laugh with the

Reviewer,

so uninteresting, and incidents so indecisive, that the history becomes dull and drawling. The rays of

Reviewer, at ' this *unknown* race of VANDALS, with their *unknown* sovereign at the *head* and at the *tail* of them." Even your letter-writer cannot assert *this* great and striking circumstance, to be true. ' I will not answer for the truth,' he honestly informs us, ' of their serving the descendant of their ancient kings;' and much less can he answer for their serving him ' with secret or voluntary allegiance,' and of his being, ' in garb and present fortunes, confounded with the meanest of his vassals.' He adds also thus: ' At least the circumstance is *unknown* to me; and I have *never* heard it *mentioned* by any one.' The letter-writer, therefore, gives up all the singular and marvellous circumstances of the story at once.

Yet he *asserts* the *general* position to be true. But how does he *prove* it to be so? By this extraordinary mode of reasoning. ' *The people* certainly exist,' he avers. Yet *what* is the people? ' A small tribe of VANDALS,' he answers; ' who inhabit part of Lusatia, and chiefly that part which is subject to the Elector of Saxony.' What then is the evidence for this tribe of VANDALS? It follows thus: ' They are called in Saxony WENDEN, *i. e.* Wendts, *or Vandals, or* Wendish.' The author thus *assumes* the one only point, which he was to prove. And the VANDALICK origin is *shewn*, by an *arbitrary* conversion of *Wenden* into *Vandals*.

Nor is this conversion merely arbitrary. It is, also, historically false. This author has not yet learned, that there was actually a tribe of VENEDI in antient Germany. Tacitus speaks of them particularly thus: ' Pucinorum, *Venedorumque*, ' et Fennorum nationes, Germanis an Sarmatis ascribam, dubito,' &c. (De Mor. Germ. 46). Those *Wendts* therefore, if their appellation be national and antient, are apparently derived from the *Venedi*. And their very language confirms this obvious etymology. ' Their language,' the letter-writer assures us, ' is—a branch of the *Sclavonian*.' In exact conformity with this says Jornandes, concerning ' *Venidarum* natio populosa—; ' quorum

of historical light in the whole, are so many, so faint, and so straggling; that they little *illuminate*

' quorum nomina, licet nunc per varias familias et loca muten-
' tur, principaliter tamen *Sclavi* et Antes nominantur.'

But were not, it may be asked by the pertinacity of disputation, the *Venedi* and the *Vandals* the same ? Certainly not, upon any principles of *historical* identity. The *Venedi* are noticed by Tacitus, as on the doubtful confines of Sarmatia and Germany. Pliny, who may be considered as a cotemporary with Tacitus, speaks to the same effect: ' quidam hæc habitari ad ' Vistulam usque fluvium, a Sarmatis, *Venedis*, Scyris, Hirris, ' tradunt' (iv. 13). And yet Pliny himself speaks of the *Vandals*, as totally different: ' Germanorum genera v, *Vindili*, quo- ' rum pars Burgundiones, Varini, Carini, Guttones' (iv. 14). These two names, we see, were cotemporary. That of *Vandals* was a generick appellation, including the Guttones, the Carini, the Varini, and the Burgundiones. And that of *Venedi* was a specific one, totally distinct from it and from all.

Your letter-writer, then, has failed egregiously in his attempt to assist Mr. Gibbon in this moment of distress. But, what is very remarkable, Mr. Gibbon himself declines his assistance. The writer was not at all aware of this. Yet it is very certain. Mr. Gibbon acknowledges expressly in a note at the end, as the Reviewer has observed, that ' the veracity—of ' Tollius,' the relater of the story, ' may *justly* be *suspected*.' He thus dashes the whole anecdote at once, out of the system of *real* history; and ranks it among the dubious and suspected incidents of man, those thin shades and spectres of history, that float in a kind of neutral state between existence and non-entity. And, by this movement of dexterity, he steals out at the back-door, while the letter-writer is waiting for him at the fore-door; and slips off from him, and from his own assertion, together.

Rebus omissis,
Atria servantem postico fallit *amicum*.

Jan. 4, 1789.   I am, Sir, yours,
Temple.

Another Reader of the English Review.

the reader, and never *warm* him. Nor have we a single trace of the main subject, the decline and fall of the empire; except in sudden incursions of hostility and in temporary cessions of territory. But we mark a plain consciousness in the author, that he is deviating from the prescribed and proper line of his history in all this. He accordingly apologises for his conduct, in one part of it thus. ' This narrative ' of *obscure* and *remote* events,' he says, ' is not fo-' reign to the decline and fall of the Roman empire'.' And he assigns a reason for it, which refers to his account of the Abyssinians: ' If a Christian power ' had been maintained in Arabia,' by the Abyssinians marching into it; ' Mahomet must have ' been crushed in his cradle, and Abyssinia would ' have prevented a revolution, which has changed ' the civil and religious state of the world.' But surely this reason is as poor in itself, as it is narrow in its extent. If the Christians of Abyssinia *had* marched into Arabia, *had* reduced the country, and *had* kept possession of it; *then* they would *either* have crushed Mahomet, *or* been expelled by him. This is all the consequence that would have ensued. That they *must* have crushed Mahomet, is an assertion equally without authority, and without probability. Mahomet would probably have assumed a new shape. And he, who propagated his religion with the sword, would with his sword have first vindicated the *freedom* of his country, and then

¹ P. 270.

given

given it his religion, with a higher authority and a quicker efficacy. The spirit of philosophising in history, is often asleep in those who profess it most. But even if the prevented invasion of Arabia, *had* it taken place, *would* have crushed Mahomet, and prevented all his operations; is this a sufficient justification of Mr. Gibbon, for entering into a ' narrative of obscure and remote events?' Are all the incidents, however ' remote' and however ' obscure,' that would have prevented (if they had happened) the main object of any history; to be recorded in the history itself? Is the war of Cæsar in Gaul, for instance, to be described in a ' narra-' tive of events,' by the historian of his expedition into Britain? Had Ariovistus's invasion of Gaul been successful, Cæsar ' must have been crushed ' in his cradle;' and Germany ' would have pre-' vented a revolution, which changed the civil ' and religious state of our island world.' An historian therefore, who had undertaken to delineate the *decline* and *fall* of the *British* empire in this island, would upon Mr. Gibbon's principles and performance be fully justified; if he should give a ' narrative of' those ' remote' events, and even step still further aside, to describe the court of Ariovistus and the country of Germany. And no one period of the Roman history could be written, without a ' narrative' of the period or periods immediately preceding; exactly as many of our old chroniclers cannot enter upon the history of their own country, without giving us all the general history of man preceding, and going previously

from

from Adam down to Caffivelaun. All indeed, that
is requisite to be done in every history, is to generalise the incidents that happen before the commencement of it, and have any influence, either preventive or operative, upon it. If their influence is operative, they should be placed in a direct point of general
view; if it is only preventive, they should be very
slightly touched, or indeed not touched at all. And,
as Mr. Gibbon could not but see this, because it is
what we may justly call the *common sense* of historical composition; so he actually saw it, and therefore promised to give us only ' the important
' circumstances,' and (which is more) only ' the
' most' important, in the ' decline and fall' of the
empire. He was to cut off all the circumstances,
even in the immediate history of its decline and fall
that were not *peculiarly* important. He was doubly
therefore, to cut off all circumstances of ' obscure
' and remote events,' that only affected the decline and fall of the empire distantly. And he was
tenfold more to cut off all such, as merely carried
a *preventive* influence with them; as would certainly, if they had happened, have prevented a formidable enemy from rising; or as *might probably*
have done so. But Mr. Gibbon has neglected
equally what he saw, what he promised, and what
he should have done. He ranges like a great
comet, without line or limit. And he has so far
formed a history, that, considered in its executed
plan, is wild, excentric, and extravagant.

In it the Goths ' affect to blush, that they
' must dispute the kingdom of Italy with a nation

E   ' of

'of tragedians, pantomimes, and *pirates*[1].' Yet a note adds, that ' this laſt epithet of Procopius ' ναυΐας λωποδύΐας, is too nobly tranſlated by *pi-* ' *rates*; *naval thieves* is the proper word.' Why was it not then uſed?——It is ſaid, that Coſrhoes ' formed a temporary bridge' over the ' Euphrates,' ' and *defined* the ſpace of three days for the entire ' paſſage of his numerous hoſt[2].'——There is often a Latin and often a French idiom, obſervable in the language of Mr. Gibbon. *This* is a Latin one; the Engliſh is, *fixed*.——And the River Phaſis ' deſcends with ſuch *oblique* vehemence, that, ' in a ſhort ſpace, it is traverſed by one hundred ' and twenty bridges[3].'

The FIFTH,

or forty-third chapter contains the hiſtory, of loſing and recovering Italy to the eaſtern empire; and an account of the comets, the earthquakes, and the plagues in the Eaſt. We are thus tranſported on the wings of this Hippogryffin hiſtory, to a ſphere that lies beyond the orb of its preſent deſign, and to one that we have ſeen torn down from its place. We have already ſeen the Vandals, tearing down the weſtern empire from its ſtation in the hiſtory. Yet we were carried, in the firſt chapter of this volume, to the ruins of it; and obliged to attend the conflict of a ſecond ſort of Vandals with the firſt, one ſtriving to maintain, and the other to acquire, the privilege of trampling upon thoſe ruins. We were

[1] p. 213. [2] p. 246. [3] p. 250.

then

then called upon to go with the Romans of Constantinople, and war with them for those very ruins. And we are now dragged into Italy a third time, to see it again lost to the barbarians, and again recovered to the eastern empire. We thus find the western giving us and our historian, almost as much trouble after its death, as it did in its life-time.

> ——————The times have been,
> That, when the brains were out, the man would die,
> And there an end; but now they rise again
> With twenty mortal murthers on their crowns,
> And push us from our stools: this is more strange
> Than such a murther is.

All this indeed, as a part of the eastern history, might have been told in a *full* history of the eastern empire. But it ought not to have been told, in a history only of its decline and fall. And it peculiarly ought not, when reason required and the author had promised, that we should have only 'the 'most important circumstances, of its' very 'decline and fall.' But the author is continually on the strain, in exerting a minuteness of diligence, and in exercising an obscure laboriousness, to swell the history beyond its natural size. He has not that happy power of genius within him, to grasp ' the ' important,' points of the history, to seize peculiarly ' the most important,' to detatch them from the rubbish of littleness and insignificance, and to make them the constituent parts of his history. He saw that this was his duty; but he could not act up to it. He drew the outline of his work with a critical hand; but he went beyond it on every side, in the excurfivenefs of his licentious pencil. And his plan only ferves at prefent, to unite with found criticifm in condemning him; to point out the *dropfical* fpirit of writing, by which he has dilated the fubftance of two volumes into fix; and to brand that accumulation of adventitious matter, with which his hiftory is fo heavily loaded, that it is breaking down under its own bulk.

In one page we have thefe words, ' Nicopolis, the *trophy* of ' Auguftus ';' becaufe he obtained a victory near it, and built it in honour of the victory. In the fame page we have a general's ' *want* of *youth* and ' experience.'——In another ' the extreme lands of ' Italy' are faid to have been, ' the *term* of their ' deftructive progrefs².' And let us add, what this chapter forces us to feel, that the hiftory frequently *reads like a riddle*, from the obfcurity of it.

The Sixth

or forty-fourth chapter is an account, no lefs than *eighty-five* pages in length, of the Roman jurifprudence; traced through the regal, the confular, and the imperial times, to the days of Juftinian; and containing a particular detail of the provifions made by it, for the various objects of law. The chapter is long and tirefome, from the ample nature of the fubject, and from the neceffary drynefs of the difquifition. Yet it has much learning, much good fenfe, and more *parade* of both. But nothing can fubdue the native barrennefs, of fuch a field as this.

¹ p 296   ² p. 309.

And, if any thing could, what has a disquisition on *all* the laws of *all* the Romans, to do with a history of the decline and fall of the empire? Even if it had the legal knowledge of Trebonius, Papinian, and Ulpian united together; if it had also the *philosophy*, of all the formers of polity and remarkers upon man, that these modern times have produced; and if both were set off with the energy of a Tacitus, and the brilliancy of a Burke; we should only point at the whole as a set of more splendid absurdities, and cry out with disdain,

Beauties they are, but beauties out of place.

A treatise on the domestic life of the Romans; a dissertation on the buttons, the strings, and the latchets of their military dress; on any thing more trifling (historically considered,) among the many trifles of antiquarianism; would have been almost as proper for the history, as such a disquisition upon their laws. That Justinian should have the honour attributed to him, of compiling the code, the institutes, and the pandects; is very reasonable. But it is very unreasonable, that a long and laboured dissertation on the laws of all the periods of the Roman history, with an enumeration of its particular provisions, should be given as a part of the history; and the essence of the statute-book served up, as an historical dish. In the fullest history of the empire, such literary cookery as this would be very absurd. It is still more absurd, in a history only of the decline and fall of the empire. And it is most of all absurd, when we had been so expressly assured,

that

that we should have only 'the circumstances of its
'decline and fall.'

We are told to 'appreciate the labours' of Justinian¹. The author is fond of the word in this harsh application of it; we have seen him using it before; and we shall see him again. After noticing Cato the censor and his son, as men skilled in the law; he remarks, that 'the kindred appellation of 'Mutius Scævola was illustrated by three sages of 'the law².' How obscure! He means, that this family had the honour of producing three good lawyers.—In the same page he mentions 'a *century* 'of volumes.'—In a farther we have, 'the *exposition* 'of children³,' for the *exposing* of them; 'the tame 'animals, whose nature is tractable to the arts of '*education*⁴;' 'the agreement of sale, for a certain 'price, *imputes*,' instead of *reckons*, 'from that mo- 'ment the chances of gain or loss to the account 'of the purchaser⁵;' 'the pain or the disgrace of a 'word or blow cannot easily be *appreciated* by a pe- 'cuniary equivalent⁶;' 'the extirpation of a *more* 'valuable tree⁷,' where the comparative is used for the positive degree, very absurdly in a list of legal punishments; and 'a prudent legislator *appreciates* 'the guilt and punishment⁸.'

We have noticed before the propensity of Mr. Gibbon to obscenity. It was then, however, covered mostly under a veil of Greek. But, in p. 375, his obscenity throws off every cover, and comes

¹ p. 333.   ² p. 350.   ³ p. 373.   ⁴ p. 384.   ⁵ p. 396.
⁶ p. 398.   ⁷ p. 401.   ⁸ p. 406.

stalking

stalking forth in the impudence of nakedness. A
soul, deeply tinctured with sensuality, loves to brood
over sensual ideas itself, to present sensual objects to
others, and so to enjoy its own sensuality of spirit
over again.

But, in p. 414, he is still more vicious. He then
mounts up into an avowed advocate—for what?
for no less an enormity than MURDER; and even
for that which, of all murders, is the only one that
precludes repentance, precludes pardon, and ends
the life with the crime of the murderer. ' The ci-
' vilians,' says this champion for self-murder, ' have
' always respected *the natural right* of a citizen *to*
' *dispose of his life*;——but the precepts of the
' *gospel*, or the *church*, have at length *imposed* a pious
' *servitude* on the minds of Christians, and *condemn*
' them to expect, *without a murmur*, the *last* stroke
' of disease or the executioner.' So boldly is Mr.
Gibbon here treading, in the steps of his honoured
acquaintance the late Mr. Hume! With all Mr.
Hume's spirit too, he arraigns the ' precepts of the
' gospel;' if they be (he hints) the precepts of the
gospel, and not the mere injunctions ' of the church;'
for prohibiting self-murder. With a similar spirit,
in the text of p. 380, he speaks of ' the wishes of
' the church;' when his note makes them to be,
the *laws of Christ* and the *precepts of St. Paul*. And
as it is highly to the honour of our religion, that
these patrons of self-murder are compelled to set
aside the dictates of the gospel, and the admoni-
tions of the church, before they can vindicate their
profligate speculations; so does Mr. Gibbon's spe-
culation

culation here, seem to tell us with a melancholy energy, to what a dreadful relief he may perhaps have recourse hereafter. May repentance anticipate distress; and the light of Christianity break in upon his mind, to stop the uplifted arm of suicide!

The SEVENTH

or forty-fifth chapter, relates principally to the invasion of Italy by the Lombards, and the separation of it again from the eastern empire. This is therefore, in all its principal parts, a mere digression. We have shewn this sufficiently before; nor need we to say more upon the subject. We have only to observe, that there is one link more added to the chain of absurdity; that to the digressional account of the Goths and Vandals, of the Goths and the eastern emperors, is now subjoined a long history of the Lombards, the emperors, and the Goths; that all these continued events of the Italian history, cannot have the least relation to the *western* empire, because *this* has long since vanished from the earth; and that they equally cannot form *any* circumstances of the decline and fall of the *eastern*, because Italy was the seat of the *western*. In every light, the narrative of events in Italy, after Italy has been so formally swept away from the stage of the history, is all impertinence.

A faint and tremulous kind of light, too, is all that is thrown over the narrative. This sometimes breaks out and engages the attention. But it is generally too tremulous to cast a steady illumination, and too faint to furnish a strong one.

And it serves only, like the natural twilight, to present the shadows of objects to our view. The whole scene of history before us, therefore, is dark, broken, and uninviting.

But digression is the great feeder of Mr. Gibbon's history. 'I should not be apprehensive,' he says, 'of deviating from my subject, if it was in my 'power to delineate the private life of the con'querors of Italy,' the Lombards[1]. Italy, having been once a grand object of his history, is for ever to remain so, it seems. It is not merely to remain, as long only as it is connected with the eastern empire. This the first chapter of this volume proves decisively. The transactions of the Goths in it have no relation to the eastern at all, and have a relation only to the Vandal settlers of Italy. Italy, therefore, is the connecting line of the history. And, upon the same principle, he may pursue the history to the coming of the Normans into the south of Italy; and then give us an account, of *their* domestic life, *their* civil laws, and *their* military transactions.

We have the court of Justinian arranged, on the formal reception of some ambassadors, 'according 'to the military and civil order of'—what? of 'the *hierarchy*[2].' This is extraordinary. Were then the persons who held 'civil and military' offices about the court, arranged in some order, similar to that of archbishops, bishops, &c. in the church? No! They were arranged in the military and civil

---

[1] p. 149.   [2] p. 149.

order of the hierarchy itfelf. And the word hierarchy is only ufed, with a ridiculous mifapplication of it, for the very court.

The EIGHTH,

or forty-fixth chapter relates principally, the fuccefses of the Romans under Tiberius, and the extenfion of the eaftern bounds of their empire, 'beyond the example of former times, as far as the banks of the Araxes and the neighbourhood of the Cafpian fea'[1];' and the great victories of Heraclius over Perfia, when ' the return of Heraclius from Taurus to Conftantinople was a perpetual triumph[2].' Thefe glorious events, undoubtedly, make a proper part of the hiftory of the eaftern empire. But they do not of the prefent hiftory. This, we muft ever remember, is a hiftory only of its *decline and fall.* And when the author planned his work, we muft equally recollect, he was to give us only ' the circumftances of its decline and fall,' ' only the important' too among them, and only, ' the moft important.'

The Cafpian fea, we are told, ' was explored, *for the firft time,* by an hoftile fleet' under Pompey. But ' in the hiftory of the world,' adds Mr. Gibbon in a note, ' I can only perceive two navies on the Cafpian, 1. of the Macedonians— 2. of the Ruffians[3].' The very fleet of the text, is moft unaccountably fhut out of the Cafpian by

[1] p. 480. [2] p. 579. [3] p. 468.

the note.——We are also told, 'the *city* and *palace*
'of Modain had already *escaped* from the *hand* of
'the tyrant¹.'——We find, that 'the ruin of the
'proudest monument of Christianity, was vehe-
'mently urged by the intolerant spirit of the
'Magi².' But what is this 'proudest monument
'of Christianity?' Is it that noblest edifice of
Christian, or even of Pagan, architecture, the church
of St. Peter at Rome? No! The words mean, as
the context shews, either Jerusalem or some build-
ing within it. 'The conquest of Jerusalem—was
'atchieved by the zeal and avarice of' Chrosroes;
'the ruin,' &c. And, on again examining the
context critically, we see it means the church of the
Holy Sepulchre at Jerusalem. So obscure is this
writer at times! He says afterwards, that 'Jerusa-
'lem itself was taken by assault,' and that 'the se-
'pulchre of Christ, and the stately churches of He-
'lena and Constantine, were consumed, or at least
'damaged, by the flames.' The stately churches
of Helena and Constantine are only *one*, that over
the Holy Sepulchre. And is this then, in Mr. Gibbon's opinion, 'the proudest monument of Chris-
'tianity;' when he knows St. Peter's to be existing
at Rome? Or could this be 'the proudest monu-
'ment of Christianity,' in the opinions of the Magi;
when they knew St. Sophia's to be existing at Constantinople?—Some cavalry are said 'to hang on
the *lassitude* and *disorder* of Heraclius's rear³.' The
expression is artificial and affected. The natural

¹ p. 473.   ² p. 502.   ³ p. 511.

language is, *to hang upon his haraffed and diforderly rear.* But nature was turned out to make way for art.——Mr. Gibbon, with the fame fpirit of affectation, '*educates* the new recruits in the knowledge ' and practice of military *virtue*'.'——We fee the fame fpirit at work, though lefs offenfively, in making Heraclius ' by a juft gradation of magni-' ficent fcenes,' that is, in the language of propriety and eafe, *through fcenes gradually rifing in magnificence,* ' to penetrate to the royal feat of Daftagerd².'—— And in p. 530 we have another oppofition, between the text and the notes. The text records ' the ' lofs of two hundred thoufand foldiers, who had ' fallen by the fword' in the wars of Heraclius againft Perfia. But a note adds this obfervation: ' Suidas—gives this number; but *either* the *Perfian* ' muft be read *for* the *Ifaurian* war, *or* this paffage ' *does not belong* to the emperor Heraclius.' He thus applies a paffage to the hiftory, without any hefitation; when he is obliged at the very moment, either to *alter* or to *reject* it; and when he even *owns,* that he is.

' The general independence of the Arabs,' he fays, in a note, ' which cannot be admitted with-' out many limitations, is blindly afferted in a fepa-' rate differtation of the authors of the Univerfal ' Hiftory, Vol. XX. p. 196—250. A perpetual ' miracle is fuppofed to have guarded the prophecy, ' in favour of the pofterity of Ifhmael; and thefe ' learned bigots are not afraid, to rifk the truth

¹ p. 512.   ² p. 524.

' of

'of Christianity on this frail and slippery founda-
'tion¹.' With such a tone of insolence, can Mr.
Gibbon abuse a champion of Christianity! Like
Virgil, he throws about his *dung* with an air of
majesty. He did so to Mr. Davis, in the very moments in which he was complaining of Mr. Davis's
rudeness. Mr. Davis indeed had provoked him,
with the rudeness of refutation and detection.
And the present author has also provoked him, by
producing an historical argument in favour of Judaism and Christianity, which he could not refute
and yet would not believe. He therefore took the
natural course, of ridiculing what he could not
answer, and of abusing what chagrined and gra-
velled him. But he had been much wiser to have
said nothing, to have never noticed the dissertation,
and so to have concealed his own impotence of malice against it. It was written by the late Mr. Swinton of Oxford, and proves the continued independency of the sons of Ishmael, by such a long train
of historical evidences; as is very wonderful in itself, as unites most powerfully to support the point
asserted, and as terminates in an argument of force and
weight for the *divinity* of our religion. But the author
is ' a learned bigot,' and ' a blind assertor,' with Mr.
Gibbon. And yet what is very wonderful, Mr.
Gibbon himself allows the continued independency
of the Arabs, takes this ' blind assertor' for his oracle, and unites with this ' learned bigot' in his belief.
This is perhaps almost as wonderful, as the inde-

¹ P. 465.

pendency

pendency itself. 'The general independence of the 'Arabs,' he owns, 'CAN—be ADMITTED with—'many limitations.' Mr. Swinton has accordingly p...ted from time to time, the 'many limitations' ver.. which the independence is to be asserted; in ... all the Arabs not to have been reduced, whi... most were; in shewing the *Bedoweens* (who are peculiarly the sons of Ishmael) not to have been, when the rest were; and in shewing even *these*, when obliged for a moment to submit, never to have been thoroughly subdued like the nations around them, and never, like them, incorporated into the substance of the Assyrian, the Persian, the Macedonian, the Roman, or even the Turkish empires. Mr. Swinton thus states the limitations, and Mr. Gibbon thus acknowledges the assertion. He acknowledges it, in the very moments in which he reprobates it. He 'admits' the point with the requisite 'limitations.' In all this long chain of historical arguments too, which stretches out to the amazing length of nearly four thousand years, which is therefore assailable (if weak) in so many different points, and in which the weakness of a single link would have destroyed the whole; Mr. Gibbon, with all the obvious desire to shew, and with all the apparent capacity to discern, does not point out *one single link of weakness* in the whole. And, what is more, in the *text* he *asserts* the doctrine, which he *admits* in the *note*; asserts it without hesitation; and asserts it, even without stating Mr. Swinton's or his own limitations. 'The sovereign of Persia 'and India,' he says, 'aspired to reduce under his 'obedience

'obedience the province of Yemen or Arabia Fe-
'lix, the distant land of myrrh and frankincense;
'WHICH HAD ESCAPED, rather than opposed, THE
'CONQUERORS OF THE EAST.' He thus acknowledges the *fact* in the plainest manner. The Arabs
of Yemen in every age to *this* period, he owns,
' had escaped' all subjection to the various and successive ' conquerors of the East.' So confused in
his ideas does Mr. Gibbon here appear, as to assert
in his text what he denies in his note, even there to
admit in reality what he rejects in appearance, and
to adopt the whole *history* of Mr. Swinton even while
he abuses him for it. So grossly disingenuous also does
he appear, in attempting to discredit an historical
evidence for Christianity, which he could not refute;
so wildly indiscreet, as to attack when he could not
hurt it; and so daringly bold, as to treat with insolence and abuse the very man, to whom he is obliged
to submit even while he is spurning at him. And
we have entered the farther into the point, because
the conduct of Mr. Gibbon in it, serves strongly to
shew the impregnable nature of Mr. Swinton's argument; to add one ray more, to the glory of this
honest champion for Christianity; and to secure the
strong ground which he wisely took, in this incidental defence of our religion.

The NINTH
or last chapter of this volume, the forty-seventh in
the series, is one of the wildest and most extravagant digressions, that even Mr. Gibbon has yet
made. It is a dissertation of no less than *eighty-nine*
pages,

pages, upon what? upon *the disputes among the Christians concerning the nature of Christ, and the opinions of the eastern churches on the point from the beginning.* Could we think it possible, if the fact was not apparent before our eyes; that a man of judgment, that a writer even of common sense, could ever have introduced such a dissertation into such an history? Any dissertation of a *length like this*, would have been absurd in any history whatever. But such a long dissertation upon a point of *theology*, must be *very* absurd. And such a long and theological dissertation, in a history only of the ' decline ' and fall' of the empire, and when we were to have only ' the circumstances of its decline and ' fall,' only the ' important' too, and only ' the ' most important;' is infinitely absurd. It would be a wildness worthy only of a Whiston and a Priestley, in *any* history; but it is a madness calculated merely for the meridian of deism, in the *present.*

The whole also is very dull. It is enlivened only, and dreadfully enlivened, by the wickedness of it. And nothing keeps the historical mind, from slumbering over the pages of it; but the bold sallies of blasphemy in it.

' The seeds of the faith, which had slowly arisen
' in the rocky and ungrateful soil of Judea, were
' transplanted, in full maturity, to the happier climes
' of the Gentiles; and the strangers of Rome or
' Asia, who never beheld the manhood, were the
' more readily disposed to embrace [he should have
                                          ' said

'said, *to believe in*] the divinity, of Christ[1].' We have selected this passage, as a full specimen of the confusion, which hangs upon Mr. Gibbon's understanding, and defeats all his theological efforts. The doctrine of our Saviour's divinity is here acknowledged, to have been preached originally to the Jews, by our Saviour and his apostles. This doctrine, we see, 'had slowly arisen—in the soil of 'Judea.' It had even arrived at last, to a 'full 'maturity' there. And it had so done, *before* the preaching of the gospel to the Gentiles. It was '*transplanted* in full maturity to the—climes of the 'Gentiles.' This therefore overthows all that he has said before, of the Jews not knowing and not believing in the divinity of our Saviour. So peculiarly unfortunate is he, in annihilating his allegations by his assertions! But he is still more so. This passage stands as a middle point, betwixt the future and the past. It looks forward to the Gentiles, as well as backward to the Jews. And it acknowledges the doctrine of our Saviour's divinity, to have been 'transplanted in full maturity' from 'the soil of Judea', into 'the happier climes 'of the Gentiles.' It acknowledges the doctrine to have been received there, even with more readiness than in Judea. The 'soil of Judea' had proved 'rocky and ungrateful' to it. It had therefore risen 'slowly,' though it reached a 'full maturity,' at last. But 'happier' were 'the climes of the 'Gentiles.' '. And the strangers of Rome and A-

[1] P. 537.

'sia—

'sia—were—more readily disposed to embrace the
'divinity of Christ.' So plainly does Mr. Gibbon
here assert the divinity of our Saviour, to have been
preached to the Jews, to have been preached to the
Gentiles, and to have been believed in by both, from
the very beginning of Christianity! He thus dashes
aside, all that he afterwards *insinuates* rather than *a-
vers*, against the Gentile reception of the doctrine.
And he stands forward in this memorable passage,
a Deist refuting the Arians, a reasoner wounded
with the two-edged sword of his own positions, and
a singular monument of literary suicide.

In p. 569 we have another evidence, of Mr.
Gibbon's love of obscenity. I will not repeat the
offence, by producing the passage. Modesty must
for ever reprobate this strange tendency of his pen.
And I cannot pass these gross eruptions of sensuality from it, without a proper censure.

'The synod of Chalcedon,' we are told, 'would
'perhaps have restored Nestorius to the honours,
'or at least to the communion, of the church; the
'*death* of Nestorius *prevented* his *obedience to the
'summons*'.' This we take from the text. But
let us look at the notes. 'The invitation of Nes-
'torius to the synod of Chalcedon,' it says, 'is re-
'lated by Zacharias—and the famous Xenaias,—
'denied by Evagrius and Asseman, and stoutly
'maintained by La Croze—: *the fact is not impro-
'bable*; yet it was the *interest* of the Monophysites,'
as friends to Nestorius, 'to *spread the invidious re-*

* P. 562—3.

'*port;*

'*port*; and Eutychius—affirms, that *Nestorius died
'after an exile of *seven* years, and consequently *ten*
'years *before* the council of Chalcedon.' In what a
state of conflict are the note and text here! *This* affirms without doubt and hesitation, that Nestorius
was *summoned* to the council, and that 'death pre-
'vented his obedience to the summons,' and that,
if death had not thus interposed, 'the synod—*would*
'perhaps *have restored* him to the *honours*, or *at least*
'to the *communion*, of the church.' But *that* tells
us another story, though with great uncertainty and
confusedness. What is so positively asserted in the
text, we find disputed in the note, maintained by
some and denied by others. Mr. Gibbon, however,
interposes to arbitrate between the disputants; and
by his arbitration inflames the dispute.

Chaos umpire sits,
And by decision more embroils the fray.

'The fact,' he says, 'is not improbable;' when he
has already asserted it to be more than probable, e-
ven actually true. But, at the very next step, he
recedes even from this faint assertion of its probability. For 'it was the interest of the Monophysites,'
he adds, 'to spread the invidious report.' He
therefore doubts even the *probability*, of what he
himself has asserted *positively*. And he instantly goes
on to show the very *falsehood*, and even the very *im-
possibility*, of the fact asserted by himself. He produces the sweeping testimony of Eutychius, that
Nestorius *died* no less than *ten* years *before* the coun-

cil fat. And in this ftate of the evidence he *leaves
the point*, oppofing his own intimated probability in
the note, and giving the lie direct to his own afferted reality in the text. We have feen already fuch
contradictions in the notes to the text, that we have
been tempted to afk, Whether the text and notes
could be written by the fame hand? But the prefent paffage fufficiently affures us, that they could.
The note is not more in oppofition to the text, than
it is to itfelf. And the oppofition in all, arifes from
the turn of Mr Gibbon's mind; brilliant, excurfive,
and ftrong, but not clear, difcriminative, and precife;
having the wing of the eagle to fupport its long
flight, but not poffeffing the eye of the eagle for its
keen refearches, only poffeffing indeed the eye of a
common bird, and fo led the more illuftrioufly
aftray by its eagle's wing.

CHAPTER THE THIRD.

I HAVE already expofed the prepofterous arrangement, which Mr. Gibbon has made of his materials in the preceding volumes of his hiftory. I now
come to his FIFTH volume. Here he fpeaks of his
previous arrangement. ' I have now deduced,' he
fays, ' from Trajan to Conftantine, from Conftantine
' to Heraclius, the regular feries of the Roman em-
' perors; and faithfully expofed the profperous and
' adverfe fortunes of their reigns [1].' Such has been

[1] P. 1.

the *execution* of the work, according to Mr. Gibbon himself! And yet, according to himself, the *plan* was very different. ' It is the design of *this* and *the two* ' *succeeding* chapters,' he told us in the first page of his first volume, ' to describe the *prosperous* condi-
' tion of the empire; and *afterwards*, from the
' death of Marcus Antoninus, to deduce the most
' important circumstances of its *decline* and *fall*.' So very opposite is the plan and the execution, according to Mr. Gibbon's *own* account! He who, after the death of *Marcus Antoninus*, was to give us only ' the circumstances,' and ' the most important' too, ' of the *decline* and *fall*' of the empire; here *confesses* he has given us ' the *regular* series of the Ro-
' man emperors,' from ' Trajan to Constantine,
' from Constantine to Heraclius;' and has ' expos-
' ed the *prosperous*,' as well as ' adverse, fortunes of
' *their* reigns.' Mr. Gibbon thus stands convicted upon his own confession, of a wild and devious aberration from his own plan. And all that we have urged upon this point, against his four volumes preceding; is here justified by himself, at the commencement of his fifth.

But he is now determined to reform his execution. ' Should I persevere in the *same* course,' he adds, ' should I observe the *same* measure, a *prolix*
' and *slender* thread would be *spun* through *many a*
' *volume*; nor would the patient reader find an a-
' dequate reward of instruction or amusement [1].'
This is again an acknowledgment of his trespasses.

[1] Page 1—2,

Mr. Gibbon, kneeling at the chair of confession, is very ingenuous. He owns the 'prolix and slen-'der thread' of history, which he has 'spun' already through four volumes. Yet, as his spiritual father or his critical, I can only consider his ingenuousness to fix his sin more fully upon him. And I proceed to consider his reformation.

The mode of execution, which he means now to adopt, is this. 'It is in the *origin* and *conquests*,' he remarks, 'in the *religion* and *government*,' of the 'new colonies and rising kingdoms,' which immediately filled the lost provinces of the empire; 'that 'we must explore the causes and effects, of the de-'cline and fall of the eastern empire¹.' This is certainly no *new* mode of execution. It is the very same, that he has pursued before with regard to the western. 'In the origin and conquests, in the reli-'gion and government,' of the Franks, the Vandals, the Goths, and the Lombards, &c.; has he 'explored the causes and effects,' of *its* decline and fall. We are *therefore* to '*persevere* in the same course,' and to '*observe* the same measure,' of writing. And Mr. Gibbon is confounding himself and his reader, by an inattention to his own conduct. 'Nor,' he adds, 'will this scope of narra-'tive, the riches and variety of these materials, *be* '*incompatible* with the *unity* of *design* and composi-'tion.' They will not be *more* incompatible than they have been, if only *so* pursued. But they will be greatly incompatible, as we have already seen

¹ P. 4.

they have been. And this intimation from Mr. Gibbon, shews us at once his suspicion that they have been, and prepares us to expect that they will be more. ' As, in his daily prayers, the musulman ' of Fez or Delhi still turns his face towards the ' temple of Mecca,' an allusion so replete with levity, that we cannot think it seriously applied; ' the historian's eye shall be always fixed on the ' city of Constantinople.' Nor is *this* a *new* mode of execution. Mr. Gibbon has always professed surely, to keep his eye upon the central point of his whole history; and, however large he may draw the circumference, still to make it move round its centre. But he has professed, and not performed. His history has moved in no regular orbit. And we shall soon find it moving so again. ' The ex-' cursive line may embrace the wilds of Arabia and ' Tartary, but the circle will be ultimately reduced ' to the decreasing limit of the Roman monarchy.' Here the *new* mode opens faintly upon the mind. We can hardly discern the meaning through the metaphor. The one is incongruous, and the other is obscure. But we discern enough to see, that Mr. Gibbon is preparing us for wilder excursions than ever. And he accordingly pushes his digressional extravagances, in the two next volumes; to a length even beyond that of all the preceding. Such is his *reformation!*

F 4   Chapter

Chapter FIRST

or forty-eighth.——Mr. Gibbon here gives us, in a courfe of *eighty-feven* pages, 'a period of fix hundred years,' and the reigns of 'fixty emperors';' defcribed in fuch a manner, that, as he himfelf allows, ' our reafon—difdains the fixty *phantoms* of kings, who have paffed before our eyes, and *faintly dwell on our remembrance*[2].' The whole indeed is cold, dull, and uninterefting, becaufe it is vague, general, and incomplete. It prefents a quick fucceffion of incidents and characters, too quick to enforce our attention or compel our regard. We are prefented with the various faces of a diamond, each of which cafts a little luftre, but all do not unite in one general effulgence. And we foon turn away, tired with the tedious and unimpreffive variation of faintnefs.

The whole chapter, alfo, is equally *without notes* and *without references*. Mr. Gibbon *profeffes* to give only 'a rapid abftract, which may be fupported by a *general* appeal to the order and text of the original hiftorians[3].' We therefore go on, entirely at the mercy of our conductor. He is equally left to the mercy of his own difcretion. And we know his conduct too well already, even when he was harneffed in the trammels of reference and authentication; to truft this hiftorical Pegafus, without either bit or bridle.

[1] p. 85.   [2] p. 86.   [3] p. 4,

But there is a much greater fault behind. 'In
'this introduction,' says Mr. Gibbon, concerning
the present chapter, 'I shall *confine* myself to *the re-*
'*volutions of the throne*, the *succession of families*, the
'*personal characters* of the Greek princes, the *mode*
'*of their life and death*, the *maxims and influence of*
'*their domestic government*, and the *tendency of their*
'*reign to accelerate or suspend the downfal of the east-*
'*ern empire* [1].' This is a very ingenious way of *con-*
fining himself. He will *confine* himself to *six* points,
when he ought to confine himself to *one* of them. The
last is the only point, that carries any relation to the
decline and *fall* of the empire. He therefore promised formally at the beginning, to confine himself to
the 'circumstances,' and 'the most important'
circumstances 'of its decline and fall.' And the
plain good-sense of criticism, the eternal laws of
composition, require that he should adhere to his
promise. Yet so much has the habit of rambling
gained the ascendant, over the suggestions of reason, the convictions of his mind, and the promises
of his pen; that he professes *now* to dwell *only* upon
six points, of which five are all extraneous to the
purpose. He will not fly to the fixed stars. He
will go *only* to the moon. And yet, all the while,
his business is wholly upon earth.

'Such a chronological *review*,' as the present
chapter gives of the imperial history, 'will serve to
'illustrate the various argument of the subsequent

[1] P. 5.

'chapters;

' chapters; and each circumstance of the eventful
' history of the barbarians, will adapt itself in a pro-
' per place to the Byzantine annals'. We are
thus to have the history of the empire detached and
entire by itself, and then the history of its invaders
equally entire and detached. This is surely a most
strange and absurd disposition, of the parts of his
history. It is such as was never projected and
never executed, we believe, by any *sound* understanding before. The subsequent chapters *may* be
' illustrated,' by the present; but the narration in
them would have been infinitely more illustrated,
by the *natural* union of this with that. The circumstances in the history of the barbarians, *may*
adapt themselves to their proper places in the
annals of Byzantium; but they would have been
infinitely better adapted, by an *actual* assignment of
them at the moment. Mr. Gibbon has robbed the
domestic and foreign history, of all their reciprocal
connexion; and so has deprived each of all the *seen*
and *apparent* illumination, that each casts upon the
other. He has thrown the history of all the events,
into great and independent masses of narration.
He has ranged them in a number of parallel lines,
that never meet. And the grand sun of historical
information, he has cut and carved into a multitude
of twinkling stars. Nor is this conduct less injuri-
ous to the unity of Mr. Gibbon's history, than it is
contrary to the principles of sense. Those parts of
the domestic history, which should connect the foreign

¹ P. 5.

with

with it, and so unite to form one long and regular chain of history; are all formed into a little chain by themselves, and leave the rest to be equally formed into little chains, all unconnected with each other. And instead of that golden chain, which should be linked to the head of the first chapter, spread thro' all the chapters subsequent, and form one universe of harmonious history; we are presented with a few links in one chapter, a few in another, all detached from all, and forming only the fragments of a disordered and broken system. Yet all this was necessary, to the prosecution of Mr. Gibbon's purposes. He found the regular and orderly sphere of history, too narrow for his excursions. He therefore frames a new one! It is indeed a disgrace to his own judgment, and an affront upon his reader's understanding. Yet he risks the affront and he incurs the disgrace, rather than not indulge himself still farther in his flights. And we must prepare our minds for extravagances of digression, beyond all the extravagances that we have seen before. From the strong and violent beating of its wings, we see the eagle is anticipating a higher and a wider range, than it has taken yet.

There are many instances of *harshness*, in the language of this chapter. ' I have now *deduced—* ' the—*series* of the Roman *emperors*[1],' ' the pompous *ceremonies*, which formed the *essence* of the ' Byzantine state[2];' ' Martina reaped the *harvest* of ' his *death*[3];' ' their *silence respects* the wisdom of his

---

[1] p. 1.   [2] p. 8.   [3] p. 9.

' administration

' administration and the purity of his manners¹,'
where the double sense of the word *respects* confounds the reader, and where the language should have been, *their silence of reprehension shews a respect for*, &c.; ' when *he* was *extinguished* by a timely ' death²;' finally vanished *in*,' read *at* ' the presence of a soldier³;' ' naval armies' for a fleet⁴; ' the *ceremony* of his funeral was mourned,' read *was attended*, ' with the unfeigned tears of his sub-' jects⁵;' and ' a promise—was *stolen* by a dex-' terous emissary from the—patriarch⁶,' read, *drawn artfully*, as the context shews the author means.

There are several instances of *obscurity*. ' The ' chances of superior merit in a great and populous ' kingdom, as they are proved by experience, ' would excuse the imputation of imaginary mil-' lions⁷;' ' the tyrant, a law of eternal justice, was ' degraded by the vices of his subjects⁸;' '*public* ' *method*,' of what? ' secured the interest of the ' prince and the property of the people⁹;' ' Con-' stantine died before his father, whose grief and ' credulity were amused by a flattering impostor ' and a vain apparition¹⁰,' an instance of Mr. Gibbon's rapid way of writing history *at times*, as no more is said, and as this only serves to

> Fling half an image on the straining eye;

' some evasion and perjury were required to silence

¹ P. 21. ² p. 45. ³ ibid. ⁴ ibid. ⁵ p. 47.
⁶ p. 60. ⁷ p. 3. ⁸ ibid. ⁹ p. 42. ¹⁰ p. 43.

' the

'the scruples of the clergy and people¹, another instance of the same; 'the first in the front of battle was thrown from his horse by the stroke of poison or an arrow²,' another instance; and 'a promise, which would have betrayed her falsehood and levity, was stolen by a dexterous emissary from the ambition of the patriarch; Xiphilin at first alleged the sanctity of oaths and the sacred nature of a trust, but,' &c³.

There are even some *contradictions*. Leo the emperor beholds Michael his successor, 'released from his chain⁴;' and yet Michael has 'the fetters remaining on his legs, several hours after he was seated on the throne of the Cæsars⁵.'—— 'Theophano,—after a reign of four years,— *mingled* for her husband the same deadly draught, which she had composed for his father⁶.' Yet all that we have heard of this before, was merely in these words: 'the death of Constantine was imputed to poison⁷.' He was then *supposed* to be poisoned; it is now *certain* that he was, and *by whom*; even by Theophano. And '*his son Romanus*,' as Mr. Gibbon told us *before*, was the person '*suspected* of anticipating his inheritance⁸.' *Then* Romanus is *suspected* of poisoning his father; *now* his wife Theophano is *asserted* to have poisoned him. ——' The promise—was *stolen* by a dexterous emissary from the ambition of the patriarch; Xiphilin

¹ p. 50.   ² p. 53.   ³ p. 60.   ⁴ p. 30.
⁵ p. 31.   ⁶ p. 48.   ⁷ p. ibid.   ⁸ ibid.

'at

' at first alleged,' &c.; ' but a whisper—relaxed
' his scruples, and he—*resigned the important paper*¹.'
How could he *resign*, what had been previously *stolen*
from him?

There are also some *absurdities*. ' By the im-
' position of *holy orders*, the grandson of Heraclius
' was disqualified for the purple; but this ceremo-
' ny, which seemed to profane *the sacraments* of the
' church,' &c.²; where the PAPIST unites with the
deist, in making *orders* to be one of the *sacraments*,
and in sneering at them. ' To her bloody deed,
' superstition has attributed a darkness of seventeen
' days,—as if the sun—COULD sympathise with the
' *atoms* of a revolving planet ³;' where the author
plainly betrays himself to be, what he so much endeavours to conceal, an actual and absolute ATHEIST.
—' Nor can we blame his pusillanimous resigna-
' tion, since *a Greek Christian was no longer master of
' his life*⁴. This is another vindication of that
horrible doctrine of SELF-MURDER, which this historian has so formally justified before. And we
thus see him mounting in this single chapter, by a
natural gradation of profligacy, from popery to
deism, to atheism, and to self-murder.

Chapter the SECOND,

or forty-ninth.—This contains the history of what?
of the *western empire* again. We have an account

¹ p. 60.   ² p. 11.   ³ p. 27.   ⁴ p. 84.

of the Lombards, of the Romans, and of the Franks. We see the Romans renouncing the sovereignty of Constantinople, the Lombards supporting it and attacking Rome, and the Franks marching over the Alps, crushing the Lombards, giving the popes a sovereignty over Ravenna, and erecting for themselves a new empire in the west. And we have the general history of this, of France, of Germany, and of Italy, to the fourteenth century. Thus doth the ghost of the western empire, continue to haunt us still.

> The tomb, in which we saw it quietly in-urn'd,
> Hath op'd its ponderous and marble jaws
> To let it out again.

And we need only repeat what we have said so often before, that Mr. Gibbon was merely to give us, according to his own acknowledgment, ' the most ' important circumstances of the decline and fall' of the *eastern* empire. Indeed in all this long detail of things foreign and adventitious, we lose sight of the eastern empire almost entirely. We have only now and then a solitary and incidental mention of it. Our eye was very lately promised, to be ' always fixed upon the city of Constantinople ;' yet we have merely one or two squinting looks at it. And Mr. Gibbon forgets equally his first and his last promises, in his overbearing love of the excentric and the extravagant.

The *harsh* or *false language* in this chapter, may be thus exemplified : ' the *ample measure* of the ex-
                                                ' archate,'

' archate¹,' for the *largeſt dimenſions;* ' he ſecretly
' *edified* the throne of his ſucceſſors²;' ' his corona-
' tion-oath *repreſents* a promiſe to maintain³,' &c.
inſtead of contains; ' the *foundation,*' meaning the
erection, ' of eight biſhopricks—*define* [defines]' for
marks, ' on either ſide of the Weſer, the bounds of
' ancient Saxony⁴;' and ' each city *filled* the *meaſure*
' of,' for *was commenſurate with,* ' her *dioceſe* or *diſ-
' trict⁵.*'

The following paſſages are proofs of *obſcurity.—*
P. 90. ' the gracious and often ſupernatural fa-
' vours, which, in the popular belief, were ſhower-
' ed round their tomb,' that of ſaints and martyrs,
' *conveyed an unqueſtionable ſanction* of the devout
' pilgrims,' &c.   What does this mean?——
P. 116, ' at the next aſſembly, *the field of March or*
' *of May,* his injuries were,' &c.——P. 134, ' the
' reign of Adrian the Firſt ſurpaſſes the meaſure of
' paſt or ſucceeding ages,' in what? in *profligacy,*
we ſuppoſe from the context, but in *number of years,*
as the note intimates.——P. 159, ' their revenue,
' *from minute and vexatious prerogative,* was ſcarcely
' ſufficient,' &c.

Nor are theſe paſſages more dark in the tranſcript,
than they are in the original.

Contradictions.——In this chapter we come back
to thoſe ſubſtantial pillars of hiſtory, notes and references. For want of them, the hiſtorical edifice before was only like a fairy fabric, reared upon a foundation of air, and glittering with the colours of the

¹ P. 123. ² p. 134. ³ p. 136. ⁴ p. 143. ⁵ p. 160.

rainbow.

rainbow. But, as we recover our notes, we return also to the old opposition between them and the text. 'The inhabitants of the dutchy of Spoleto 'sought a refuge from the storm, declared *themselves* 'the servants and subjects of St. Peter, and *com-* '*pleted*, by this voluntary surrender, *the present circle* '*of the ecclesiastical state*¹.' This is peremptory, for the surrender of *themselves* and of their *country* to the popes. Yet the note, after citing the passage on which the text is founded, contradicts the latter in this manner: '*it may be a question*, whether 'they gave *their own persons* or their *country*.'——
'The king of the Franks and Lombards asserted 'the inalienable rights of the empire; and, in his 'life and death, *Ravenna*, as well as Rome, was 'numbered in the list of *his* metropolitical cities².' Ravenna then was considered by Charlemagne, as *his* city. Yet the note says thus of him: '*Charle-* '*magne* solicited and obtained from the *proprietor* '*Adrian the First*, the mosaics of the *palace* of *Ra-* '*venna*.'——'A synod of three hundred *bishops* was 'assembled at Frankfort³.' But the subjoined note says, that this number 'must include, *not only* the '*bishops*, but the *abbots*, and even the *principal lay-* '*men*.'—So much are the notes and the text, playing at cross purposes with each other!

Absurdity.—' Both Selden—and Montesquieu— ' represent Charlemagne, as the first *legal* author of ' tithes. Such obligations have country gentle- ' men to his memory !' Country gentlemen have

¹ p. 124.   ² ibid.   ³ p. 131.

G   neither

neither obligation, nor disobligation, to the memory of Charlemagne, for this; unless Mr. Gibbon thinks that there are any of them, who possessed their estates *before* Charlemagne imposed the payment of tithes. If they bought or inherited them, with the burden already upon them; they are not injured. But indeed it is only ignorance, in Mr. Gibbon, Montesquieu, and Selden; that could attribute the first payment of tithes to Charlemagne. He reigned from the middle of the eighth century, to the beginning of the ninth. And Boniface, archbishop of Mentz but a native of England, who was born in 670; testifies tithes to have been paid by the *English* in his time, *one whole century* at least before Charlemagne. They were paid undoubtedly; and *legally* too, or they would not have been paid at all; from the first legal establishment of Christianity, in the island and on the continent [1].

Chapter the THIRD,

or fiftieth.—This proposes to give us ' the genius
' of the Arabian prophet, the manners of his na-
' tion, and the spirit of his religion;' which ' in-
' volve the causes of the decline and fall of the east-
' ern empire [2].' We have accordingly, up to p. 196, an account of Arabia, its geography, its manners, its history, &c. To p. 219 we have Mahomet's parentage, life, and Koran, described; to p. 237 the success of Mahomet in converting his own family, his expulsion from Mecca, his reception at

[1] Hist. of Manchester, II. quarto, 438—439.
[2] p. 170.

Medina, and his plundering expeditions in the deserts of Arabia; to p. 240 his reduction of Mecca; and to p. 256 his history to his death. We thus have *eighty-six* quarto pages, one *eighth* of the whole volume, laid out in what is merely the *private* history (as if it were) of Mahomet. That the great and striking principles of Mahometanism, and the marking features of Mahomet's character and life, should have been produced before the reader; was requisite to the illumination of the history. But nothing more was requisite. And as this might have been executed in a quarter part of the space actually taken, so would it have made a deeper impression on the reader. But Mr. Gibbon has always an unhappy propensity to dissertation. He loves to spin his long web of threads, that are ready to break at every touch; while he lays his history fairly to slumber. He forgets, in his travels through Arabia, and during his residence in it, that he is writing the history of the decline and fall of the Roman empire; that, if one foot of his historical compasses may be stretched with propriety, for a short time, into the deserts there, it can only be for a short time, and the other must remain centered and fixed at Constantinople all the while; and that his own reason has prescribed, and his own pen has promised, to dwell only upon the ' important,' and the ' most important,' circumstances of its decline and fall.

But Mr. Gibbon has inflamed the absurdity of this devious chapter, by giving us a list and an account of Mahomet's successors, Abubeker, Omar, Othman,

Othman, and Ali, to p. 262; with an account of the civil war between the Mahometans, p. 262—265; the fucceffion of Moawiyah, and the change of government from elective to hereditary, p. 266—271; all 'anticipated' confeffedly, and therefore containing a hint in p. 262, that the Mahometans had now reduced 'Perfia, Syria, and Egypt,' and in p. 267, that they were even befieging Conftantinople; when we have hardly feen them yet breaking out from Arabia. This ' anticipation' feems to be purely the refult of wantonnefs, as we are afterwards to attend the progrefs of the Mahometan arms, and to accompany the armies of thofe very men, Ali, Othman, Omar, and Abubeker, in their reduction of the countries. And the only reafon, which he has affigned for this act of wantonnefs, is this; ' that the merit and misfortunes of Ali ' and his defcendants lead him to *anticipate*, in this ' place, the feries of the Saracen caliphs.' The reafon appears as trifling, as the conduct is extravagant.

The hiftory in this chapter carries a peculiar air of *obfcurity* with it. It is very frequently unintelligible. And we are ready to invoke Œdipus, to come and explain the enigmatic paffages. But we pafs over the *obfcure expreffions*, and alfo the *falfe language*, in order to mark more fully fome *contradictions* and fome *abfurdities*.

' Mahomet *placed* himfelf, with Abubeker, on a ' *throne* or *pulpit*[1].' So fays the text. But what adds the note? ' The *place*, to which Mahomet *retired*

[1] p. 232.

' during

' during the action, is styled by Gagnier—*umbra-*
' *culum, une loge de bois avec une porte.* The same
' Arabic word is rendered by Reiske,—by *folium,*
' *suggestus editior*; and the difference is of the ut-
' most moment, for the honour both of the inter-
' preter and the hero.' Yet without settling or attempting to settle, by arguments in the note, this
' difference of the utmost moment;' Mr. Gibbon
has decided it without any argument in the text,
and fixed it to be ' a throne or pulpit.' And then
the note comes to decide *against* this decision, to in-
timate the place may be some shed or cabin of
wood, and to say that Mahomet 'retired' to it
during the action.

Text. The ' *dream* of a nocturnal journey is se-
' riously described, as a real and corporeal transac-
' tion¹.' Note. ' The nocturnal *journey* is *cir-*
' *cumstantially related* by Abulfeda,—who *wishes* to
' think it a vision.—Yet the Koran, without nam-
' ing either heaven, or Jerusalem, or Mecca, has
' only dropt a mysterious hint, *laus illi qui transtulit*
' *servum suum ab oratorio Haram ad oratorium remo-*
' *tissimum.*—A slender basis for the aerial structure
' of tradition!' Mr. Gibbon first makes the journey
to be a *dream*. He then refers to Abulfeda, who
makes it a *reality*; circumstantially relating it, and
only wishing, from the gross absurdity, to resolve it
(if he could) into a dream. And he next produces
a passage from the Koran, which shews it decisively to be a *reality*. He produces it in confirmation of
the text, and in evidence of its being a *dream*. Yet

¹ p. 211.

it proves it *not* to be a dream, in the plainest manner. The paſſage praiſes God, for *tranſlating* his ſervant *from the oratory Haram*, &c.; ' *tranſtulit* ' ſervum ſuum *ab oratorio Haram*,' &c. And Mr. Gibbon, who ſays the Koran mentions not Mecca, is deceived by his inattention; the ' oratorium Haram' being the temple of Mecca, which is called in Arabic *Masjad al Haram*, or ſimply *Al Haram* and *Haram*, the ſacred temple '; and Mr. Gibbon himſelf accordingly carrying Mahomet in the text, ' from ' the' very ' temple of Mecca².

This *dream*, as Mr. Gibbon calls it, he thus deſcribes in ſhort. ' A myſterious animal, the Borax, ' conveyed him from the temple of Mecca to that ' of Jeruſalem; with his companion Gabriel, he ' ſucceſſively aſcended the ſeven heavens, and re- ' ceived and repaid the ſalutations of the patriarchs, ' the prophets, and the angels, in their reſpective ' manſions.' But let us dwell a little more particularly on this ſubject, than Mr. Gibbon chuſes to do. The *dreams* of ſuch a Homer as this in theology, are worth our attention. And as a narrative of this nocturnal journey will uſefully expoſe the credulity of thoſe, who, like Mr. Gibbon, think ' a ' philoſophical theiſt might ſubſcribe the popular ' creed of the Mahometans³; ſo I ſhall ſoon ſhew it to be a reality, even in the opinions of the Mahometans themſelves, and to form a fundamental article in that very creed. Al Borak then was an

---

[1] Modern Univerſal Hiſt. 1. 207, 74, and 28, octavo.
[2] p. 211. [3] p. 204.

animal

animal, which had a man's face, a horse's jaws, eagle's wings, and eyes like stars; which could move as swift as the lightning, but *was informed with a rational soul,* yet had not naturally *the power of speech*; which begged of Mahomet *to be introduced into heaven* at the day of judgment, and to which Mahomet actually *promised a place* there. This hippogryffin of Mahomet's carried him to the *temple* of Jerusalem, where he met Abraham, Moses, and OUR SAVIOUR, with a number of prophets and angels. These all went to prayer with him. He then ascended without the beast, and with only the angel Gabriel, to the first heaven; where he saw angels of all sorts and shapes. Some were in the form of *birds*, and some in that of *beasts*, being the angels that interceded *for birds and beasts* respectively. One of the former was a *cock*, being the *angel of cocks*; and of so prodigious a size, that with his *head* he *touched* the second heaven, though a *journey of five hundred years* above the first. In the second heaven he saw another angel, *whose head reached up to the third*, though equally a *journey of five hundred years distant from it*. In the third, he saw another, who was so large and big, that the space *between* his *eyes* only, was a distance equal to a *journey of seventy thousand days*; an angel, according to the proportions of *this* part of his body, that could not *possibly* have stood *within any one, even of Mahomet's heavens*. In the fourth heaven he saw an angel, as tall as any before, and reaching equally in height a *journey of five hundred years*. In the fifth and sixth he saw no more

more of these tall angels. But, in the seventh, he saw one with *seventy thousand heads, seventy thousand tongues in every head,* and *seventy thousand distinct voices* coming at the same time from *every tongue;* and another with a *million* of *heads,* a *million* of *tongues,* and a *million* of *voices.* And, as he saw Abraham, Moses, and our Saviour, at Jerusalem; so he saw Adam in the first heaven, our Saviour *again,* and John, in the second, David and Solomon in the third, Aaron and Enoch in the fifth, Moses *again* in the sixth, Abraham *again,* and *again* our Saviour, in the seventh; and *recommended himself to the prayers of* our Saviour, though all the other prophets and saints recommended *themselves* to Mahomet's prayers. So truly in its *substance* is this nocturnal journey a *vision* and a *dream,* even the dream of sickness, and the vision of insanity! Yet it was all related by Mahomet, as a reality. *He related it the next morning.* But it was received, even by the credulous Arabs, with a general burst of contempt. Some laughed at the extravagance of the fiction. Some were indignant at the effrontery of the imposture. Mahomet was very properly challenged therefore, to ascend up to the heavens again, not by night but by day, and in the sight of them all. Yet this bold fiction was the grand hinge, upon which the prophetic character of the impostor turned. Could he not induce them to swallow such fictions as these, he would have resigned his title of a prophet, and have sunk into a mere warrior. But they did swallow it. Their credulity was even as

gigantic,

gigantic, as his falsehoods. And as Abubeker vouched *at the time*, for the *truth* and *reality* of all that Mahomet had related, when (according to Mr. Gibbon himself in a *distant* passage) 'the *veracity* of 'Abubeker *confirmed* the religion of the prophet[1];' and as Mahomet introduces God in two parts of the Koran, swearing by the stars, &c. to the truth of Mahomet's admission into his presence: so, even in the early days of Omar the second successor to Mahomet, a Mahometan general alleges for the surrendery of Jerusalem to him, that 'Mahomet himself went from it in one night to heaven;' all the Mahometans in general have ever since considered a disbelief of this journey, to be a disbelief of the Koran itself; and all the Turks in particular observe a grand festival to this day, on the twentieth night of their month Rajed, for the very night in which this journey was performed[2]. To such sottishness of credulity are those reduced, who would fly from the mysteries of Christianity to the monsters of Mahometanism!

Mahomet, says Mr. Gibbon, in this nocturnal journey, 'passed *the veil of unity*, and approached 'within *two bowshots* of the throne, and felt a cold 'that pierced him to the heart, when his *shoulder* 'was touched by the *hand* of God[3].' What is this 'veil of unity,' and whence did Mr. Gibbon derive

---

[1] P. 220.

[2] Prideaux's Life of Mahomet, p. 53—66, 2d Edit. 1697; and Modern Univ. Hist. 1. 65—81, and 424.

[3] p. 211.

it?

it? There is no such 'veil,' I apprehend, in the Mahometan accounts of this journey. Nor what a 'veil of unity' means, is it easy to guess. And I suspect Mr. Gibbon to have borrowed it, by some strange misconception, from *the seventy thousand veils*, that this madman represents to have been before the face of God[1]. As to the 'two bow-shots,' these have been corrected by a late author into *two bow-lengths*[2]; though this very author has forgot to adopt his own correction, in the progress of the history[3]. And, as to the *hand* of God applied to the *shoulder* of Mahomet, God is said to have put *one* of his hands upon the *shoulder*, and *another upon the breast*, of Mahomet[4].

'In *the prophetic style*, which uses *the present or past for the future*, Mahomet had said, *appropinquavit hora, et scissa est luna*.—This figure of rhetoric has been converted into a fact, which is said to be attested by the most respectable witnesses.—The festival is still celebrated by the Persians[5].' Mr. Gibbon here, and in the passage preceding, mistakes totally the nature of the Koran. The hints in it have *not* been made 'the basis of traditions.' The traditional is the *full* story, and the Koran contains only the *abstract* of it. We see this very evident in the passage before. The whole history of Mahomet's nocturnal journey, from the temple of Mecca to the seventh heaven; was *related*

---

[1] Prideaux, p. 63. [2] Modern Univ. Hist. 1. 76.
[3] Ibid. 1. 424. [4] Ibid. 1. 76.
[5] p. 212.

by himself the very next morning, to his countrymen of Mecca. Yet the Koran contains no more account of it, than this general one; that God 'transtulit servum suum ab oratorio Haram ad oratorium remotissimum;' not as Mr. Gibbon has wildly asserted before, 'without naming either Heaven, or Jerusalem, or Mecca,' which would make the whole most amazingly ridiculous; but naming *Mecca* (as I have already shewn) by its customary appellation among the Arabs, *Masjed al Haram*, or temple Haram; and equally naming *Jerusalem* assuredly, by its equally customary appellation among them, of *Masjed al Aksi* or *Aksa*, the farther temple, or the temple most remote, as the temple of Jerusalem *is actually denominated by the Arabian Abulfeda himself*[1]. In the ideas of Mahomet himself, and of his followers for ages, there were only two temples in the world worthy of their notice, that of Mecca, and this of Jerusalem; that they called the Holy Mosque, and this they denominated the Farther one. This passage in the Koran, therefore, is actually posterior in time, to the recital of the story the next morning; is to be explained by the tradition of it; and is accordingly explained so by the Mahometans themselves, to this day. And the case is nearly similar, with the present passage. It is no prophecy. It is merely, like the former, an intimation of a story related by himself. Only here the intimation is as full as the relation, and the Koran *therefore* is a sufficient witness of its own

[1] Modern Univ. Hist. 3. 304.

meaning.

meaning. The Koran itself relates the incident, not as a future, but as a past, fact. 'The hour 'hath approached,' it says, 'and the moon *hath* '*been* split asunder; but *if they see a sign*, they turn 'aside, saying *this is a powerful charm*; and they 'accuse of *imposture*,' &c.'. Here the context proves demonstrably, that the *prophetic* interpretation of the passage is only a sorry subterfuge of Mr. Gibbon's, equally against grammar and good-sense. Mahomet here appears, actually alleging such a miracle to have been wrought by him, and confessing the people not to have believed it. Even one of his *personal* followers, Ebn Masud, affirmed he beheld the miracle with his own eyes; and even saw mount Hara, one of the hills near Mecca, appear at the time between the two divisions of the moon[2]. Accordingly 'it is said,' Mr. Gibbon himself tells us, 'to be attested by the most respectable eye-wit-'nesses.' And, as the fact is believed by the Mahometans in general[3]; so Mr Gibbon again allows 'the festival' of it, to be, 'still celebrated by the 'Persians' in particular. So unhappy is Mr Gibbon, in all his attempts to strip Mahometanism, of its pretended miracles of action, and its real prodigies of absurdity!

Text. 'A small portion of ground, the patri-'mony of two orphans, was acquired by *gift* or *pur-*'*chase*.' Note. 'Prideaux—reviles the wicked-'ness of the impostor, who despoiled two poor or-

[1] Modern Univ. Hist. 1. 62.   [2] Ibid. ibid.
[3] Ibid. ibid. and 84.

' phans, the sons of a carpenter; a reproach which
' he drew from the Disputatio contra Saracenos,
' composed in Arabic *before* the year 1130; but the
' *honest* Gagnier—has *shewn*, that *they were deceived*
' *by* the word *Al Nagjar*, which signifies in this
' place, not an obscure trade, but a noble tribe of
' Arabs. The desolate state of the ground is de-
' scribed by Abulfeda; and his *worthy* interpreter
' has proved, from Al Bochari, the *offer of a price*;
' from Al Jannabi, *the fair purchase*; and from Ah-
' med Ben Joseph, *the payment of the money by the*
' *generous Abubeker*. On these grounds *the prophet*
' *must be honourably acquitted*[1].' We here see the
zeal, with which Mr. Gibbon, taking the *honest* and
worthy Gagnier for his associate in the work, labours
to prove the innocence of Mahomet in this transac-
tion. But the evidence of Gagnier in favour of Mahomet, had been fairly stated before in Modern
Universal History[2]; and the reader too candidly left
to judge, between the accusation and the defence.
Mr. Gibbon therefore has only the merit, of producing the evidence at second hand. Nor can we
after all say with Mr. Gibbon, that Mahomet 'must
' be honourably acquitted.' To assert that Prideaux and his author ' were deceived' into the story, by mistaking the name of an Arab tribe for the
name of a business; is only to trifle with the reader.
A *circumstance*, like this, cannot in the remotest degree affect the *substance* of the story. And, even in
the point itself, whether a writer, who (as we shall

[1] p. 227.   [2] Vol. 1. p. 95, 96.

instantly

inftantly fhew) 'lived in the court of a Saracen caliph, was likely to confound the name of a Saracen tribe, with that of a particular profeffion, and to know the very language of the country, *worfe* than an European of the prefent century; or whether Peter of Toledo, who tranflated the Arabic original into Latin, was likely to know it *worfe* than Gagnier, who *never faw the original*, and only guefled at it *through* and *againft* the tranflation; let common-fenfe decide. ' It is recorded as an inftance of his [Ma-
' homet's] injuftice,' fays Prideaux on the authority of Difputatio Chriftiani, c. 4, ' that he violently
' difpoffeffed certain poor orphans, the children of
' an inferior artificer a little before deceafed, of the
' ground on which it,' a mofque at Medina, ' ftood;
' and fo founded this firft fabric for his worfhip,
' with the like wickednefs as he did his religion [1].'
The work here alleged by Prideaux, fays Mr. Gibbon, was written ' before the year 1130.' It was in all probability written *very long* before, as it was *then* tranflated out of Arabic into Latin. It was written too, by one who actually held an office in the court of a Saracen caliph; and was addreffed by him to his friend, a Mahometan [2]. It forms therefore a very important authority. Againft it, is produced Al Bochari, who died in 869, Al Jannabi, whofe hiftory comes down to 1588, and Ahmed Ben Jofeph, who finifhed his in 1599 [3]. The only witnefs

[1] Prideaux's Life of Mahomet, p. 76.
[2] Prideaux's Letter to Deifts, p. 163.
[3] Ibid. ibid. p. 157, 159, and 154.

of moment against him, therefore, is Al Bochari. And he attests only 'the *offer* of a price;' which is very consistent with the relation of Prideaux's author, and indeed implies it. A price being only *offered*, and not *given*; it being inadequate, I suppose, and therefore refused; the ground was taken away by violence. Nor, even if we admit all the three witnesses in favour of Mahomet, can he be acquitted. Al Bochari alleges, that a price was *offered*. But Al Jannabi denies this, says a price was *given*, and so 'a fair purchase' was made by Mahomet. And then Ahmed Ben Joseph comes, contradicts Al Jannabi, and avers no purchase to have been made by *Mahomet*, but the purchase to have been actually made by *Abubeker*, he paying the money. Thus do Mahomet's witnesses confound themselves, and confirm the accusation. But let us consider the story, upon the face of all these testimonies united. From Al Bochari we learn, that a price was offered by Mahomet, and not accepted by the owners. From Prideaux's author we find, that the land was *then* taken away by Mahomet. From Ahmed Ben Joseph we understand, that this violence was urged against Mahomet, as it is actually urged by Prideaux's author; and that *therefore* Abubeker paid for it the money, *which the owners had demanded for it*. For this *reason* Al Jannabi declares the ground to have been fairly purchased. And, as this appears to be nearly or wholly the real state of the case, from Mahomet's living *ten* years after he had seized the ground, and built

x his

his mosque upon it [1], and from Abubeker's *then* succeeding Mahomet, and *then* paying the money; so the whole reflects all the disgrace upon Mahomet, that Prideaux had cast upon him for it. Mr. Gibbon thus appears unfortunate again, in his zeal for the honour of Mahometanism! Nor is it worth while perhaps to notice his confusedness of ideas, in all this. His text speaks of the land being 'acquired by *gift* or *purchase.*' Yet his note endeavours to disprove all '*gift*,' by proving the whole a '*purchase.*' And, even though he brings several authorities, for a price being either offered or given for the land; he intimates the land to be worth no price at all, as ' the *desolate* state of the ground,' he says ' is described by Abulfeda.' So much has the Mahometan here confounded the critic, in Mr. Gibbon!

' A friendly tribe, instructed *(I know not how)* in
' the art of sieges, supplied him with a train of bat-
' tering *rams* and *military engines*, with a body of
' five hundred *artificers* [2].' He should have said in propriety, just as the Mod. Univ. Hist. says, ' with
' battering rams, *catapults*, and *all other* military
' machines employed in such operations; together
' with *the most skilful engineers to play them*; with
' which he was supplied by the tribe of *Daws*, the
' *the most famous of all the Arabs for such artificers* [3].'
This would have resolved his difficulty at once, concerning the derivation of such knowledge to the

[1] Prideaux's Life of Mahomet, p. 88.   [2] p. 241.
[3] Mod. Univ. Hist. 1. 185.

tribe. It was common to *all* the Arabs. Only *this tribe* was *the moſt famous* among them for it. And accordingly Mahomet appears upon *another* occaſion, and in *another hiſtory*, to have ' battered ' the wall' of a town ' ſome days, with his *rams* ' and *other* military engines¹.'

P. 233. 'Drams of ſilver.' Mr. Gibbon has here, and in 246, &c. &c. &c. confounded a *weight* with a *coin*. Theſe 'drams of ſilver' were *ſilver drachmæ*, current among all the orientals, and denominated *dirhems* by the Arabs².

Note. ' The *diploma ſecuritatis Ailenſibus* is at-
' teſted by Ahmed Ben Joſeph, and the author *Li-*
' *bri ſplendorum* (Gagnier, Not. ad Abulfedam, p.
' 125); but Abulfeda himſelf, as well as Elmacin
' (Hiſt. Saracen. p. 11), though he owns Maho-
' met's regard for the Chriſtians (p. 13), *only* men-
' tion *peace* and *tribute*. In the year 1630, Sionita
' publiſhed at Paris the text and verſion, of Maho-
' met's patent in favour of the Chriſtians; which
' was admitted and reprobated by the oppoſite taſte
' of Salmaſius and Grotius (Bayle, MAHOMET.
' Rem. AA). Hottinger doubts of its authenticity
' (Hiſt. Orient. p. 237); Renaudot urges the con-
' ſent of the Mahometans (Hiſt. Patriarch. Alex. p.
' 169); but Moſheim ſhews the futility of their o-
' pinion, and inclines to believe it ſpurious. Yet
' Abulpharagius quotes the impoſtor's treaty
' with the Neſtorian patriarch (Aſſeman. Bib-
' liot. Orient. tom. 11. p. 418), but Abul-

¹ Mod. Univ. Hiſt. 1. 152.   ² Ibid. 1. 118, 194, 223, &c.

' pharagius

'pharagius was primate of the Jacobites¹.' I have cited this long note with all its pomp of erudition, in order to exhibit Mr. Gibbon *just as he would wish to be exhibited*; and to point out what he would *not* wish to have pointed out, the solemn trifling of all. What is the conclusion of this *parade* of authorities, and this *pageantry* of arguments? Who can tell? Is the diploma genuine or spurious? Reason encounters reason, authority clashes with authority, and ' man drives man along.' This is very ridiculous in itself. But it is more ridiculous, when we consider the intention of the note. It was drawn up *in order* to decide. And it is still more ridiculous, when the note was to decide *in favour of the text*, and to *corroborate what it had said*. ' To ' his Christian subjects,' says the text, ' Mahomet ' readily granted *the security of their persons*, the *freedom of their trade*, the *property of their goods*, and ' *the toleration of their worship*.' The note was then to prove as the text asserts. But Mr. Gibbon forgot his purposes, in the predominance of his learning. The note left the text in the lurch. And, opposing the text by alleging Elmacin and Abulfeda for only peace and tribute, it produces nothing ultimately in favour of it. The text is undoubtedly wrong, and the diploma is undoubtedly spurious. Mr. Gibbon, amidst all his authorities and reasons, has forgotten to produce a decisive one of either. There is a ' particular in it,' says Prideaux concerning the diploma, ' which manifestly discovers the forgery. ' It makes Moawias, the son of Abu Sophian, to be

¹ p. 245.

' the

'the *secretary* to the impostor, *who drew the instru-* '*ment*; whereas it is certain, that Moawias, with his 'father Abu Sophian, was *then in arms against him*; 'and it was not till the taking of Mecca, *which was* '*four years after*, that *they came in unto him*, and to save 'their lives embraced the imposture [1].' But let me add what is still more decisive perhaps, that it is dated in the fourth month of the *fourth* year of the *Hegira*, or flight of Mahomet; when the *Hegira* was *not* made an æra of computation, till *eighteen* years after the flight [2]. The instrument is thus proved to be a forgery, by those strongest signatures of a forgery, two false dates! Mr. Gibbon's text, therefore, is entirely overthrown, and his note is completely superseded. His remark too, concerning this diploma, from 'Abulpharagius quoting the 'impostor's treaty with the Nestorian patriarch;' and his reply to it, from 'Abulpharagius being 'the primate of the Jacobites;' is all confusion. Abulpharagius was not 'primate of the Jacobites.' He was merely a *physician* among them [3]. And the treaty with the Nestorian patriarch, was *six years after* the date of this diploma [4].

'*The perpetual independence* of the *Arabs* has been 'the theme of *praise*, among *strangers* and *natives*; 'and the arts of controversy transform this singular '*event*, into a prophecy and a miracle, in favour of 'the posterity of Ishmael. *Some exceptions*, that can 'neither be dissembled nor eluded, render this

[1] Prideaux's Life of Mahomet, p. 157—158.
[2] Compare Prideaux's Life, p. 158 with p. 78.
[3] Ibid. Letter to Deists, p. 153.
[4] Modern Univ. Hist. 1. 205, 206.

'mode

'mode of reasoning as indiscreet as it is superflu-
'ous.' He then mentions the exceptions, and adds:
'yet *these exceptions* are *temporary* or *local*; the BODY
'OF THE NATION HAS ESCAPED THE YOKE OF THE
'MOST POWERFUL MONARCHIES; the arms of *Sesos-*
'*tris* and *Cyrus*, of *Pompey* and *Trajan*, *could never*
'*atchieve the conquest of Arabia*; the present sove-
'reign of the *Turks* may exercise a *shadow* of ju-
'risdiction, but his pride is reduced *to solicit the*
'*friendship of a people*, whom it is dangerous to pro-
'voke and *fruitless to attack*[1].' Thus does Mr.
Gibbon, like a child at play, knock down his own
fabrication of cards with his own hand! But, as he
adds in a note, ' a nameless doctor (Universal Hist.
' Vol. XX. octavo edition) has formally *demonstrat-*
'*ed* the truth of Christianity, by the independence
' of the Arabs. A critic, besides the exceptions of
' fact,' which Mr. Gibbon has already allowed to
be only *temporary* and *local*, and not to relate to *the*
main body of the people; ' might dispute the meaning
' of the text (Gen. xvi. 12.),' when he allows the
fact to be *strictly consonant* to the *interpretation*, ' the
' extent of the application,' when his own allowance
shews this, ' and the foundation of the pedigree,'
when he does not dare to deny it, and when the very
Arabs themselves have always affirmed, and do still
affirm it. Mr. Gibbon, we see, could not be quiet
because he was beaten. He therefore returns to assault the baffling writer, a second time. He thus a
second time proclaims his own rage, and betrays his
own convictions, in the same instant. And the ser-

[1] P. 178—179.

pent, still gnawing upon the file, and still unable to break it, exposes his folly in his feebleness, and shrinks into his hole covered with blood and shame.

' The writers of the Modern Universal History
' (Vol. I. and II.) have compiled, in 850 folio
' pages, the life of Mahomet and the annals of the
' caliphs. They enjoyed the advantage of reading,
' and *sometimes correcting*, the Arabic texts; yet,
' notwithstanding their high-sounding boasts, I can-
' not find, after the conclusion of my work, that
' they have afforded *much* (if any) additional infor-
' mation. The dull mass is not quickened by a
' spark of philosophy or taste; and the compilers
' indulge the criticism of acrimonious bigotry, a-
' gainst Boulainvilliers, Sale, Gagnier, and all who
' have treated Mahomet with favour, or *even jus-*
' *tice*[1].' The author of this arraigned portion of the Modern Universal History, I can inform the public, was the same who asserted the independence of the Arabs, in so substantial a manner; the late Mr. Swinton of Oxford. Mr. Gibbon is angry at both these works, for the same reason; the honourable zeal for Christianity and for truth, that pervades them. Yet in the Mahometan history, it seems, Mr. Gibbon has not derived *much*, if *any*, information from Mr. Swinton. If he has derived *any*, he has certainly *stolen* it; for he has made no acknowledgments. That he has however derived *much*, I am inclined to think from his own expres-

[1] p. 275.

fions. And indeed how can it be otherwife, when (according to Mr. Gibbon himfelf) Mr. Swinton had ' the advantage of reading, and *fometimes cor-* ' *recting*, the Arabic text?' But I could mention many paffages, in which Mr. Gibbon has apparently copied Mr. Swinton. I fhall haftily cite one. In p. 221 Mr. Gibbon ufes the word ' vizir,' as an appropriate term among the Arabs, for a deputy and fupporter; and fays in the note, that he ' endea-
' vours to preferve the Arabian idiom, as far as he
' can feel it himfelf in a Latin or French tranflation.'
But he had the idiom preferved before, and the word adopted in an Englifh hiftory. Mr. Swinton in 1. 47—48, at this very point of the hiftory, had ufed the term; and even fubjoined a note to explain the meaning. ' Who,' fays Mahomet there to his few followers, ' will *be* my *wazir* or affiftant—and be-
' come my brother and my vicegerent?' and ' the
' word *wazir* or *vifir*,' adds a note,—' properly
' fignifies a *porter* or *carrier of burdens*; but, in a
' more noble fenfe, it is taken for a *privy counfellor*,
' or rather a *prime minifter*, who is the perfon that
' *bears the whole burden* of the adminiftration.' At
' the commencement of the Turkifh empire,—the
' office of *vifir* was finally eftablifhed, and conti-
' nues to this day. *None of thofe authors who have*
' *favoured* the public with a hiftory of *wazirs, feem*
' *to have traced this fupereminent dignity to its original*
' *fource.*' But I could point out alfo many paffages of Mr. Gibbon's hiftory, in which he might have borrowed to his advantage from Mr. Swinton. I have

have actually pointed out a remarkable one before.
And upon the whole, and after examining both the
histories, I am compelled to say; that the darkness,
the abruptness, and the unfairness of Mr. Gibbon's,
render the reading of Mr. Swinton's absolutely necessary, to the investigation of the history and the acquirement of the truth. Mr. Swinton indeed *does* take
pains, to expose the folly and to repel the effrontery
of Sale, Gagnier, and Boulainvilliers, those half-renegadoes from Christianity and from reason. This
was requisite to the purity of the history. But I
could produce many instances of his candour and
fairness. I have actually produced a striking one
before. And, as to his 'acrimony,' I am glad that
Mr. Gibbon *feels*, and I am sure that he *retorts*, it.
But THAT history, it seems 'is not quickened by a
'spark of philosophy and taste.' It certainly is
wanting in vivacity and sentiment. Mr. Swinton
was *weak* enough, to give us substantial criticisms
for 'taste,' and to substitute solid truths for 'philo-
'sophy.' And, with all this *weakness*, he has actually given us a *body* of history, that wants indeed
some nice proportions, some graces of movement,
and some brilliancy of aspect; and that yet will be
surveyed with profit and satisfaction, when the dressed and painted *dolls* of the present day, will be cast
away with the fantastic fashion that produced them.

I have more than once before noted the strong
turn of *obscenity*, that runs through Mr. Gibbon's
history. I have too much occasion, to notice it here
again. I will venture to cite a couple of passages.

H 4 'Seven

'Seventy-two *houris*, or black-eyed girls,' says Mr. Gibbon concerning the fenfual paradife of the Mahometans, 'of refplendent beauty, blooming youth, virgin purity, and exquifite fenfibility, will be created for the ufe of the meaneft believer; a moment of pleafure will be prolonged to a thoufand years, and his facuities will be increafed an hundred fold to render them worthy of his felicity [1].' Mr. Gibbon, we fee, dwells upon the picture with peculiar relifh. I even fufpect him to have added from his own pencil, two of the ftrongeft ftrokes in it. But in the next page he returns to his feaft of fenfuality. 'Ufelefs would be the refurrection of the body,' he fays in his own character or in that of a Mahometan, *and perhaps the difference is very little*; 'unlefs it were reftored to the poffeffion and exercife of its *worthieft* faculties; and the union of *fenfual* and intellectual *enjoyment* is *requifite*, to complete the happinefs of the *double animal*, the perfect man.' This is fufficient for a tafte of Mr. Gibbon's *libidinous* fpirit. I need only *refer* to a flight quotation of obfcenity in p. 253, and to a very impudent quotation and paffage in p. 254. And Mr. Gibbon feems to be equally happy, in any opportunity of fhewing his infidelity, and in any occafion of exhibiting his lafcivioufnefs.

Chapter FOURTH

or fifty-firft.——In this chapter, after fome prefatory matter, we have the reduction of Perfia by the

[1] P. 218.

Saracens (p. 283—295), a point of hiſtory, totally foreign to the decline and fall of the Roman empire; and ſtill more foreign (if poſſible) to a work that is to confine itſelf to the ' circumſtances,' the ' im-
' portant,' and even ' the moſt' important, in the account of this decline and fall. We have then the reduction of Syria (p. 296—331), and of Egypt (p. 331—349), by them. We have next their conqueſt of Weſtern Africa, to the Atlantic (p. 349—363); all as foreign as that of Perſia, becauſe the hiſtory of it was finiſhed, when we cloſed the career of the weſtern empire. And we have finally the reduction of Spain, equally foreign with both (p. 364—381); and ſome remarks at the cloſe, to ſhew the triumph of the Arabick religion over that of Chriſtianity (p. 381—391). Had Mr. Gibbon materials, he would ſwell every chapter of digreſſion into a volume; and expand and dilate the hiſtory of the decline and fall of the empire, into a large library. Give me but a foot to ſtand upon, ſays this hiſtorical Archimedes, and I will ſhake and agitate the whole globe at my pleaſure. And he writes, and writes, and digreſſes, and includes one hiſtorical *parentheſis* within another, in an almoſt infinite ſeries.

From p. 276 to p. 296, we never think of the empire or emperor at all. In p. 303 we have the firſt mention of the latter. We then find him ' in ' his palace of Conſtantinople or Antioch.' And we ſee him, like the reader, ' awakened' to a feeling for the empire. In p. 296—331 the ſun of hiſtory riſes and ſhines upon the empire. But it then

then sinks in the *west*. And it goes to shine *in other worlds*.

There is also great confusion, in the series of the history. The reduction of Persia comes *first*, and is placed by Mr. Gibbon himself in p. 290, 'A. D. 637 —651.' We are *next* presented with ' the con-' quest of Transoxiana,' as p. 294 tells us, ' A. D. ' 710.' But we have *then* ' the invasion of Syria, ' A. D. 632.' We thus, like a crab, go backwards in our course. And what shews the absurdity of such an irregular arrangement at once, we see the emperor in p. 303, ' awakened by the invasion of ' Syria, the loss of Bosra, and the danger of Damas-' cus;' when, in the previous part of the history, e-vents a thousand times more formidable to him have happened, and the whole empire of the Persians has been subdued by the Saracens.

Contradictions.—P. 287. ' The walls of Ctesi-' phon or Madayn, which had resisted the battering-' rams of the Romans, would not have yielded to ' the *darts* of the Saracens.' Mr. Gibbon forgets, that he has already given them battering-rams *once*; and he knows not that he ought to have given them *twice*. But this strange forgetfulness concerning himself, and this gross mistake concerning the A-rabs, who had all the Greek engines of war; as we have already seen them, and shall see them still more, having the Greek *coins* among them; runs through his whole history here, and lends a false co-louring to it. Thus he says in p. 305, concerning the siege of Damascus: ' the art, the labour, the mi-
' litary

' *litary engines*, of the Greeks and Romans, are sel-
' dom to be found in the *simple*, though succefsful,
' operations of the Saracens; *it was sufficient for*
' *them*, to inveft a city with arms rather than with
' trenches, to repel the fallies of the befieged, to at-
' tempt a ftratagem or an affault, or to expect the
' progrefs of famine or difcontent.' Yet he himfelf in p. 307 fpeaks thus, concerning this very fiege:
' Elmacin—notices the ufe of *Baliftæ* by the Sara-
' cens (Hift. Saracen. p. 25, 32).' This is in A. D.
634. And A. D. 638 he notices ftill in oppofition
to all, that ' the military engines, which battered
' the walls' of Alexandria, ' may be imputed to
' the art and labour of—Syrian allies' (p. 335.).

We have already feen Mr. Gibbon, making
ftrange miftakes about the *coins* of the Arabians.
We fee him making ftill more, in this chapter.
P. 289 he fpeaks of ' twenty thoufand *drams*,'
p. 293 of ' *drams* of filver,' and p. 280 of ' *drams*
' or pieces of filver;' when he fhould have faid,
drachmæ or *dirhems* of filver'! P. 327 he mentions
' two hundred thoufand pieces of *gold*;' and p.
279 ' five pieces of *gold*;' when he fhould have
mentioned as many *dirhems* of *filver*[2]. P. 338 he
notices ' two *pieces of gold*,' p. 349 ' four millions
' three hundred thoufand *pieces of gold*,' p. 288
' thoufands of *pieces of gold*,' p. 294 ' two thou-
' fand *pieces of gold*,' and p. 325 ' three hundred
' thoufand *pieces of gold*;' when he fhould have
fpoken more fpecifically, have turned his pieces of

---

[1] Mod. Univ. Hift. 1. 433.   [2] Ibid. 1. 471 and 379.

gold

gold into *denarii* or *dinars*[1], and given us the correspondent value in English money. We should then have had some idea of the sums intended; and not been left, as we now are, totally in the dark about them. And in p. 381, at last recovering the specific name, he reckons ' twelve millions and forty-five thousand *dinars* or pieces of gold,' to be ' about *six* millions of sterling money;' when the *dinar* appears to have been about 13*s*. 6*d*. in value[2], and the sum consequently is above *eight* millions.

P. 345. Mr. Gibbon notices a point, as not discovered by ' the self-sufficient compilers of the ' Modern Universal History.' This is another stroke at Mr. Swinton. But it cannot hurt his reputation. I may very safely say still, that for truth, for facts, and sometimes even for *characteristic* facts, we must refer to Mr. Swinton; though, for brilliancy and pointedness, we must go to Mr. Gibbon. And I cannot refrain from marking with surprise, the charge of ' self-sufficiency' from such a writer as Mr. Gibbon. He who comes forward in his text, with such an air of superior observation; he who fills his notes with an hundred references, quotations, sneers, sarcasms, and caricatures; and he, who appears in his notes and text, like another Briareus, wielding his hundred arms against heaven itself; even he taxes the *self-sufficiency* of Mr. Swinton. And the fact presents us with a wonderful

---

[1] Mod. Univ. Hist. 1. 488, Renaudot, 334 ' aurei denarii,' Mod. Univ. Hist. 1. 433, Ibid. 11, 76, ' 2000 dinars,' and ibid. 1. 455. [2] Ibid. 1. 196.

picture, of the blindness incident to the human mind, and of the partiality fostered in the human heart. Mr. Gibbon would otherwise have never presumed, to charge another with his own darling sin. The giant, in compliment to himself, would have spared the pigmy. And Sir John Cutler, that king of misers, would not have had the effrontery to accuse a prudent œconomist, of avarice.

P. 344. 'Renaudot answers for versions of the 'Bible, Hexapla, *Catenæ Patrum*, Commentaries '(p. 170).' This gives us an instance, of what I have previously dwelt upon, the unfaithfulness of Mr. Gibbon in his references. He has marked in Italics the Italicised words above. Yet *these very words* are not in Renaudot, p. 170. The passage runs thus: 'Versionum sacræ scripturæ, com- 'mentariorum, hexaplorum, et aliarum ejusmodi 'lucubrationum.' And this serves strongly to confirm, all that I have said of Mr. Gibbon before; such a falsification of the passage as this, being either merely the result of his habitual carelessness, or the wilful suggestion of his sarcastic genius.

P. 299. The text mentions 'the ringing of 'bells.' But the note says: 'I much doubt, whe- 'ther this expression can be justified, by the text of '*Al Wakidi* or the practice of the times.' So far I note the passages, only to shew the contradiction between them. But the contradiction is heightened, as the note goes on. And I wish to ascertain the point denied in it, and so to vindicate the text in opposition to the note. 'Ad Græcos, says Du-
'cange

'cange (Gloffar. med. et in fin. [infimæ] Græ-
'citat. tom. 1. p. 774) campanarum ufus fe-
'riùs tranfit [tran*fiit*], et etiamnum rariffimus.
'The oldeft example, which we can find in
'the Byzantine writers, is of the year 1040;
'but the Venetians pretend, that they. intro-
'duced bells at Conftantinople, in the ninth
'century.' This is a ftriking fpecimen of that
fpirit of learning, which overlooks the object directly under its feet, while it is gazing for it among the
ftars. At the very furrender of Jerufalem to the
Arabs, one of the articles impofed by the conquerors on the Chriftians, is this; that, ' they fhall not
' *ring*, but only *toll*, their *bells*[1].' Very foon after
this event, one Kais being afked by the emperor
concerning *Mahomet*, how at the time he had per-
ceived himfelf infpired; faid that ' fometimes he
' heard a found refembling *that of a bell*, but
' ftronger and fharper[2].' Then comes ' the ring-
' ing of bells' in the text, at the fiege of Bofra.
And, what is a remarkable conclufion to the whole,
only *fix* pages after Mr. Gibbon has adopted in the
text, and *refuted* in the note, this early ufe of bells;
and in his account of the clofely following fiege of
Damafcus; he himfelf fays, that ' the fignal was
' given by a ftroke on the great *bell*[3].'

P. 312. Mr. Gibbon in the text fpeaks of ' the
' fair of Abyla, about thirty miles from Damafcus.'
' *Dair Abil Kodos*,' fays a note, ' after retrenching

---

[1] Mod. Univ. Hift. 1. 429.   [2] Ibid. 1. 449—450.
[3] P. 307.

'the last word, the epithet *holy*; I *discover* the A-
'bila of Lysanias, between Damascus and Helio-
'polis; the name (*Abil* signifies a vineyard) con-
'curs with the situation to justify my conjecture
'(Reland Palestine. tom. 1. p. 307, tom. 11. p.
'525—527).' This is all a series of errors. The place is *not* a *town*. It is only a monastery. Mr. Gibbon's own narrative shews this plainly, ' The 'hermit,' he says himself p. 314, ' was left alive, in 'the *solitary* scene of blood and devastation.' Dair Abil Kodos, therefore, *cannot* be the *town* of *Abila Lysaniæ*, mentioned by Ptolemy [1].' Even if it could, *Mr. Gibbon* did not ' *discover* the Abila of 'Lysanias' in the name of Abil; D'Anville's map of the country discovering it for him, by making the modern name of ' Abyladys,' to be ' Abel.' Nor does the name signify the Holy *Dair* or House of Abila, but the house of *the Holy Father*; the words at full length being *Dair Abi Al Kodos*, and only by elision contracted into *Dair Abi'l Kodos*. And, even if the *present* vines of Abila could anyways relate to its *ancient* name, the signification of *Abil*, a vineyard, can have no relation to the monastery; the *town* confessedly lying ' between Damascus and Heliopo-
' lis,' and is about *thirty* miles ' from the former;
' when Abil is not more than *twelve*; and the *mo-*
' *nastery* being, not between Tripoli and *Harran*,' as Mod. Un. Hist. places it, an interval of region too large for any local discrimination, but (as I suppose was intended to be said) betwixt Tripoli and

[1] Lib. v. p. 160. Bertius.

Scurura

Scurura or Caraw, and being probably the present monastery of *Der Mar Jacob* to the west of Caraw, and far to the north of Abila [1].

I have noticed before, the mean and wretched love of *obscenity* in Mr. Gibbon. He has yet to learn,

> That want of decency is want of sense.

And he most shamefully breaks in upon all decency, in this chapter; wounding the delicacy of his reader in p. 278, with a long and impudent quotation in Latin, concerning a scene of Mahometan sensuality. Sensuality is the life and soul of Mahometanism. ' In the eyes of an inquisitive polytheist,' says Mr. Gibbon *for that very reason*, I doubt not, ' it must ' appear worthy of the human and the divine na- ' ture [2].' ' It must appear' peculiarly ' *worthy* of ' the *human*—nature;' because it ' restores' this nature even in paradise, as we have seen before, ' to ' the possession and exercise of its *worthiest* facul- ' ties [3].'

There is an air of *obscurity* in the narration too, that frequently distracts the reader. We cannot understand the history, unless we are previously acquainted with it. This obscurity often lies also, in single and detached sentences.—' Perhaps the Persians,' he says, ' who have been the masters of the Jews, ' would assert the honour, a poor honour—of being ' *their* masters [4].' I give the passage as the press

---

[1] Mod. Univ. Hist 1. 392—394. D'Anville's map, and map in Pococke, vol. 2d; corrected the one by the other.
[2] p. 382.   [3] p. 219.   [4] p. 383.

gives

gives it me. Nor is the context more clear, than the extract. And what is the poffible meaning of it?——Once the proverb of a diamond cutting a diamond, is very indifcreetly ufed in the hiftory. But the vulgarity is at once covered and betrayed, by this pedantry of learning: ' *it was a maxim among* ' *the Greeks*, that, for the purpofe of cutting a dia' mond, a diamond was the moft effectual[1].' ' In ' the name of the city,' Jerufalem, ' the profane ' prevailed over the facred[2].' He fhould have faid in propriety, that the modern and the Roman prevailed over the ancient and the Jewifh. ' *Jerufa*' *lem* was known to the devout Chriftians—; but ' the *legal* and *popular* appellation of *Ælia*—has ' paffed from the Romans to the Arabs.' The name of *Jerufalem* was known equally to the Arabs, as to the Chriftians. Nor was the appellation of *Ælia*, the *legal* and *popular* one. The town indeed is called only *Ælia*, in Omar's *fecond* addrefs to the patriarch[3]. But it is called ' Ælia *or* Jerufalem,' in his *firft*[4]. And as in the nocturnal journey of Mahomet, we apprehend it is denominated *Jerufalem* only[5]; fo is it certainly denominated only *Jerufalem* by the Roman hiftorian Ammianus Marcellinus, about *two centuries and an half* after Adrian had impofed the name of *Ælia* upon it[6]. *Ælia* therefore was the *legal* name, but *Jerufalem* the *popular*

---

[1] p. 317.   [2] p. 320.
[3] Mod. Univ. Hift. i. 431.   [4] ibid. i. 430.
[5] Prideaux's Life, 54 and 64, and Mod. Univ. Hift. 1. 67 and 77.
[6] L. xxiii. c. 1. p. 350. Valefii ' apud Hierofolymam templum.'

one;

one; among the very Romans firſt, and conſequently among the Arabs afterwards.

We have ſeveral inſtances of *falſe language,* in this chapter: p. 349, ' two authentic liſts, of the pre-
' ſent and of the twelfth century, *are circumſcribed*
' *within,*' that is, *contain only,* ' the reſpectable
' number of two thouſand ſeven hundred villages
' and towns' in Egypt; p. 325 ' the *luxury* of An-
' tioch,' for *the luxurious Antioch,* ' trembled and
' obeyed;' p. 327, ' bidding an eternal farewell
' to Syria, he—*abſolved the faith* of his ſubjects,'
or, as he ſhould have ſaid, *he abſolved his ſubjects—
from their fealty;* p. 318, they ' overturned,' for *o-
verthrew,* ' a detachment of Greeks;' p. 355, ' the
' well-known cities of Bugia and Tangier *define,*'
for *mark* ' the—limits of the Saracen victories;'
p. 372, ' the maritime town of Gijon was the *term*
' of the lieutenant of Muſa;' and p. 375, ' from
' his *term* or column of Narbonne he returned.'

We have alſo one *contradiction.* P. 374. ' The
' Goths *were* purſued *beyond* the Pyrenean moun-
' tains.' So ſays the text. But the note *doubts* this. ' I much queſtion,' ſays the author *there,*
' whether Muſa ever paſſed the Pyrenees.' And yet the text in p. 376 repeats this much queſtioned aſſertion; and ſays poſitively, ' he was preparing to
' *re*-paſs the Pyrenees.'

The deſtruction of the Alexandrine library, is partly denied and partly excuſed. If it was only a library of divinity, it is *excuſed;* as ' a philoſo-
' pher may allow with a ſmile, that it was ulti-
' mately

' mately devoted to the benefit of mankind [r].'
Into what a mere Vandal and Goth, does the
leaden weight of infidelity sink Mr. Gibbon! It
is *denied*, because two writers, both Christian, both
Egyptian, and both earlier than the relater himself,
one of whom too has amply described the reduction
of Alexandria; have *not* noticed the fact. But a
negative argument is of no moment, in opposition
to a *positive* one. The fact is positively related, and
by an author of unquestionable merit, Abulpharagius. No accumulation of testimonies merely negative, can countervail this. Nor is the destruction
said by him to have been done, *at* the reduction of
Alexandria, but *some time afterwards*. Yet, as Mr.
Gibbon farther argues, this destruction ' is repug-
' nant to the sound and orthodox precept of the
' Mahometan casuists;' a weak argument in itself,
and annihilated by its own allowance immediately
afterwards, that ' a more destructive zeal may per-
' haps be attributed to the first successors of Maho-
' met.' ' In this instance' however, adds Mr. Gibbon, ' the *conflagration* would have speedily expired
' in the deficiency of materials;' when, even according to his own account from Abulpharagius, the
library was not burnt in *any general conflagration*;
but ' the volumes of paper or parchment were dis-
' tributed to the six thousand baths of the city, and,
' such was their incredible multitude, that six
' months were barely sufficient for the consumption

[r] Page 343—345.

' of

' of this precious fuel;' and when the parchment or paper was used only for *lighting* the fires, not for forming them, and *therefore* lasted so long a time. The Roman writers too, says Mr. Gibbon, ' Aulus Gellius (Noctes Atticæ, vi. 17), Ammianus Marcellinus (xxii. 16), and Orosius (L. vi. c. 15),—all speak in the *past* tense; and the words of Ammianus are remarkably strong, *fuerunt*,' &c. But this is only another instance of that *dishonest management*, with which Mr. Gibbon garbles his quotations and references. All these writers speak only, of *the library destroyed in Cæsar's time*. They may well therefore speak ' in the past tense.' Gellius (vi. 17), says, ' ea omnia bello priore Alexandrino—incensa sunt.' Orosius says (vi. 15), that the ' regia classis' was ordered to be burnt by Cæsar; ' ea flamma—quadraginta millia librorum—exussit.' And Marcellinus (xxii. 16) adds, in the words cited by Mr. Gibbon, ' bibliothecæ fuerunt in-æstimabiles.' or *innumerabiles*, as Mr. Gibbon reads them; ' et loquitur monumentorum veterum concinens fides,' &c. *What* does this consenting testimony say? Mr. Gibbon *chose to suppress it*. But it says, ' septingenta voluminum millia— *sub dictatore Cæsare* conflagrasse.' Mr. Gibbon thus quotes the authors for the *later* library, when they speak only of the *former*; and, in Marcellinus, wilfully suppresses the very words that would have betrayed they did. Another library was formed after the destruction of this. Epiphanius, Tertullian, and

Chrysostom,

Chryfoftom, prove decifively its exiftence[1]; as A-
bulpharagius fhews us its termination. And the
evidence of fuch an hiftorian as the latter, 'an au-
'thor of eminent note in the Eaft, as well among
'Mahometans as Chriftians[2];' the coincidence of
his teftimony with that of Chryfoftom, Tertullian,
and Epiphanius; the vacuity that there would be in
the hiftory, from the want of it; its pointednefs, and
its circumftantiality; leave us no room to doubt of
the fweeping deftruction, that thefe friends and fa-
vourites of Mr. Gibbon's, thefe fanatic Goths and
Vandals of Arabia, made of the collected literature
of the world.

Chapter FIFTH,

or fifty-fecond.—In this chapter we have an account, of the firft fiege of Conftantinople, and of the
fecond, by the Arabs, and of their failure in both
(p. 392—405); of the invafion of France by them
(p. 405—412), a point quite foreign to the fubject;
of the civil wars among the Saracens (p. 412—
416), all equally foreign as *particular* hiftory; of
the revolt of the Saracens in Spain from the caliphs
(p. 416—418), equally foreign; of the magnificence of the caliphs (p. 418—420), and its confe-
quences on their private and public happinefs
(p. 421—422), equally foreign; of the introduction

---

[1] See a very ufeful note in Reimar's Dion Caffius, p. 327; and another as ufeful in A. Marcellinus, Valefii, p. 343.

[2] Prideaux, Letter, p. 15.

and progress of learning among the Saracens (p. 423—431), equally foreign; of their invasion of the empire and reduction of Crete (p. 431—436); of their reduction of Sicily (p. 437—438), equally foreign; of their expeditions against Rome (p. 438—443), equally foreign; of their invasion of the empire again (p. 443—447); the disorderliness of the guards of the caliphs (p. 447—449), equally foreign; the rise and progress of the Carmathians among the Saracens (p. 449—452), equally foreign; the revolt of the provinces from the caliphs (p. 452—458), equally foreign; and the successes of the empire over them (p. 458—463). Mr. Gibbon is strangely slumbering in this chapter, over his own scope and aim in the history. He forgets, that he is writing the history of the decline and fall of the eastern empire. He dreams that he is writing a history of the *Saracens*, and tracing the *caliphate* to its decline and fall. And, in consequence of this delusion, out of seventy-two pages in this chapter, there are only twenty-eight, that have a connexion with the history. The rest is all the very impertinence of digression.

The history of the introduction and progress of learning among the Saracens, is endeavoured to be connected with the general history, by this argument. ' The sword of the Saracens,' we are told at the close, ' became less formidable, when their ' youth was drawn away from the camp to the col-
' lege '.' But, *had* this been the case, the introduc-

¹ P. 431.

tion

tion and the progress should have been only *noticed*, not *dwelt upon*. And it is *not* the case, even upon the face of Mr. Gibbon's own history. For, on resuming the narrative after this account, we find not, as we have a right to expect, this observation exemplified in the conduct of the Saracens. We find indeed the reverse of this. We find them *more* triumphant than ever, over the empire; even imposing a tribute upon it [1], even insulting the emperor most grossly [2], and even impressing ' the ' coin of the tribute with the image and superscription,' of the caliph [3]. Crete and Sicily, too, are subdued by that very king 'Almamon,' who was ' engaged in the introduction of foreign science [4].' The Arabs also defeat the army of the empire, in a grand battle afterwards [5]. And the *future* weakness of the caliphs is actually ascribed by Mr. Gibbon himself, to ' the disorders of the Turkish ' guards [6],' to ' the rise and progress of the Car- ' mathians [7],' and to ' the revolt of the provinces [8].' With such a stumbling pace does Mr Gibbon proceed in his history!

He says thus concerning Crete: 'I cannot con- ' ceive that mountainous island, to *surpass*, or even ' to *equal*, in *fertility* the *greater part* of Spain [9].' So speaks the note. But, in the very next page, the text tells us of some *Spanish* Arabs, whom he calls ' a band of Andalusian volunteers [10];' that

[1] p. 432.   [2] p. 433.   [3] p. 434.
[4] p. 434—438.   [5] p. 444—445.   [6] p. 447—448.
[7] p. 449—452.   [8] p. 452—456.   [9] p. 435.
[10] p. 435.

' they

'they saw, they *tasted*, they *envied*, the *fertility* of
'Crete.'——'In the—city of Mopsuestia,' says
the text, '—two hundred thousand Moslems were
'destined to death or slavery; a surprising degree
'of population, which must at least include the
'inhabitants of the dependent districts [1]. But the
note adds: 'yet I cannot credit this extreme po-
'pulousness.' Then why did he insert in it his
text?——We are told, 'that the liberal Alma-
'mon was *sufficiently* engaged in the restoration
'of domestic peace, and the introduction of foreign
'science;' and in *the very next* words are further
told, that, 'under the reign of Almamon,—the
'islands of Crete and Sicily were subdued by the
'Arabs [2].'

'They breathed at Dorylæum, at the distance
'of three days [3];' that is, three days after their
flight they rested at Dorylæum. 'Their retreat
'*exasperated the quarrel* of the townsmen and mer-
'cenaries [4],' that is, occasioned a quarrel between
them, as we *have heard of none existing before.*
'From—Elmacin and the Arabian physicians, some
'dinars as high as two dirhems—may be *deduced* [5],'
that is, *it may be deduced that there were such.*
'Three thousand pieces of gold [6]' should be as in
Mr. Swinton, we apprehend, 'three thousand
'pounds weight of gold [7].' 'The gold dinars,'
which the Saracens now coined in their own mints,

---

[1] p. 460. [2] p. 435. [3] p. 444. [4] p. 461.
[5] p. 397. [6] p. 395.
[7] Mod. Univ. Hist. 11. 78.

'may

'may be—equivalent to eight shillings of our ster-
'ling money¹:' when there are nine very fine dinars, at this time preserved in the Bodleian col-
lection at Oxford; and there was another lately in
that of the Rev. Mr. Brown, fellow of Trinity college there; ' whose *value*,' says Mr. Swinton exprefsly, ' according to *weight*, amounts to about
' *thirteen shillings and sixpence*,' English money². ' I
' have reckoned the gold pieces,' meaning (as he
should have *said*) the *dinars*, ' at eight shillings³;'
when he ought to have reckoned them *at least*, 'for
thirteen shillings and sixpence. ' One million of
' pieces of gold,' he should again have said *dinars*,
' about four hundred thousand pounds sterling⁴;' a-
bove seven hundred and fifty thousand pounds.
And a person ' *consecrates* a sum of two hundred
' thousand *pieces of gold*, to the foundation of a col-
' lege at Bagdad, which he endowed with an ample
' revenue of fifteen thousand *dinars*⁵;' when the
dinars and the pieces of gold are the same in reality,
though they are distinguished so much by name.

Chapter sixth,

or fifty-third.——This chapter contains an account,
of the ' royal volumes of Constantine Porphyroge-
' nitus' (p. 464—468), and of ' the Legatio
' Liutprandi, Episcopi Cremonensis ad Nicepho-

¹ p. 397   ² Modern Univ. Hist. 1. 196.
³ p. 419.   ⁴ p. 438.   ⁵ p. 424.

' rum

'rum Phocam' (p. 468), as the sources of intelligence for Mr. Gibbon's present chapter; of the present state of the provinces of the empire (p. 468—470); of the general wealth and populousness of the empire (p. 471—472); of the particular state of Peloponnesus (p. 472—478); of the revenue of the empire (478—479); of the pomp and luxury of the emperors (p. 479—483); of the honours and titles of the imperial family (p. 483—485); of the titles and names for the officers of the palace, the army, and the state (p. 485—487); of the adoration paid to the emperor, reception of ambassadors, processions, and acclamations (p. 487—490); marriage of the Cæsars with foreign nations, imaginary law of Constantine forbidding it, first exception, second, third, &c. (p. 490—494); despotic power and coronation-oath of the emperor (p. 495—496); military force of the Greeks, Saracens, and Franks (p. 496—499); tactics and character of the Greeks (p. 500—502); tactics and character of the Saracens (p. 502—504); the Franks or Latins (p. 504—506); their character and tactics (p. 506—508); the disuse of the Latin language (p. 508—511); the period of ignorance (p. 511—512); the revival of Greek learning (p. 512—515); decay of taste and genius (p. 515—517), and want of national emulation (p. 517—518). These are points, some more proper for a note than the text, some so wildly devious from his subject, and all so petty and uninteresting; that I need only contrast them with the often cited promise, of

giving

giving merely ' the circumstances,' the ' impor-
' tant' circumstances, and the ' most important,'
of the decline and fall of the empire. And we
cannot censure this labyrinth of digressions and mi-
nutiæ with more severity, than by thus contrasting
it and the promise together.

Obscure. ' At length the approach of their hos-
' tile brethren extorted a golden bull, to define the
' rights and obligations of the Ezzerites and Milen-
' gi[1].' This is darker than the Delphic oracle.——
' Yet the maxims of antiquity are still embraced
' by a monarch formidable to his enemies;' who is
this? ' by a republic respectable to her allies[2];'
which is this?——' The Franks, the Barbarians,
' and the *Varangi or English*[3];' who are these? We
know not and we cannot guess, till we come *two
chapters afterward*, to find some Scandinavian pirates
' saluted with the title of *Varangians* or corsairs[4];'
and till in the page *following* we see, that ' the new *Va-*
' *rangians* were a colony of *English* and *Danes*, who
' *fled from the yoke of the Norman conqueror*[5].'——
' This scholar should be likewise a soldier; and
' alas! Quintus Icilius is no more[6].' We understand not this, till we come to a very distant
page; where we find that ' Q. Icilius (M. Guis-
' chard)' analysed the operations of Cæsar's cam-
paigns in Africa and Spain[7]. So strangely does
Mr. Gibbon write, to use singular and extraordinary
appellations without any explanation, and then to

[1] p. 473.   [2] p. 479.   [3] p. 486—487.   [4] p. 561.
[5] p. 562.   [6] p. 467.   [7] p. 616.

re-use

re-ufe them with one. His hiftory is thus like a *glow-worm*, and carries its light in its tail.

Falfe Englifh. He mentions ' a golden bull to
' define the rights and obligations of the Ezzerites
' and Milengi, whofe annual tribute was *defined*,'
for *fixed*, ' at twelve hundred pieces of gold ',' that
is, *dinars*, fomething more than our old *marks*.——
' By this impious alliance he *accomplifhed*,' for *compleated*, ' the meafure of his crimes².'——' No con-
' fideration could difpenfe *from*,' read *with*, ' the
' law of Conftantine ³.'——' Difcern and opprefs the
' *laffitude* of their foes ⁴.'

Contradiction. After various intimations in the text, concerning the fcandalous conduct of Hugo's family; and after feveral references to and quotations from Bifhop Liutprand in the note, as a decifive authority for them; Mr. Gibbon fweeps away at once the note and the text from the face of *authentic* hiftory, by this dafhing ftroke at the clofe; ' yet it muft not be forgot, that the Bifhop
' of Cremona was a lover of fcandal⁵.' Such an unlucky hand has Mr. Gibbon, in fetting afide *his own* authorities, and in overthrowing *his own* narrative!

Chapter SEVENTH

or fifty-fourth.—This chapter propofes to be ' fome
' *inquiry* into the doctrine and ftory,' of whom? ' of

¹ p. 473.   ² p. 492.   ³ ibid.
⁴ p. 504.   ⁵ p. 493.

' the

'the *Paulicians*' (p. 520). These, ' I am confident,' says Mr. Gibbon, ' gloried in their affinity to ' the apostle of the Gentiles' (p. 521). He accordingly recounts their origin (p. 522); their scriptures (p. 523); their not worshipping images, relics, or saints; their considering the true cross as a mere piece of wood, and the body and blood of Christ as mere bread and wine (p. 523); their quaker-like rejection of baptism and communion (p. 523); their condemning the Old Testament, as the invention of men and dæmons (p. 524); their allowing the godhead, but denying the personality, of Christ; giving him a body merely spiritual, that was not bound and could not be crucified (p. 524); and holding a god of goodness and a god of malignity (p. 524); their loosely spreading over the provinces of Asia Minor (p. 525), the persecution of them (p. 526—528), their revolt (p. 528—530), their decline in one part of the empire (p. 530), and their transplantation from another (p. 531); their continuance in their new settlement (p 531—533), their dissemination from thence into the West (p. 533—534), their persecution there (p. 534—536), and their being the beginners of the Reformation (p. 536); with an essay at the end of all, on the character and consequences of the Reformation (p. 536—540). This is obviously such a detail of little and insignificant points, so far as it relates to the empire at all; and such a mere dissertation on ecclesiastical history, in all the great remainder; as is equally contrary to his promise,

promise, and repugnant to his purpose. The pope claims all temporal authority '*in ordine ad spiri-* '*tualia.*' And Mr. Gibbon, like an infallible monarch in history, absolves himself from the obligations of his promises, absolves himself from all proprieties of conduct, and arrogates every part of history, ecclesiastical or civil; *in order to* the history of the Roman empire, the history only of its decline and fall, and the history only of the most important circumstances in either.

' We cannot be surprised, that they should have
' found in the gospel, the orthodox mystery of the
' trinity;—the rational Christian—was offended,
' that the Paulicians should dare to violate the
' unity of God;—their belief and their trust was in
' the Father, of Christ, of the human soul, and of
' the invisible world'.'——This seems to me as contradictory, as it is absurd.——' They likewise
' held the eternity of matter, a stubborn and re-
' bellious substance, the origin of a second prin-
' ciple, of an active being, who has created
' this visible world,' &c[2]. Is the strangeness here, the result of folly in these Paulicians, or of injudiciousness in their historian?

Chapter EIGHTH

or fifty-fifth.—This chapter relates the transactions of the Bulgarians with the empire (p. 542—547);

[1] p. 524.   [2] ibid.

547); the origin of the Hungarians (p. 548—551); the tactics of the Hungarians and Bulgarians (p. 551—553); the inroads of the Hungarians into Germany, Eastern France, and Italy (p. 553—556), all foreign to the history of the empire, and doubly foreign to the history of its decline and fall; the Hungarian reduction of the Bulgarians, and inroad up to the gates of Constantinople (p. 546); the expulsion of the Hungarians from Germany (p. 556—559), all equally foreign; origin of the Russians (p. 560—563), geography and commerce of Russia (p. 563—566), the wars of the Russians with the empire (p. 566—574), and the conversion of the Russians to Christianity (p. 574—579). The chapter therefore contains many parts, that have not the slightest connexion with Mr. Gibbon's subject. And, even in such as have a connexion, the thread of history is evidently spun too fine and long. The *facts* bear little proportion to the *disquisitions*. A large fabric is reared upon a slender pillar. And Mr. Gibbon's vast system of history, like that of the universe, moves for ever upon an imaginary pole.

'If in my account of this interesting people 'the Saracens,' says Mr. Gibbon, '*I have deviated* '*from the strict and original line* of my undertaking, 'the *merit* of the subject will *hide my transgression,* 'or *solicit my excuse*'.' I have already shewn him to have 'deviated' most wildly from 'the strict,' and also from the 'original, line of his undertaking.' He here acknowledges in effect, that he has. But

¹ P. 541.

he hopes his 'tranfgreffion' will be hid, or at leaſt his 'excufe' will be 'folicited,' by 'the merit of 'the fubject.' Yet his 'excufe' may be 'foli-
'cited,' and his 'tranfgreffion' will ſtill not be 'hid.' He has even pleaded 'the *merit* and mis-
'fortunes of Ali and his defcendants' before, for confeffedly '*anticipating*—the feries of the Saracen 'caliphs¹.' But no 'merit of a fubject' can alter the unchangeable law of propriety. And whatever Mr. Gibbon may wiſh to fuggeſt in extenua-
tion of his conduct, it is not one particular fubject that has carried him off in a *parabola*; it is many an one, it is almoſt every one. The *centripetal* power in him is very weak. The *centrifugal* is very ſtrong. And he is perpetually flying off in a tangent, and running away into the wilds of fpace.

Contradictions. Text. 'The Hungarian lan-
'guage—bears a cloſe and clear affinity to the 'idioms of the Fennic race².' Note. 'I read in 'the learned Bayer—, that although the Hungarian 'has adopted *many* Fennic words (*innumeras* voces), 'it *effentially* differs, *toto genio et naturâ.*' Where then is, or where can be, the 'cloſe and clear affi-
'nity,' in it 'to the *idioms* of the Fennic race;' when 'the whole genius and nature' of *that* is 'ef-
'fentially' different from *this?*

Falfe language. P. 552. 'Their fole induſtry was 'the *band* of violence and rapine;' p. 554 'their—
'fettlements extended—beyond the *meafure*,' read *bounds*, 'of the Roman province of Pannonia;' p.

¹ p. 256—271.   ² p. 550.

557, 'prevent their second discharge by the—*career*
'of your lances;'—'Otho *dispelled* the conspiracy;'
p. 558, 'the *resources* of discipline and valour were
'*fortified* by the arts of superstition;' p. 574, 'Con-
'stantinople was *astonished to applaud*,' read *with astonishment applauded*, 'the martial virtues of her sove-
'reign;' and p. 577 'a religion—different—from
'the worship of their native idols,' *worship* made a
religion!

Chapter NINTH,

and fifty-sixth.—This gives us the wars of the Greeks,
Latins, and Saracens in Italy (p. 580—587), all foreign; the wars of the Normans with all three in
the same country (p. 587—594), all equally foreign; the wars of the Normans with the Latins
only (p. 594—598), still more foreign; the pedigree and character of Robert Guiscard the Norman
(p. 598—601); his general success against the Latins, the Greeks, and the Saracens, in Italy and
Sicily (p. 601—603), still foreign, as still within
the ground of the late empire of the West; his particular successes in Italy (p. 603—604), still foreign; the learning of Salerno, one of his new ac-
quisitions (p. 604), a digression upon the back of a
digression; the trade of Amalphi, another of his ac-
quisitions (p. 605—606), another digression upon
the back of the first; the conquest of Sicily from
the Saracens by his brother Roger (p. 606—609),
still foreign; Robert's invasion of the empire (p. 609
—620); the expedition of Henry the emperor of
Germany against Rome (p. 621—623), still foreign;

reign; Robert's re-invasion of the empire (p. 623
—626); the conduct of Robert's brother Roger,
against his Norman brethren, the pope, and the Pisans, in Sicily and Italy (p. 626—629), still foreign; his successes over the Saracens in the West
of Africa (p. 629—631), still foreign; his invasion
of the empire (p. 631—633); the invasion of Italy by the emperor (p. 633—637), still foreign;
the last invasion of the empire by the Normans
(p. 638—644); and the wars of the Normans and
Germans in Italy and Sicily (p. 638—644), again
foreign. The chapter thus gives us a lively picture, of the digressional spirit of the author. Out
of the seventeen points which I have here enumerated, five only relate even distantly to his subject,
and twelve are the mere supplement of injudiciousness and extravagance. And Mr. Gibbon's history is become like the great whirlpool of Norway,
that is so terribly denominated *the navel of the sea*;
and sucks into its eddy, bears, whales, ships, and
every thing, that come within any possible reach of
its engulphing streams.

False language. P. 612. ' The *provisions* were
' either *drowned* or damaged;' p. 631, ' the ve-
' nerable *age* of Athens—was *violated* by rapine and
' cruelty;' and p. 639, ' *the ascendant* of the eu-
' nuchs,' for *the principal* of them.

Contradiction. The pope ' *conferred* on Robert and
' his posterity—all the lands,' &c. ' This *apostolic*
' *sanction* might justify his arms, but ',' &c. The

---

[1] P. 601—602.

text

text thus says positively, that the pope *did* confer these lands. The note accordingly adds, that ' Baronius—*has* published *the original act.*' Yet, after all, Mr Gibbon remarks with equal weakness and contradictoriness, that Baronius, ' professes to ' have copied it from—a Vatican M. S. ;' but that ' the names of Vatican and Cardinal awaken the ' *suspicions* of a protestant, and even of a philoso- ' pher.' Mr. Gibbon thus *suspects* the truth, of what he himself has asserted peremptorily. And he often throws in a dash of his sceptical pen, as we have seen before, in this self-confounding manner. Indeed *he* may well doubt the evidence of *others*, who is often doubting the testimony of *himself*.

Chapter TENTH,

or fifty-seventh.————This exhibits to us the history of that greatest of the Turkish princes, who reigned in the eastern provinces of Persia, and subdued Hindostan (p. 645—651), all foreign as *particular* history; general manners of the Turkmans, east and west of the Caspian (p. 651); first emigration of the eastern to their reduction of Persia (p. 652—653), all foreign; their history in Persia (p. 654—656) still foreign; their conduct to the Saracen caliphs (p. 656—658), still foreign; their invasion of the empire (p. 658—666); the death of their sovereign (p. 666—667); the general successes of the next sovereign, in Turkestan, in the Tartary adjoining

joining to China, in Arabia Felix, and in the empire (p. 667—669), still foreign for every part but the last; the manners of this sovereign (p. 669—670), his death (p. 670—672), and division of his empire into three parts (p. 672—673), all foreign as particular; reduction of Asia Minor by the Turks (p. 673—677); and state of Jerusalem under the caliphs and under the Turks (p. 677—684), still foreign, as respecting a city that had long been rent from the empire. Thus does Mr. Gibbon persist to the end of the volume, in that extravagant spirit of rambling with which he began it. He promised indeed at his outset, to give us only ' the most im-
' portant circumstances' of the decline and fall of the *empire*. He promised also, at the commencement of *this* volume, *not* to spin such a prolix and slender thread of history, as he had spun through the four volumes preceding. And he has kept both his promises, by giving us the most *un*-important circumstances in that of the *empire*, by giving us the circumstances of the decline and fall of *every* empire connected with it, by spinning his thread of history still more slender and more prolix, and so making his very reformation the cause and cover of greater transgressions. Nor must we censure Mr. Gibbon very sharply, however sharply we may censure his history, for this. *He cannot help it.* He has a clear and strong judgment. This shews him the right line, in which he should move. But he has a powerful principle within him, that is always carrying him off from it, and twisting his course into
obliquities

obliquities upon one side and into curvatures on the other. And his right line, as traced by a critical eye through the long range of his volumes, is nothing but a series of zigzags.

CHAPTER THE FOURTH.

HAVING gone over the fourth and fifth volumes of this extensive history, we now come to the SIXTH and last.

Chapter FIRST,

or fifty-eighth.———In this we have the preaching up of the first crusade by Peter the Hermit, 1—3; the pope calling a council to promote it, 3—5; his calling a second council, 5—8; an inquiry into the justice of the crusade, 8—11; the spiritual motives to it, 11—14; the temporal, 14—17; the march of the vanguard of crusaders to Constantinople, 16—21; the leaders of the main body, 21—26; the march of this to Constantinople, 26—32; the conduct of the emperor towards them, 32—34; their doing homage to him, 34—37; the insolence of one of their officers to him, 37—38; the numbers, nations, and character of their army, when reviewed in Asia, 38—40; Nice, the capital of the Turks, taken by them, 40—42; their defeat of the Turkish sultan, 42—44; their march through Asia Minor, 44—45; one of them founding a principality *beyond the bounds of the empire,* 45; their reduction of Antioch, 46—48; their being besieged in it themselves, 48—49; their sallying out and defeating the besiegers, 49; their distress before they sallied out, 49—51; their sallying out in consequence of a pretended miracle, 51—53; their defeating the Mahometans in consequence of this and another, 53—54; the former endeavoured to be proved a fiction, 54—55; the state of the Turks and Saracens at this period, 55—56; the slow proceedings of the crusaders, 56—57; their march towards Jerusalem, 57; their siege and reduction of Jerusalem, 59—61; their appointment of one of them to the throne of Jerusalem, 61—62; their defeating the Saracens of Egypt, 62; the extent and strength of their kingdom of Jerusalem, 63—66; its feudal tenures, 66—67; its feudal courts, 67—68; its mode of determining suits by combats, 68—70; its court of burgesses, 70; its Syrian subjects, 70—71; and its villains and slaves, 71. From this detail, therefore, the chapter appears to be all a string of digressions. In a history of the *crusades,* perhaps in a *full* history of the *empire* or of *Mahometanism,* Mr. Gibbon might allowably take this ample sweep of particular narration. But in a history of the *decline* and *fall* of the empire, he is only adding digression to digression; and piling one mountain upon the head of another, that he may lose himself in the clouds.

None of these accounts marks any symptom of decline, or shews any tendency of falling, in the empire. They all indeed unite to note the very reverse. The empire, the extinction of which was threatened in the danger of the capital, is rescued from every danger, and saved from every threat. The narrow dimensions of the empire are enlarged. The lost provinces are recovered, by the homagers of the empire. The internal power of it is augmented, by strong colonies of foreigners. And the two great kingdoms of the Mahometans, that had successively menaced the destruction of it, are now humbled by the armies of its spirited auxiliaries from the West. Yet all this is related, with a circumstantial minuteness of narrative, and with digressional dissertations concerning the justice of the expedition, its spiritual and temporal motives, the falsehood of one of the miracles in it, the extent and strength of the kingdom erected in it at Jerusalem, and its laws and customs; in a history, that professes to give us *only* the *decline* and *fall* of the empire, and that promises to produce *merely* the *important* circumstances of it. The decline of the empire is shewn—in the restoration of it. The fall is exhibited—in the enlargement. And the appearance behind the mirrour, is totally different from the figure before it.

Mr. Gibbon inquires into the justice of the crusade. He urges, that the Christians of the West might equitably preserve the endangered empire of Constantinople, and relieve their oppressed brethren

of the eastern churches; 'but this salutary pur-
'pose might have been accomplished by a mode-
'rate succour; and our calmer reason must disclaim
'the innumerable hosts and *remote operations*, which
'overwhelmed Asia and depopulated Europe.'
Their resolution also to recover *Jerusalem*, was a
wild one, he adds: as 'Palestine could add nothing
'to the strength and safety of the Latins, and fana-
'ticism alone could pretend to justify the conquest
'of that distant and narrow province[1].' And he
farther adds, that the Mahometans had as good a
right to their conquered territory in the East, as the
Christians themselves had to theirs in the West; both
being equally the result of conquest. With these arguments does Mr. Gibbon mean to condemn the
crusades. He who, at the eruption of the Saracens
from the deserts of Arabia, institutes no inquiry into the justice of *their* proceedings, and throws no
formal stain upon the honesty of *their* arms; institutes one of condemnation against the Christians.
But the crusades may be justified, upon the plainest
principles of honest policy.

A nation had burst from the wilds of Tartary,
had embraced the religion of Mahometanism, had
in the course of a few years reduced all the European side of Asia, and now menaced the immediate
destruction of the empire. In these circumstances
of alarm and danger, well might the nations of the
West be apprehensive for themselves. They had
recently seen their own folly in their own suffer-

[1] P. 9—11.

ings;

ings; when they had permitted the first flight of these Mahometan locusts, to make the same settlements unresisted. The Saracens had then reduced Africa, to its western frontier; had subdued Sicily and Spain; and had ravaged France and Italy. The Turks were the Saracens revived, with *their* religion, *their* enthusiasm, and *their* victoriousness. And the same consequences would be sure to result, from the same inattention to their progress in the nations of the West. Thus reflecting; and they could not but reflect in this manner, if they thought at all; they must naturally wish to prevent the re-invasion of Europe, by dispossessing these formidable Tartars of their nearer conquests in Asia. The long line of coast, that ranges from the Euxine to Egypt, would be their object. And to beat back these fanatic savages into the inland countries, perhaps beyond the Euphrates, and perhaps into Tartary; would be their wish. They would thus think as HANNIBAL thought, and thus act as HANNIBAL acted, with the spreading conquerors of Rome. So indeed every man must act and think, who has discernment enough, to apprehend clearly the future from the past; and who has vigour enough, to resolve upon preventing the evils by his resolution, which he cannot but foresee in his sagacity. Even Mr. Gibbon objects not to the principle. He only makes exception to the numbers, with which it was pursued. But the exception is surely a very poor one, the petty effort of a mind, that *would* make exceptions though it *could* not object. The principle
of

of Hannibal's warfare, on this mode of reasoning, was equally just and wise; *but* why should he carry such a large army with him, for the execution of his views? His ' salutary purpose' of keeping the Romans from Africa, by invading their own country of Italy; ' might have been accomplished by a ' moderate succour' to the Gauls of Italy. ' And ' our calmer reason must disclaim;' *not* indeed, as Mr. Gibbon disclaims in the crusaders, ' the remote ' operations' of Hannibal in Italy, because the ' o-' perations' there would be equally ' remote,' either with a large or with a moderate army; but ' the innumerable hosts' of Africans and Spaniards, ' with which' he ' overwhelmed' the regions of Italy, ' and depopulated' those of Carthage. So truly ridiculous does Mr. Gibbon's exception appear, when applied to an expedition, projected upon a similar principle, and executed nearly in the same manner.

Yet the resolution of wresting *Palestine* out of the hands of the Mahometans, adds Mr. Gibbon, was very fanatic. It was not so in itself, as I have already shewn. And, if it was made so by the leaders or by accident, it was so made very usefully. Those elder brothers in fanaticism, the Saracens, who had become so truly formidable from the military genius of Mahometanism; and their younger brothers, the Turks, who had imbibed their spirit, and were treading in their steps; could only have been encountered by an equal principle of fanaticism or of religion, in the endangered kingdoms of the West.

Nothing

Nothing less than such a strong principle as this, which by the novelty, the grandeur, and the affectingness of its object, would strike powerfully upon the soul, push with a vigorous fermentation through all the substance of its hopes and fears, and even rouse them to an energy unfelt before; could possibly have done this. And the introduction of recovering Palestine from the Mahometans, and rescuing the sepulchre of our Saviour out of the polluting hands of the infidels; was certainly one of the happiest strokes of policy, or one of the luckiest incidents of chance, that could come in aid of such a rational policy. It became the active spirit, that vivified the whole mass. In vain would the remote concerns of futurity have been held up, to the generality of the world. They would have heard, have been convinced, and still slept over the danger. But when an object of their religion was exhibited along with it; when the sepulchre of Him, in whom they all believed, and from whom they all hoped for salvation, was exhibited to them, as polluted by the hands of his and their enemies; and when to rescue this was considered as an act of high religion, a glorious exertion of faith, and a deed of Christian heroism; all were struck, all were wrought upon. The wicked had still their inward reverence, for all that was sacred in their religion. This reverence was now touched in its tenderest string. It vibrated therefore very feelingly from the impulse. And the heart, which would not be holy in order to gain heaven, and yet still fostered the vain

hope

hope of gaining heaven without holiness; readily caught at this surer way of gaining it, by the easier mode of fighting for it. Nor was this delusive kind of reasoning peculiar to those times. We see the same continually in our own; external deeds substituted for internal rectitude. But the good felt the impulse much more powerfully. Their practice continually cherished the vital flame in their heart. Their spirits were ready to kindle, at any offered incentive of religion. And Shakespeare has accordingly stated in an age of commencing protestantism, this motive for a crusade in such a manner; as is *felt* (we believe) by our own age, and was more felt probably in his:

> ——————————therefore, friends,
> As far as to the sepulchre of Christ
> (Whose soldiers now, under whose blessed cross
> We are impressed, and engaged to fight)
> Forthwith a power of English shall we levy;
> Whose arms were moulded in their mothers' wombs
> To chase these pagans in those holy fields,
> Over whose acres walk'd those blessed feet,
> Which, fourteen hundred years ago, were nail'd
> For our advantage, on the bitter cross.

Yet Mr. Gibbon objects, that the Christians had no more right to dispossess the Turks of Palestine, than the Turks had to deprive them of their dominions in the West; and that they fanatically supposed Palestine to be theirs, because of their Saviour's sufferings in it. So supposing, they were only thinking with a portion of that over-religious-ness or fanaticism, which was requisite to the general undertaking. This was only a mark of the height, to which the necessary spring-tide of religion was risen. Nor was there any injustice in it. The Turks had no right, and the Saracens had none; except what the sword of conquest had given them. To this right of theirs, might with equal justice be opposed the right of a *new* conquest. But the only nation besides, that claimed the country, the Romans, urged more equitably against it their long possession, their recent loss, and their present claim. On this footing stand all the national rights in the world. Take away this; and the world becomes one great scene of national scrambles, without right, or possibility of right, in any of the nations. And the Romans SOLICITED the assistance of their brother Christians of the West, for the preservation of the empire and the recovery of its provinces. What then, but the rank and fœtid fanaticism of the Koran, can pretend to doubt the right of the Christians, to assist the reduced empire, and to wrest back its provinces from the plunderers?

On these solid and substantial grounds of justice, and with this strong body of policy animated with that lively soul of religion; did the nations of the West come gallantly forward to the crusade. Their conduct forms a very wonderful object of curiosity, to the philosopher, the politician, and the historian. The disunited kingdoms of the late empire of the West, that had been overwhelmed with a deluge of barbarians from Germany and the Baltick; that had

however

however subdued this wild accession of foreign soil, had incorporated it into its own substance, and had risen at last the stronger and the more luxuriant from it; now united into a kind of loose republick again, under the seeming sovereignty of the ecclesiastical king of Rome too, and in order to relieve and restore the remaining half of the empire. They thus shewed an attention to that grand principle of modern policy, of which we feel the want in all the progress of the Roman arms, and which we vainly fancy to be the refinement of these latter days. They also carried their attention to a length, to which the poor and feeble policy of modern times has never been capable of going. And this extraordinary display of policy, and this astonishing eruption of religion, unite to make one of the most singular epochas in the history of human nature; and served, with wisdom and with justice, to save the empire of Constantinople for ages, and to keep the Turks out of western Europe for ever.

'If the reader will turn to the first scene of the 'First Part of Henry the Fourth, he will see in 'the text of Shakespeare the natural feelings of 'enthusiasm; and in the notes of Dr. Johnson, the 'workings of a bigotted though vigorous mind, 'greedy of every pretence to hate and persecute 'those who dissent from his creed¹.' The reader has already turned to the text; let him now turn to the notes. 'The lawfulness and justice of the holy wars,' says Dr. Johnson, ' have been much disputed; but

¹ P. 9.

' perhaps

'perhaps there is a principle, on which the question
'may be easily determined. If it be part of the
'religion of the Mahometans, to extirpate by the
'sword all other religions; it is, by the law of self-
'defence, lawful for men of every other religion,
'and for Christians among others, to make war
'upon the Mahometans, simply as Mahometans,
'as men obliged by their own principles to make
'war upon Christians, and only lying in wait till
'opportunity shall promise them success.' Are these
then *all* 'the workings of a bigotted though vigo-
'rous mind,' that we were to see here? Is this
then *that* striking evidence to which we were referred, for Johnson being '*greedy* of *every* pretence, to
'*hate* and *persecute* those who *dissent from his creed?*'
The charge recoils forcibly upon the bringer of it.
And the *bigotry*, the *hatred*, and the *persecution*, are
beaten back in the face of the accuser. Mr. Gibbon evidently *caught* at this opportunity of insulting
the *dead* lion, for the many triumphs which it had
made in its life, over the prostrated carcase of infidelity. He thus defeated his purpose by his eagerness. There is *not* much 'vigour,' in the short
passage. Nor is there *one* particle of 'bigotry,' of
'hatred,' or of 'persecution,' in it. There is only one mistake, in supposing it to be 'part of the
'religion of the Mahometans, to *extirpate* by the
'sword all other religions.' This indeed was *actually* practised, on the *first* ground of their religion.
'Under the reign of Omar' the second successor of
Mahomet, says Mr. Gibbon himself, 'the Jews of
'Chaibar

'Chaibar were *transplanted* to Syria; and the caliph
'alleged the injunction of his dying master, that
'*one* and *the true* religion should be professed in his
'native land of *Arabia*¹.' But the Mahometans
necessarily refrained from practising it, in their other
conquests. And Dr. Johnson only produces the allegation as a *conditional* one, though Mr. Gibbon
chooses to consider it as *positive*. ' *If* it be part of
' the religion of the Mahometans,' he says, ' to ex-
' tirpate,' &c. But let us change the word *extirpate*
into *subdue*, and then the allegation may become *absolute*, and the argument will be decisive. ' *As it is* part
' of the religion of the Mahometans,' Dr. Johnson
would then say, ' to *subdue* by the sword all other reli-
' gions; it is, by the law of self defence, lawful for
' men of every other religion, and for Christians a-
' mong others, to make war upon Mahometans,
' simply as Mahometans, as men obliged by their
' own principles to make war upon Christians, and
' only lying in wait till opportunity shall promise
' them success.' And Mr. Gibbon himself allows
us, ' that, in *peace* or *war*, they *assert* a *divine* and
' *indefeasible* claim of *universal empire*².' I thus
vindicate the character and the reasoning of Dr.
Johnson, from the abuse of a writer, who, I know,
at once hated and dreaded him in his life-time.

In all this history of the first crusade, we see a
studied design to shade the glory of the Christians,
to place their failings and vices in the fullest point of
light, and to break into the great order of narration

¹ Vol. v. p. 237.   ² Vol. vi. p. 10.

with

with the view of lessening their victories. We see all this particularly exemplified, in the history of the siege and battle of Antioch. We have first a general and rapid account of the siege; too general to catch the attention much, and too rapid to rest upon it long. Instantly as this is ended, without pausing one moment upon the greatness and importance, of winning such a town after such a resistance; we see the Christians within it, surrounded by a large army of Mahometans. The good-fortune of having entered the town, before the Mahometans came up to relieve it; is not touched upon. To have done so, would have betrayed some symptoms of remaining Christianity in Mr. Gibbon's head. And he could not be capable of such a *weakness*. But the deliverance of the Christians, is as sudden and short as their danger. They ' sallied,' out, and ' in a single memorable day annihilated ' or dispersed the host of Turks and Arabians.' Mr. Gibbon then points at ' the human causes' of their victory. ' Their supernatural allies,' he says, ' I shall proceed to consider' hereafter. He thus deprives us of the pleasure, of dwelling upon this victorious battle of the Christians. For he hastens *back*, to tell us of their intemperance from plenty, of their distress from famine, of their viciousness at the siege of the town, and during their blockade in it by the Mahometans. ' The Christians were se-
' duced,' he says, ' by *every* temptation that *nature*
' either prompts or *reprobates* ¹ ;' when his own note

¹ p. 50.

to the passage shews only *one single* incident, and that *not* of lust which 'nature reprobates,' but of 'an 'archdeacon of royal birth—*playing at dice* with a 'Syrian concubine;' and when *this* serves to refute the infamous calumny in *that*. He then tells us of a pretended miracle, that inspirited the Christians; of their marching out to attack the Mahometans; and of another miracle being supposed to be seen by them, in their march. But, just as we expect some account of the charge, the battle, the victory, and its glorious consequences; we are instantly turned off with one inquiry, into the reality of the first miracle, and with another into the state of the Turks and Saracens, &c. &c. And thus artfully lost in its effect upon the reader, by being broken into fragments, the battle being separated from the victory, and the interval filled up with invectives against the conquerors; and thus disgraced by falsehoods *more than Mahometan*, against these 'barbarians of the 'West,' as he presumes to call them'; the history must be spurned at with disdain, by every friend to truth, to honesty, and to Christianity. Indeed in all the narrative of this chapter, we see the Mahometan so rampant in Mr. Gibbon; and the love of antichristian falsehoods in him, so much stronger than a regard to himself and a reverence for honour, those two pillars of heaven and of history; that we cannot trust his word for a moment, and we cannot but despise his spirit continually.

'The mother of Tancred was Emma, sister of the

' p. 55.

'great Robert Guiscard; his father, the Marquis
'Odo the Good. It is singular enough, that the
'family and country of so illustrious a person should
'be unknown¹.' This is all a mistake, I apprehend. Tancred was not *nephew* to Robert Guiscard; and *son* to Odo. He was the *son* of Roger, Count of Apulia, *nephew* to Bohemond, Prince of Tarento, and grandson to Robert Guiscard. This a letter of Bohemond's own shews. Mr. Gibbon quotes it himself. There, he remarks, 'Tancred is
'styled *filius*; of whom? certainly not of Roger,
'nor of Bohemond².' And on this account, and because Godfrey of Bouillon and Hugh are called *brothers* in it, *sworn-brothers*, I suppose; he calls it
'a very doubtful letter.' But we have another from Bohemond to his brother Roger. 'I suppose you,' it says from Antioch, 'to have understood by the
'letters of *your sonne* Tancred,' &c.; 'I assure you
'much of the valour of *your sonne* Tancred³.' This settles at once the unknown 'family and country' of Tancred's paternal ancestors. And Tancred is accordingly called the *nephew* of Bohemond, 'Tan-
'credus nepos Boamundi;' by a very respectable historian of the time⁴.

'At the siege of Antioch,' says Mr. Gibbon,
'Phirouz, a Syrian renegado, had acquired the fa-
'vour of the Emir and the command of three

¹ p. 25.   ² p. 43.   ³ Knolles, 19.
⁴ William of Malmesbury, p. 79, edit. 1596. So also in fol.
85 concerning him and Bohemond, 'haud pudendus avunculo
'nepos.'

'towers.

'towers.—A secret correspondence, for *their mutual
'interest*, was soon established between Phirouz and
'the prince of Tarento; and Bohemond declared
'in the council of the chiefs, that he could deliver
'the city into their hands. But he claimed the so-
'vereignty of Antioch, *as the reward of his service*;
and the proposal, which had been rejected by the
'*envy*, was *at length* extorted from the *distress*, of his
'equals.' The town was taken. 'But the citadel
'still refused to surrender; and the victors them-
'selves were *speedily* encompassed and besieged' by
the Turks[1]. Here are several mistakes, which a
letter of the time decisively corrects. 'King Cas-
'sianus,' says Bohemond himself concerning the
Turkish governor of Antioch, 'had *required a time
'of truce*,' a circumstance totally omitted by Mr.
Gibbon; '*during which our soldiers had free recourse in-
'to the citie without danger*,' a striking feature in the
complexion of these crusades, that is equally unnoticed by Mr. Gibbon; 'untill that by the death of
'Vollo a Frenchman, slaine by the enemie, the
'truce was broken. But, whilst it yet seemed an
'hard matter to winne the citie, one *Pyrrhus*, a
'citizen of Antioch, *of great authority*, and *much
'devoted unto mee*, had conference with me concern-
'ing the yeelding up of the citie; yet *upon condi-
'tion*, that the *government thereof should be committed
'to me*, in whom *he had reposed an especiall trust*.
'I conferred of the whole matter, with the princes
'and great commanders of the armie; and *easily

[1] P. 48.

'obtained,

' obtained, that the government of the citie was by
' their generall consent allotted unto me. So our
' armie, entering by a gate opened by Pyrrhus, tooke
' the citie. *Within a few daies after*, the towne A-
' retum was by us affaulted, but not without some
' loffe and danger to our perfon, by reafon of a
' wound I there received [1].' Here we fee, that the
correfpondence between Bohemond and Pyrrhus began, in the extraordinary intercourfe permitted by
the truce, and then Pyrrhus had fhewn himfelf
much devoted to Bohemond; that Bohemond did
not carry it on for his *private* intereft; that Pyrrhus
made it an exprefs ftipulation of his opening the
gates to the Chriftians, Bohemond fhould have the
government of it afterwards; that he did this, unin-
fluenced by Bohemond, and purely confidering his
own intereft, he being *a citizen of great authority*,
and wanting to retain it under a governor, to whom
he was *much devoted*, and in whom *he repofed an ef-
pecial truft*; that Bohemond mentioned the propofal
and the ftipulation to the other generals, and the
latter was *not* ' rejected by their envy,' and ' at
' length extorted from their diftrefs,' but was ' eafi-
' ly obtained' from them; and that, *after* taking the
town and *before* the coming up of the Turks, *the
town of Aretum was attacked*, and *Bohemond was
wounded in the affault*. Such a number of miftakes
have we here, in this fhort paffage!

' I have been urged to anticipate *on* the ftory of
' the crufades,' p. 29; ' their portable treafures

---

[1] Knolles, 19.

' was,'

' was,' p. 29; ' had almoſt reached the firſt *term*
' of his pilgrimage,' p. 30.—' In ſome oriental tale
' I have read the fable of a ſhepherd, who was
' ruined by the accompliſhment of his own wiſhes:
' —ſuch was the fortune, or at leaſt the apprehen-
' ſion, of the Greek emperor¹.' This is the ſtyle
of a diſſertation, and not of a hiſtory. But Mr.
Gibbon is perpetually confounding the two ideas.
And his whole hiſtory hitherto is little more, than
one extenſive and amplified diſſertation.—' He was
' himſelf inveſted,' ſays Mr. Gibbon in his very
frequent obſcurity, ' with that ducal title, which
' has been improperly transferred to his lordſhip of
' Bouillon in the Ardennes,' p. 22; ' they overran
' —the hills and ſea-coaſt of Cilicia, from Cogni to
' the Syrian gates,' p. 449; &c. &c.

Abulpharagius is again ' the Jacobite primate,'
p. 53; when he was only a phyſician among the Jacobite Chriſtians.—In his firſt volume Mr. Gibbon,
from the littleneſs of his ſpite againſt the Jews, called them ' the moſt deſpiſed' portion of the Aſſy-
rian ſlaves; when he had no authority but his ſpite,
for ſaying they were deſpiſed at all. In the ſame
petty malice of infidelity he ſays here, that Jeruſalem had ' derived *ſome* reputation from its ſieges²;'
when its ſieges are the moſt memorable in hiſtory.
—Conrad's wife ' confeſſed the manifold proſtitu-
' tions, to which ſhe had been expoſed by a huſ-
' band, regardleſs of her honour and his own.'
So ſays the text p. 4. ' Yet it ſhould ſeem,' adds

---

¹ p. 32.   ² p. 57.

the note, 'that the wretched woman was *tempted by* 'the *priests*, to relate or subscribe some infamous 'stories of herself and her husband.' *It should seem* then, that the *charge* in the *text* is *not true,* or at least the *assertion* in it is *doubtful.*

'Their siege,' says Mr. Gibbon, p. 59, concerning the crusaders before Jerusalem, ' was more reasonably directed against the *northern* and *western* 'sides of the city. Godfrey of Bouillon erected his 'standard on the first swell of Mount Calvary,' which is on the north-west¹; 'to the *left*,' which is therefore to the *east*, ' as far as St. Stephen's gate,' which lies about the *middle* of the *eastern* side², ' the line of attack was continued by Tancred and ' the two Roberts; and Count Raymond established ' his quarters from the citadel,' which was (as we shall shew immediately) on the *south-west*, ' to ' the foot of Mount Sion, which was no longer included within the precincts of the city,' was not *all,* but was *in part,* even in *great* part, and lay to the *south* of Calvary³. What a labyrinth of confusion have we here! The attack is directed only against the *northern* and *western* sides. Godfrey accordingly encamps on the *north-western.* But then the attack is diverted by Mr. Gibbon's mistake, from the *right* to the *left,* and from the *western* to the *eastern* side. Yet we instantly find, that this *eastern* was meant for the *western*; as the line of attack is continued round by the *south-west*, to the

---

[1] See Pococke, 11. Part 1. 7. Plan. [2] Pococke.
[3] Pococke.

south. Where indeed ' the citadel' lies, is not explained *here* by Mr. Gibbon. But it is *hereafter*. *Two pages afterward* he makes it to be the *Pisan Castle*, which was a little to the north of the south-western angle [1]. And as we can know the true history of reducing Antioch and Jerusalem, not from Mr. Gibbon, but only from Knolles; so we may observe the accuracy of Knolles contrasted with the confusedness of Mr. Gibbon, in this very passage. ' The Christians,' *he* says, ' with their armies ap-
' proching the citie, encamped before it on the
' *north*; for that, towards the *east* and *south*, it was
' not well to be besieged, by reason of the broken
' rocks and mountaines. Next unto the citie lay
' Godfrey the duke, with the Germanes and Lo-
' ranois; *neere unto him lay the Earle of Flanders and*
' *Robert the Norman*; before the *west* gate lay Tan-
' cred and the Earle of Thouloufe [2].'

At this siege, ' the scanty *springs* and hasty tor-
' rents were *dry* in the summer season; nor was the
' thirst of the besiegers relieved, *as in the city*, by
' the artificial supply of cisterns and aqueducts [3].'
This is not true. A letter of the time, as given us by Knolles, shews it not to be so. ' After long travell,' says the writer, ' having first taken certaine townes,
' we came to Jerusalem; which citie is environed
' with high hills, without rivers or fountaines, *except-*
' *ing onely that of Solomon's*, and that *a verie little one.*

[1] Pococke.   [2] Knolles, p. 22.
[3] p. 59.

' In

in it are many cefterns, wherein water is kept, *both* in the citie *and the countrey thereabout*¹.'

In ftorming Jerufalem, fays Mr. Gibbon, ever eager to lay load upon the crufaders, ' a bloody fa-crifice was offered by his miftaken votaries, to the God of the Chriftians—; they indulged themfelves *three days* in a promifcuous maffacre.' A note adds, that ' the *Latins*—are not *aſhamed* of the maffacre;' but pretends not to point out any of them. ' After feventy thoufand Moflems had been put to the fword,' &c. ' Tancred alone betrayed fome fentiments of compaffion.' And ' the felfifh lenity of Raymond—granted a capitulation and fafe conduct, to the garrifon of the citadel.' Note adds, that *this* was named ' Caftellum Pifanum,' and ' the Tower of David².' It was, as I have noticed before, near the fouth-weftern angle of the city; and confequently upon Mount Sion, the feat of David's city. But I have produced this paffage, in order to collate it with that original letter of the time, which I have cited in part before. ' In the affault of the citie,' fays *Godfrey of Bouillon* himfelf, ' I firft gained that part of the wall that fell to my *lot* to affaile, and commanded Baldwin to enter the citie; who, having flain certaine companies of the enemies, broke open one of the gates for the Chriftians to enter. Raymond had the citie of David, with much rich fpoile, yeelded unto him. But, when we came unto the temple of Solomon, there we had a great conflict, with

¹ Knolles, 24.   ² p. 60—61.

' fo

' so great slaughter of the enemie, that our men
' stood in blood above the ancles; the night ap-
' proching, we could not take the upper part of
' the temple, which the next day was yeelded, the
' Turks pitifully crying out for mercie: and so the
' citie of Jerusalem was by us taken the fifteenth of
' July——: besides this, the princes with one con-
' sent saluted me (against my will) King of Jeru-
' salem.' This is the most authentic account of
the storm of Jerusalem, that the nature of history
can possibly furnish; because it is a cotemporary
one, given by an eye-witness, and drawn up by the
grand actor and conductor of the whole. Yet how
astonishingly does it differ from Mr. Gibbon's! The
asserted ' massacre of three days,' of which ' the
' Latins' are said to be ' not ashamed,' is shewn to
be absolutely false by the very general of the Latins.
The storm of Jerusalem was like many other storms
of cities, a progressive scene of fighting and blood
through the streets, up to the level of Mount Moriah. *There* had stood the temple of Solomon.
There now stood another temple, the present
mosqué, with ' colonades' to it, ' which have a
' grand appearance, and are of *very* good *Corin-*
' *thian* architecture¹.' It was therefore a Christian
church before, built in the time of the Romans;
and had been turned into a mosque, as it is now
turned again. To this ground, as to the most retired and defensible part of the whole town,
and into this mosque upon it, had many of the
Turks retreated. Here they were attacked by the

---

¹ Pocock, 14.

victorious

victorious Christians. Instantly there was 'a great
'conflict.' This was carried on 'with so great a
'slaughter of the enemie, that' the assailants 'stood
'in blood above the ancles.' This is a stroke most
formidably picturesque, to mark the slaughter of the
'conflict.' But the Turks, though driven from
the interiour of the temple, still maintained themselves upon the roof of it, and beat off the Christians. 'The night approaching,' they 'could not
'take the upper part of the temple.' They desisted
from their attempts, for the night. But 'the next
day' they were preparing to renew them. The
Turks, seeing this, 'pitifully cried out for mercie.'
Mercy was promised them. The roof 'was
'yeelded' up. 'And so the citie of Jerusalem
'was by them taken,' without any more blood-
shed. Such is the *certain* account of this storm!
Where then is the horrible 'massacre' of 'three
'days?' There was no massacre at all. There
was even no blood-shed, except such as is always
made in a storm, *while the opposition lasts*. Nor
was *this* 'for three days.' It was for one only.
And the very next morning, when the Turks on
the roof of the temple cried out for quarter, it was
granted them. What then shall we say, to the
bold and daring falshood in Mr. Gibbon? We
hope he was deceived by, as he actually refers us
to, 'Elmacin (Hist. Saracen. p. 363), Abulphara-
'gius (Dynast. p. 243), and M. de Guignes (tom.
'II. p. 11. p. 99) from Aboulmahasen.' But at
the best, and supposing him *not* to have falsified *their*
reports; yet he has certainly been very *credulous*,

in

in leaning upon such *secondary* authorities, when he had such a *primary* one at hand. And his credulity, every one must observe, is *never* exerted *except* on the *anti-christian* side. Nor is this all his mistake, in this description of the storm. He chose again to confound the natural course of the narration, which is all regularly given in Knolles[1], in order, no doubt, to serve the same purpose as before, of distorting the facts, breaking their unity, and diminishing their force. He thus omits all mention whatever, of the stand at the temple or mosque on Mount Moriah, of the bloody conflict held in it, and of the mercy shewn to those upon the roof of it. This grand and memorable incident in the storm, did not suit with his views of writing history. It would have precluded his ' massacre of ' three days.' It was therefore suppressed. Yet he says, immediately previous to the passages above, that ' the spoils of *the great mosch*, seventy lamps ' and massy vases of gold and silver, rewarded the ' diligence—of Tancred.' And he, who notices the spoils of the temple, and takes no notice of the sharp conflict at it, must have wilfully suppressed the latter. But Raymond, he says *finally*, ' granted ' a capitulation and safe conduct to the garrison of ' the citadel.' This is evidently said from its final position, in order to single him out as one, who shewed kindness amid the bloody spirit of his massacreing companions. Yet the fact is, that it happened in the *very beginning* of the storm. One of the gates,

[1] p. 23.

says

says Godfrey, was 'broke open—for the Christians
' to enter:' Raymond had '*the citie of David*,' that is,
all that large part of it, the ground of which was
within the walls, ' with much rich spoile, *yeelded*
' unto him;' but, when we ' came to the temple
' of Solomon,' &c. *That* was not stormed, but
yeelded to him; just as the upper part of the temple was afterwards to the rest. And Mr. Gibbon
either directly *precludes* the *yielding* of the latter, and
the *mercy* shewn at it, by declaring that, ' of these
' savage heroes of the cross, Tancred *alone* betrayed
' some sentiments of compassion,' as Raymond did
of ' selfish lenity;' or else alludes to the mercy at
the temple, in what he thus says of Tancred, and
in what he also hints of ' the spoils of the great
' mosch—*displaying the generosity* of Tancred;' and
so glances obscurely, at what he *fully knew* and
chose not to reveal. He fully knew all, no doubt.
Yet he chose not to reveal it. He *actually* has *falsified* the alleged evidence of the Latins. And, on
the whole, he appears in such a light upon the
present occasion, as must blast his historical credit
with the critical world, and annihilate his personal
reputation with the Christian, for ever.

' The expulsion of the Greeks and Syrians' from
the holy sepulchre at Jerusalem, ' was justified by
' the reproach of heresy and schism (Renaudot,
' Hist. Patriarch. Alex. p. 479)'.' We have seen
Mr. Gibbon before, making very free with the
authority of this very Renaudot; and even fixing

[1] p. 63.

special

special and marked words upon him, that he never used. We see something like this literary legerdemain, exercised here. The 'Greeks and Syrians' of Mr. Gibbon, are *neither* in Renaudot. They are merely *the Jacobite Christians* of *Egypt.* 'Mirum nemini esse debet, eâ clade tantopere per‑ 'culsos Mahomedanos fuisse, qui urbem celebrem 'sanctitate, et ad quam Christiani ex toto orbe 'confluerent, ereptam sibi deplorabant. Sed non 'minor fuit *Jacobitarum Ægyptiorum* dolor—. Inde 'factum est,' says an author quoted by him 'ut 'nos Christiani *Jacobitæ Coptitæ* non ampliús pere‑ 'grinationis religiosæ ad eam urbem instituendæ fa‑ 'cultatem habeamus.' But Mr. Gibbon has changed his *Copts* into *Greeks and Syrians,* and multiplied his *Jacobites* into *Nestorians, Jacobites,* and *Melchites.* 'Every reader conversant with the his‑ 'tory of the crusades,' says Mr. Gibbon himself upon another occasion, 'will understand by the 'peuple des *Suriens,* the *Oriental Christians, Mel‑* 'chites, Jacobites, or Nestorians' (p. 70). Yet, to make it more full, Mr. Gibbon has added the *Greeks* to the *Syrians.* And, all the while, his author speaks only of *Egyptians.* This is another instance of the *foul play,* which Mr. Gibbon practises with his references; and the point, in justice to the publick, cannot be too frequently proved to the reader.

'William of Malmsbury (who wrote about the 'year 1130) has inserted in his history (l. iv. p. '130—154) a narrative of the first crusade: but 'I wish

' I wish that, instead of listening to the tenue
' murmur which had passed the British ocean (p.
' 143), he had confined himself to the number of
' families, and adventures of his countrymen [1].'
This is a very unjust account of Malmsbury's narrative. The latter contains much and useful matter in it. Nor has the former forgotten in this and other parts of his history, to give us intimations concerning the particular crusaders of England, their ' families,' and their ' adventures.' *Edgar Atheling*, he says ' subsequenti tempore cum *Roberto Godwino*,
' milite audacissimo, Jerosolymam pertendit.' The Turks, he adds, *then* besieged King Baldwin at Rama, who broke through the host of besiegers, principally by the gallantry of Robert, ' evaginato
' gladio dextrâ lævâque Turcos cædentis. Sed
' cúm, successu ipso truculentior, alacritate nimiâ
' procurreret, ensis manu excidit; ad quem recolli-
' gendum cum se inclinasset, omnium incursu op-
' pressus, vinculis palmas dedit. Inde Babyloniam
' (ut aiunt) ductus, cúm Christum abnegare nollet,
' in medio foro ad signum positus, et sagittis tere-
' bratus, martyrium consecravit. Edgarus amisso
' milite regressus, multaque beneficia ab impera-
' toribus Græcorum et Alemannorum adeptus
' (quippe qui etiam eum retinere pro generis am-
' plitudine tentassent), omnia pro natalis soli desi-
' derio sprevit [2].' But he speaks again of this Robert, in his history of the crusades. Baldwin, he says, ' quinque militibus comitatus, in montana re-

[1] p. 39.   [2] fol. 58.

' pendo

'pendo infidiantes elufit: militum unus fuit Robertus Anglus, ut fuperius dixi; cæteros notitiæ noftræ fama tam longinqua occuluit[1].' He alfo mentions Odo, Bifhop of Baieux and Earl of Kent, as one of the companions of his nephew Robert, Duke of Normandy. He went with him to Jerufalem and died at Antioch. 'Jerofolymitanam viam ingreffus, *Antiochiæ* in *obfidione Chriftianorum* finem habuit[2].' And he hints at a *large* body of the Englifh going with Duke Robert: 'Robertus Normannorum Comes—habuit focios Robertum Flandrenfem, Stephanum Blefenfem,' &c.; 'parebant eis *Angli*, et Normanni,' &c.[3] In his narration too, he fays fome of the crufaders marched through Theffaly and Thrace to Conftantinople, but that many of the common men died of want and difeafe by the way, and 'multi in *vado*, quod pro rapiditate *diaboli* dicitur, intercepti[4].' At the fiege of Nice, 'exanimatorum cadavera Turci uncis ferreis innumerûm trahebant, ludibrio noftrorum *excarnificanda*, vel *ablatis veftibus* dejicienda.' On the furrender of Nice, the emperour 'juffit— diftribui argentum et aurum optimatibus, nummos æreos inferioribus.' At the fiege of Antioch 'omnes pariter proceres *facramento fecere*, obfidioni *non* ponendas ferias *quoad* vel vi vel ingenio prenderetur civitas.' But the Turks, putting many of the citizens of Antioch to the fword, were 'baliftis et petrariis *capita interemptorum* in caftra Francorum emittentes.' A famine came on among the be-

[1] fol. 84. [2] fol. 63. [3] fol. 75. [4] fol. 76.

siegers. ' Nondum surgentibus in altam segetem
' culmis, quidam *siliquas fabarum* nondum adultarum
' pro summis deliciis amplecterentur; alii *carnes*
' *jumentorum*, alii *coria* aquis mollita, quidam *car-*
' *duos* parúm coctos per abrasas fauces utero demit-
' tebant; quidam vel *mures*, vel *talium quid deli-*
' *ciarum*, poscentibus aliis venundabant, et esurire
' sustinebat pro lato jejunus venditor auro; nec de-
' fuerunt qui *cadavera cadaveribus infarcirent, huma-*
' *nis pasti carnibus*, longé tamen et in montibus, ne
' nidore carnis adustæ cæteri offenderentur; plures,
' spe reperiendæ alimoniæ, ignotis vagabantur se-
' mitis, et a latrunculis viarum gnaris trucidaban-
' tur.' Yet with a spirit of resolution, which does high
honour to the leaders and to the men; and, to pass
over which, Mr. Gibbon suppresses all these striking
circumstances of the famine, a famine so uncommon in an un-surrounded camp of besiegers; the
Christians persisted in spite of all, and took the town.
In taking it ' Franci per funeas scalas nocte intem-
' pestâ in murum evecti, *vexilloque Boamundi, quod*
' *vermiculatum erat, ventis in fastigio turris exposito*,
' signum Christianum lætis fragoribus ingeminant,
' *Deus vult, Deus vult;* Turci experrecti, et sopo-
' ris penuria inertes, fugam per angiportus inva-
' dunt.' The Turkish army comes, and surrounds
them in the town. Distress ensues in it. ' Qua-
' propter, *triduano* priús *cum letaniis* exacto *jejunio*,
' legatus *Petrus heremita* mittitur ad Turcos.' He
offers them the alternative, either to move away from
before the town, and return into Persia, or agree to
fight

fight them the next morning; ' fortem per *duos* vel
' *quatuor* vel *octo* experiantur, ne periculum ad to-
' tum vergat exercitum.' This singular, humane, and
wise proposal, which recalls to our minds an image
of the earliest times of the Romans, the Turkish
Sultan received in this striking manner; without
answering, ' *scacchis ludens,* et *dentibus infrendens,*
' inanem dimisit.' The Christians then prepared
to attack the Turks, the next day. But not the
least notice is taken of the holy lance, so much dwelt
upon by Mr. Gibbon, and even noticed by Florence
of Worcester, a writer cotemporary with Malmesbury[r]. Yet the appearance of St. George, and of
St. Demetrius (instead of St. Theodore and St.
Maurice), is noticed by Malmesbury though unnoticed by Florence, and is even affirmed to be true.
The order, in which the Christians marched out of
the town, is particularly told. Even one incident
of the battle is noticed, to the honour of two Englishmen.
Robert, eldest son to the Conqueror, ' vic-
' toriam pulchrâ experientiâ nobilitavit. Nam cúm
' Turci —, subitó terrefacti, fugæ se dedissent, nos-
' trique palantes vehementer impeterent; Corba-
' nach Dux,' the commander of the Turks, ' ge-
' nuinæ virtutis memor, retento equo suos inclina-
' vit, famulos ignavos et annosarum victoriarum
' oblitos vocans, ut victores quondam orientis pa-
' terentur se ab advenâ et *pene inermi* populo finibus
' excludi. Quo clamore multi resumentes ani-
' mum, Francos conversi urgere et propiores cæde-

[r] p. 467. Edit. 1592.

' re

' re cœpere; Corbanach suos animante et hostes fe-
' riente, ut imperatoris et militis officium probé ex-
' equeretur. Tum veró *Normannus Comes*, et *Phi-*
' *lippus clericus filius Rogerii Comitis de Monte Gome-*
' *rico*, et Warinus de Tanco castello Cenoman-
' nico, mutuâ vivacitate se invicem hortati, qui si-
' mulatâ anté fugâ cedebant convertunt cornipedes,
' et *quisque suum comparem incessens dejiciunt*. Ibi
' Corbanach, quámvis Comitem cognosceret, solo
' tamen corpore mensus,' Robert being (as Malmesbury says before) of a small stature, ' simul et fu-
' gere inglorium arbitratus, *audaciam congressûs morte*
' *propinquâ luit* vitali statim spiritu privatus. Cujus
' nece visâ, Turci, qui jam gloriabundi *ululabant*,
' spe recenti exinaniti fugam iterârunt. In eo tu-
' multu Warinus cecidit, *Robertus cum Philippo*
' *palmam retulit*. *Philippus* hâc militiâ præcluus
' [præclarus], *sed Jerosolymis* (ut fertur) *bono fine*
' *functus*; præter exercitium equestre *literis clarus* [1].'
This very extraordinary fact, the killing of the
Turkish general with Robert's own hand, is wholly unnoticed by Mr. Gibbon. Yet he wishes
Malmesbury had given us some accounts, of the
' adventures' of our countrymen. And though he
has given us some, Mr. Gibbon omits them all;
either ignorant of their existence, or unwilling to
dwell upon them. The Christians thus defeating
the Turks, ' reversi veró in predam, tanta in illo-
' rum castris reperiunt, quæ cujuslibet avarissimi
' exercitûs satietatem possent vel temperare vel ex-

[1] Fol. 86.

' tinguere.'

'tinguere.' Yet all these circumstances are omitted by Mr. Gibbon.

The Christians now advance by Tripolis, Berithus, Tyre, Sidon, Accaron, Caipha, and Cæsarea; there leave the sea-coast to the right; and penetrate through Ramula to Jerusalem. But here let me subjoin a circumstance, that is omitted equally by Mr. Gibbon and by Malmesbury, but is peculiarly characteristick of the spirit of these crusaders.— 'Marching from Ruma,' says Knolles, 'and draw-
'ing neere to Jerusalem, they in the *vantgard* of
'the armie, *upon the first descrying of the holy citie,*
'gave for joy *divers great shouts and outcrys*, which
'with *the like applause* of *the whole armie,* was so
'*doubled* and *redoubled,* as if therewith they would
'have *rent the verie mountaines* and *pearced the high-*
'*est heavens.* There might a man have seene the
'devout passions of these most worthie and zealous
'Christians, uttered in right divers manners: some
'with *their eies and hands cast up towards heaven,*
'called aloud *upon the name and helpe of Christ Jesus;*
'some, *prostrat upon their faces, kissed the ground,*
'as *that whereon the Redeemer of the world sometime*
'*walked;* others *joyfully saluted those holy places,*
'which they had heard so much of and then first
'beheld: in briefe, *everie man* in *some* sort *expressed*
'*the joy he had conceived* of the *sight* of the Holy
'Citie, as the end of their long travell¹.' This passage carries such a lively affectingness with it; that I well remember the impression which it made

¹ Knolles, p. 21.

upon

upon my mind, when I *last* read it, and nearly *half a century ago*. And surely such circumstances as these should be caught at with eagerness, by every history, by the *philosophy* of history particularly, if this philosophy means any thing beyond the pettiness of oratorical parade, or the monstrousness of infidel credulity; as what peculiarly catch the manners of the moment while they are rising, and reflect them back in all their vivacity and vividness to posterity. In so striking a way did the crusaders act at the first view of Jerusalem. They besiege it. 'Nor was the thirst of the *besiegers* relieved,' says Mr. Gibbon; 'nor were there any trees for the 'uses of shade;' but, as Malmesbury, with a more judicious appositeness to the months of *June* and *July*, observes, ' nec quisquam sibi *obsessor* verebatur
' in cibatu vel in *potu*, quód messes in agris, uvæ
' in vineis, maturaverant; sola jumentorum cura
' erat miserabilis, quæ pro qualitate loci et tem-
' poris nullo sustentabantur irriguo.' The commanders take their posts. ' Raimundus veró *turris*
' *Davidicæ* impiger assistebat: hæc *ad occasum solis*
' urbem muniens, ad medium feré tabulatum qua-
' dratorum lapidum *plumbo infuso compaginata*, om-
' nem metum obsidentium paucis intus defendenti-
' bus repellit.' The besiegers however assaulted the town; not, as Mr. Gibbon says, ' in the fanatic ' hope of battering down the walls without engines, ' and of scaling them without ladders¹;' but ' for-
' tunam *scalis erectis* tentarunt, in resistentes *volaticas*

¹ P. 59

' *moliti*

'*moliti sagittas.*' They were beaten off, not though, as Mr. Gibbon again says, ' by dint of *brutal force* ' they *burst* the first barrier;' but ' quia erant *scalæ* ' paucæ et ascendentibus damnosæ.' They then made two moveable turrets, one ' quod nostri ' Suem, veteres Vineam vocant.' This he describes, and adds, ' protegit in se subsidentes, qui, quasi ' more suis, ad murorum suffodienda penetrant fun- ' damenta.' The other, ' in modum ædificiorum ' facta, *Berefreid* appellant[1], quod fastigium muro- ' rum æquaret.' The assault begins. This is described by Malmesbury, with a particularity and spirit that are very engaging, and that we in vain look for in Mr. Gibbon. *This* author reserves *his* particularity for the *vices* of the *Christians*, and *his* spirit for the *victories* of the *Mahometans*. The assault continued one whole day, without effect. The next morning it was renewed, with more success. Malmesbury is still particular and spirited. He sets causes and effects, plain before our eyes. The Christians under Godfrey and the two Roberts, gain the wall and enter the city. Raymund learns the fact, from hearing the clamour of the enemy, and seeing them throw themselves headlong over the walls. He enters the town. ' Quingentos quoque *Æthiopas*, ' qui, in *arcem David* refugi, claves portarum, pol-

---

[1] A false reading for *Belfrid*, see Du Fresne's Glossary, Benedictine edition; our present *belfrey* for a church-steeple, and the French *beffrey* for a steeple and a turret; a name, not communicated from the turret to the steeple, as Dr. Johnson supposes, but, as the former half of the name, and the previous use of *bells*, concur to shew, derived from the steeple to the turret.

' licitâ

' licitâ membrorum impunitate, tradiderant, specta-
' to præsentis pacis commodo incolumes Ascalonem
' dimisit.' *Then*, says Malmesbury, but not with
strict propriety, as we have seen before, and shall
instantly see here again, the Turks had no place of
refuge, 'nec ullum erat *tunc* Turcis refugium; ita
' et supplices et *rebelles*,' a word that shews the opposition to have still continued, ' insatiabilis vic-
' torum ira consumebat.' Ten thousand took refuge in the temple of Solomon, and were slain there;
' decem millia—interfecta.' *Then*, ' post hæc,' the
dead bodies were collected and *burned*. This took
up the army two or three days, after the grand day
of the storm. ' Ita *cæde infidelium expiatâ urbe*, se-
' pulchrum Domini, quod tamdiu desideraverant,
' pro quo tot labores tulerant, supplicibus cordibus
' et corporibus petierunt.' Yet, adds Malmesbury,
concerning the day of storming the town, and the
days of burning the dead, ' illud insigne continentiæ
' in omnibus optimatibus exemplum fuit; quód
' nec *eo die*, nec *consequentibus*, quisquam respectu
' prædæ avocavit animum, quin cæptum persequeꞏ
' rentur, triumphum.' There was only *one* exception. It was made by Tancred, the very hero of
Mr. Gibbon's history, and praised by him for his
' generosity' on this very occasion. ' Solus Tan-
' credus, intempestivâ cupidine occupatus, quædam
' preciosissima de templo Salomonis extulit; sed
' postmodum suâ conscientiâ et aliorum conventus
' [convictus] colloquio, vel eadem vel appreciata
' loco restituit.' And this suspension of all the
strong feelings of avarice, for *several* days; a victorious

rious army abstaining from touching the vast booty under their hands, in the very moments of rapine; and continuing calmly and steadily to abstain, till they had cleared the city from the slaughter in it, and so had been able with propriety to make that religious procession, which they had always intended, to the tomb of their Saviour; forms one of the most striking pictures in the history of man, and is worthy of celebration by the tongue of the philosopher, and the pen of the historian, for ever. When this was all over, and not before, ' *tum* quicunque ege-
' nus vel domum, vel aliquas divitias, invasit, nun-
' quam ulteriús ullius locupletis tulit convicium, sed
' semel possessa in jus adoptavit hæreditarium.'—
Such is the full, the lively, and the curious history of the first crusade, in William of Malmesbury! So thoroughly unjust, is Mr. Gibbon's slighting insinuation against it!

He wishes Malmesbury had *not* given it, when every reader must thank him very cordially *for* it. He fancies Malmesbury had only listened, to the ' tenue
' murmur' which had passed the British sea. How could he so fancy, when Malmesbury has given us such a particular and pointed account of the crusade? But at the *end* of this *general* account, Malmesbury proposes to *enlarge* and *continue* it; to give the *particular* history, of each leader in this and the future crusades. ' *Singulorum* procerum facta et exitus
' scripto insigniam,' he says; ' nec quicquam veri-
' tati, fecundúm relatorum meorum credulitatem,
' subtraham: nullus veró, cui amplior provenit
' gestorum notitia, me pro incurioso arguat; quia
                                                  ' trans

'trans oceanum Britannicum abditos, vix tenui
'murmure, rerum Asianarum fama illustrat¹.' He
thus apologises for the *future* slenderness of his materials, in this *minute* and *succeeding* history. And he
accordingly gives us directly, the special history of
Godfrey, King of Jerusalem, of Baldwin his brother
and successor, and of the second Baldwin, the successor of both; declaring that he takes his account
of the former Baldwin, 'fidei soliditate accommo-
'datâ dictis Fulcherii Carnotensis, qui, capellanus
'ipsius, aliquanta de ipso scripsit, stilo non equidem
'agresti, sed (ut dici solet) sine nitore ac palæstrâ,
'et qui alios admonere potuit ut accuratiús scribe-
'rent².' He then proceeds to the history of Bohemund King of Antioch, and of Tancred and Roger, his respective successors. The account of Raimund follows next, and of his sons William and
Pontius, successively kings of Tripolis. And the
whole closes with the private adventures, of Robert
Duke of Normandy. Malmesbury therefore means
not to censure his preceding and general accounts,
as if they were only the effusions of a slight and slender report. They are *evidently* something, infinitely
superior to this. Indeed, I *must* say it in justice to
the truth, that they are even *superiour* to Mr. Gibbon's; being not bent by the force of 'philosophy,'
into all the little frauds of writing, the artful suppression, the dexterous distortion, and the wilful
falsehood; and exhibiting the heroes of the crusade,

¹ Fol. 80.   fol. 81.

in their *native* colours and *just* proportions, in all their *romantic majesty* of character.

Malmesbury, says Mr. Gibbon, ' wrote about ' the year 1130.' But he wrote earlier. The conclusion of his *fifth* book is dated by himself in the 28th of Henry the First, according to one copy, and in the 20th, according to the common and earlier copies. ' Hæc habui—de gestis Anglorum quæ ' dicerem,' he says to Robert Earl of Gloucester, ' ab adventu eorum in Angliam usque in annum *vicesimum* fæliciffimi regni patris vestri¹.' And, as Henry began his reign in August 1100, Malmesbury wrote the history of the crusades in his *fourth* book, on or before 1120, and about twenty or twenty-two years only after the storm of Jerusalem. As a *cotemporary* and a *dignified* writer, therefore, he ought to have been selected by Mr. Gibbon, for one of his principal authorities in the first crusade. We have already seen some errours that Mr. Gibbon would have avoided, and many beauties that he might have adopted, by doing so. His siege of Jerusalem would have been particularly improved, by the act; and his storm of Jerusalem have been saved from that accursed calumny, with which it is now polluted. But he chose to insert the calumny. He chose to take for his authors, Elmacin, Abulpharagius, and M. de Guignes from an unknown Aboul-

---

¹ Fol. 98. So in fol. 87, concerning Robert Duke of Normandy imprisoned by Henry the First in 1106, one copy says ' utrûm aliquando fit exiturus, vero vacillante, in dubio,' and another, ' nec unquam usque ad obitum relaxatus.'

mahasen;

mahasen; *because they had it.* Yet, why did not he also chuse to take Abulfeda with them; who extends *their* massacre of ' three days' over ' a ' whole week;' and makes the Christians to slay *seventy thousand* persons *in the temple or mosque on Mount Moriah*[1], when we know for certain from Malmesbury that there were only *ten thousand*, and when these surely are sufficient for the garrison of a single mosque? He was afraid to stretch the *improbable falsehood of that*, to such a straining length of incredibility. The seventy thousand persons in the mosque too, he thought proper to overlook; and makes them the amount of all, that were slaughtered in the whole town. He thus deviates from Abulfeda, while he follows authors not superiour in reputation; and corrects him though he cites him not. And he chose to wander, in the train of Elmacin, Abulpharagius, and the unpublished Aboulmahasen, for the length of the slaughter and the number of the slain; rather than follow the best authority in the world, the letter of Godfrey himself, which shews the slaughter to have continued only for one day and during the resistance; and rather than copy the next best account in the world, the narration of a judicious cotemporary, which coincides with the letter entirely, proves the slaughter in the streets to have been only during the storm and the resistance, and states the number slain at the mosque to have been only ten thousand. To the testimony of a very respectable cotemporary, and to the concurrent evidence of an

---

[1] Mod. Univ. Hist. iii. 304.   [2] p. 60.

eye-witness,

eye-witnefs, an actor, and a commander; he prefers the authority of Elmacin, who lived *near a century and a half* afterwards, of Abulpharagius, who wrote near *three centuries* from the time, and probably, though uncited, of Abulfeda, who died near *three centuries and a half* later than the fact[1].

Having faid this, I will annex the account of this part of the ftorm, which is given us by Knolles, and is all conformable to what I have faid. ' In this ' confufion,' fays the truly refpectable author, if refpectability is attached to veracity in preference to falfehood, ' a wonderful number of the better fort of ' Turks, retiring unto Salomon's temple, there to ' do their laft devoire, made there a great and ter- ' rible fight, armed with defpaire to endure any ' thinge; and the victorious Chriftians no leffe dif- ' daining, after the winning of the citie, to find ' there fo great refiftance. In this defperat con- ' flict, fought with wonderful obftinacie of mind, ' many fell on both fides: but the Chriftians came ' on fo fiercely with defire of blood, that, *breaking* ' *into the temple, the foremoft of them were by the* ' *preffe that followed after*, violently *thruft upon the* ' *weapons of their enemies*, and fo miferably flaine. ' Neither did the Turks, thus oppreffed, give it o- ' ver; but, as men refolved to die, defperatly ' fought it out with invincible courage, not at the ' gates of the temple only, but even in the *middeft* ' thereof alfo; *where* was to be feene *great heapes*,

[1] Prideaux's Letter to a Deift, p. 163, 153, and 154.

' both

'both of the *victors* and the *vanquished, slaine indif-*
'*ferently together*. All *the pavement of the temple*
'*swam with blood*; in such sort, that *a man could not*
'*set his feet*, but either upon *some dead man*, or *over*
'*the shooes in blood*. Yet, for all that, the obstinate
'enemie still held the *vaults* and *top*,' meaning the
arches within and the roof above, 'of the temple;
'when as the night came so fast on,' it being, as
Knolles has said before, ' midday' when the storm
began, ' that the Christians were glad to make an
'end of the slaughter, and to sound a retrait. *The*
'*next day* (for that *proclamation was made*, for *mercie*
'to be *shewed* unto *all such* as should *lay downe their*
'*weapons*) the Turks, that yet held *the upper part*
'of the temple, *came down and yeelded themselves*.
'Thus was the famous citie of Jerusalem with great
'bloodshed, but far greater honor, recovered by
'these worthy Christians, in the yeare 1099 [1].' And
such is the history, which is given us by the pen of
Christian probity; the very opposite of that, which
is held out to us by the hand of Mahometan kna-
very!

Text. ' The northern monarchs of *Scotland, Den-*
'*mark*, Sweden, and Poland, were yet strangers to
'the passions and interests of the south [2].' Note.
'The author of the Esprit des Croisades has *doubted*,
'and *might have disbelieved*, the crusade and tragic
'death of Prince Sueno, with 1500 or 15000 *Danes*,
'who was cut off by Sultan Soliman in Cappado-

---

[1] Knolles, p. 23.   [2] p. 21.

' cia,

' cia, but who still lives in the poem of Tasso (tom.
' iv. p. 111—115).' Yet Mr. Gibbon in a distant
page inconsistently says, that there were in the crusade ' bands of adventurers from Spain, Lombardy,
' and England; and from the distant bogs and
' *mountains* of Ireland or *Scotland*, issued some naked
' and savage fanatics, ferocious at home but unwar-
' like abroad[1].' Note says, that ' William of
' Malmesbury *expressly* mentions the *Welsh* and
' *Scots*, &c.;' and that Guibert notes ' *Scotorum*,
' apud se ferocium, alias imbellium, cuneos,' where
' the *crus intectum* and *hispida chlamys* may suit the
' Highlanders, but the *finibus uliginosis* may rather
' apply to the Irish bogs.' The Scotch of Guibert
may seem to be the Irish only, from the ' finibus
' uliginosis.' Nor would the dress be any argument to the contrary. The Irish at this period
wore the same dress, with the Highlanders. But
the Scoti of Guibert are what their name imports,
the present inhabitants of Scotland, and the same
with the Scots of Malmesbury. And it was then
as common with foreigners, to discriminate Scotland
by its *bogs*, as it now is with ourselves to denote Ireland. This is evident from the circular letter of
Frederick Emperour of Germany, to the nations
around; on the wild irruptions of the Tartars. It
is in M. Paris, p. 498, and is quoted by Mr. Gibbon himself in p. 304. There the writer speaks of
' cruenta *Hybernia* cum agili Walliâ, *palustris Sco-*
' *tia.*' &c. And, as Mr Gibbon might have saved

---

[1] P. 39—40.

at

at once the uncertainty and the contradiction, by stating the truth; so he should never have run into the new contradiction, of asserting those to be 'naked' in the text, whom he covers with a *rough mantle*, 'hispida chlamys,' in the note. This is bringing back that poetical *bull* of Blackmore's, which (I understand) is *suppressed* in the *late* edition or editions of the poem;

> A painted vest Prince Vortiger had on,
> Which from a naked Pict his grandsire won.

Nor is Mr. Gibbon's conduct less remarkable, in other points. He intimates that Scotland sent no adventurers to the crusade. Yet he cites Malmesbury, for Scotland actually sending some; and Guibert, for the character of the sent. He cites Guibert in the note, as confirmed by Malmesbury, for the *Scots* actually going; and yet in the text states them to be *either* Scots *or* Irish. But let us also observe Mr. Gibbon's conduct about Denmark. This, we are told, equally sent no men to the crusade. Yet afterwards Mr. Gibbon cites a passage from Malmesbury, that proves it did send some. He however quotes *only* till *he comes to the proving words*, and then laps up the sentence with an *&c.* 'William of Malmesbury expressly mentions the 'Welsh and Scots, *&c.*' This pregnant *&c.* produces these words in William: 'tunc Wallensis 'venationem saltuum, tunc Scotus familiaritatem 'pulicum, *tunc Danus continuationem potuum, tunc* 'Noricus

'*Noricus cruditatem reliquit pifcium* [1].' And the whole gives us a remarkable proof, of Mr. Gibbon's aftonifhing inattention to his own affertions and evidences. The Norwegians, the Danes, and the Scots appear as crufaders in the very paffages to which Mr. Gibbon has referred, in the very quotations which Mr. Gibbon has produced, and in his own notes and text. But Mr. Gibbon's management of this laft reference fhews us fomething more. He cites Malmefbury for the *Welfh* going to the crufade; and then, either ftrangely omits them in his text, or more ftrangely comprehends them under the *Englifh*. In this paffage alfo, Malmefbury fpecifies the *Dane* and the *Norwegian* as equal crufaders with all. Mr. Gibbon, however, ftops fhort in his quotation from it, fhuts them both out of his note, and excludes them both from his text; becaufe he recollects what he has faid before of Denmark fending *no* crufaders, and forefees the authority clafhing with his affertion. He thus fhews us his memory, at the expence of his probity. And he keeps the reft of the paffage under his thumb, becaufe it will encounter what he has faid before; and fuppreffes the contradicting authority, rather than turn back, and correct the falfe affertion by it. Nor is the ftory of Sueno the Dane, which the author of Efprit de Croifades *doubts*, and which Mr. Gibbon *difbelieves*, improbable in itfelf, or unfounded (I apprehend) on a fact. In Norway fays Malmefbury, ' filii ultimi Magni, Haften et Si-

[1] Fol. 75.

' wardus

' wardus, regno *adhuc* divifo imperitant: quorum
' pofterior *adolefcens fpeciofus et audax, non multûm eft*
' quód *Jerofolymam* per *Angliam* navigavit; *innumera*
' *et præclara facinora* contra Saracenos *confummans*,
' præfertim in obfidione Sydonis, quæ pro confcien-
' tiâ Turcorum immania in Chriftianos fremebat¹.'
This is, in all probability, the very hero of Taffo.
He was indeed a Norwegian. But Norway having
fome time before been reduced by Denmark², the
Dane and the Norwegian would eafily be confounded in the South. We have indeed an actual King
of Denmark, engaged in the crufade; but he died
at fea before he reached Jerufalem. Henry, ' Je-
' rofolymam adiit medioque mari fpiritum evo-
' muit³.' And all ferves to fhew the exiftence, in
the frequency, of Danifh and Norwegian crufaders;
very decifively againft Mr. Gibbon.

Chapter SECOND

or fifty-ninth.——This gives us the fuccefs of the
Greek emperor with his own troops over the Turks,
in confequence of the crufade, 72—73; the anger
of the crufaders at the emperor, for leaving them,
73; one of their leaders paffing back into Europe
for fuccours againft the emperor, 73—74; his inef-
fectual return with them, 74; a fupply fent to the
firft crufaders, 75; fecond crufade, 75; third, 75;
the general numbers and character of each, 75—77;

¹ Fol. 60.   ² fol. 59.   ³ fol. 60.

the conduct of the emperours towards them, 77—80; the general hiftory of the fupply fent to the firft crufade, 80; that of the fecond crufade, 80—81; that of the third, 81—82; the perfeverance of Europe in the crufades, 82—83; the character of St. Bernard, 83—84; his fuccefs in preaching up the fecond crufade, 84—85; fuccefs of the Turks againft the crufaders, 84—87; the character of him who was the caufe of their fucceffes, 87—88; the taking of Egypt from the Saracens by the Turks, 88—89; the calling in of the crufaders by the Saracens, 89; the expulfion of the Turks by the crufaders, 89; their return, 89—90; their fecond expulfion, 90; their return and reduction of Egypt, 90—91; the revolt of Egypt from the Turks under the commandant of their mercenaries, 92—93; the general fuccefs of his fon, Saladin, over the Saracens, the crufaders, and the Turks, 93; the character of this fon, 94—95; his reduction of the holy land up to Jerufalem, 95—97; his taking Jerufalem, 97—100; the third crufade, 100—101; his being beat off from Tyre by the crufaders, 101; their befieging Acre, 101; their battles with Saladin before it, 102; their taking it, 103; the conduct of the kings of France and England refpectively in Paleftine, 103—104; the particular exploits of the king of England, 105—107; his treaty with Saladin and departure for England, 107—108; the civil wars among the Turks on Saladin's death, 108; the character of Innocent III. Pope of Rome, 108—109; author of the fourth and fifth crufades, 109; an account of the fourth referved for the next chapter,

chapter, 109; an account of the fifth, 109; its ill succefs, and the reafons, 109—110; a new crufade under Frederic III. Emperor of Germany, 110—111; his general fuccefs, though oppofed and betrayed by the eaftern Chriftians, 111—113; the irruption of the Carizmans into Paleftine, 113; the fixth crufade, that of St. Louis into Egypt, 113; his character, 113—114; his forces, 114; his ill fuccefs, 115—116; the feventh crufade, the fecond under St. Louis, 116; his death at Tunis, 117; the ftate of Egypt under the Mamalukes, 117—118; our Firft Edward in Paleftine, 118; reduction of almoft all Paleftine by the Mahometans, 119; the ftate of the only town left, Acre, 119; its fiege by the Mamalukes, 120; and its furrendery to them, 120. Such are the contents of this chapter. Nor let any one of my readers be too much ftartled, when I rudely awaken him from his dream of reading, by telling him; that this *was to be* the hiftory of the eaftern empire's decline and fall. *That* it *was to be*, and *this* it *is*. And the reader, who has been awake to the digreffions from the beginning of the chapter, muft have gone on ftep by ftep in the turnings and windings of the whole labyrinth, expecting that every turn would be the laft, and that he fhould then recover the original line of the hiftory. Yet he has found himfelf to his amazement, ftill going on in the winding courfe; one turn coming after another, till he has been involved in mazes upon mazes, loft in the inextricable labyrinth, and obliged to advance with his author and with ' confufion worfe ' confounded,' to the end of the whole.

In this history of events, either *totally* irrelative to the history of the decline and fall of the eastern empire, or affecting it only *in a point or two* of the whole; Mr. Gibbon has passed over some incidental touches of the times, that are peculiarly pleasing in themselves, and ought to have been studiously selected by him. Concerning *sugar* says Pliny: 'Saccharon et Arabia fert, sed laudatius India; est autem mel in harundinibus collectum, gummium modo candidum, dentibus fragile, amplissimum nucis avellanæ magnitudine, *ad medicinæ tantùm usum*[1].' But this plant had been brought in the days of the crusades, into other countries of Asia. Baldwin the second, King of Jerusalem, marched by Antioch to Laodicea towards Jerusalem; but was much distressed in the way between Jerusalem and Laodicea, by the want of provisions, &c. 'At vero famem nonnihil levabant,' says an historian of the times, 'ARUNDINES MELLITAS continué dentibus terentes, quas *Cannamellas*, composito ex cannâ et melle nomine, vocant: sic hi, omninó a *Tripolitanis* et *Cæsariensibus* immenso ære necessaria nacti, Jerosolymam venêre[2].' And this was in all probability the first time, that the sugar-cane, hitherto applied only to *medicinal* purposes, was *now used as food*; and the juice of it, which now constitutes so important an article in the food of the western Europeans, *began to be so* in all probability, from this adventure of the cru-

[1] Nat. Hist. xii. 8.   [2] Malmesbury, fol. 81.

saders.

saders. This eastern *honey-cane* was now brought into Europe, was afterwards carried by the Portuguese to Madeira with those vines which constitute the great commerce of that island, and was thence transplanted to the grand nursery of the cane for Europe at present, the West Indies. The Portuguese, says a Jew who wrote in Italy about the year 1502, in discovering Madeira ' in eâ plantâ-' runt—*cannas pro melle*,' he using nearly the very language of Malmesbury, ' ad faciendum saccharum,—et vinea ex *vitibus Candiæ et Cypri*.'—The origin of that corrosive disease in Europe, which, for these three centuries nearly, has been so strikingly the scourge of GOD upon promiscuous whoredom; is much disputed. Long before the West Indies could possibly have compensated the cruelties of Europe, by imparting this pestilential bane to the European nations; evident symptoms of its commonness among us, appear in the regulations of our licensed brothels. And that higher stage of this disorder, which makes it act as a *cancer* upon all the affected parts of our frame, is now supposed therefore to have been the only part of the plague, which was imported from the West-Indies. Yet even this is not true. The disease appears to have been in Europe, and with this sharpest acrimony of it; ages before the discovery of America. This a very remarkable passage in a cotemporary history of the crusades, sufficiently

[1] Peritsol's Itinera Mundi, latinized by Hyde. Oxon 1691, p. 113—114. ad 179.

shews. Baldwin abovementioned married. 'Ad
' legitimum connubium non multò post *Comitissa*
' *Siciliæ* Jerosolymam venit—; et tunc quidem illam
' thoro recepit, sed non multò post dimisit. Aiunt
' *incommodo tactam*, QUO EJUS GENITALIA CANCER,
' MORBUS INCURABILIS, EXESIT [1].' And as this lady
came from Sicily, which had long been in the possession of the *Arabs*; we apprehend the disorder
to have been derived from the same quarter, from
which the small-pox is known to have been, even
from *Arabia*; and so to have formed with that,
two of the curses which Mahometanism inflicted
upon Europe, which perhaps have outdone in mischief the ravages of its arms, and have certainly
survived them in their consequences. This historical argument, too, is apparently corroborated by
the *relative* appellations, with which these two diseases are distinguished by us Europeans; the *great*
and the *small* pox, ' la *grosse*' and ' la *petite* verole,'
&c. plainly denoting the one to be *cotemporary* with
the other, in the knowledge of Europe.—The *black
woolly hair* of the natives on the coast of Guinea, is
a very striking circumstance in the aspect of them.
The general blackness of their appearance they so
far share in common with others, as not to be
blacker than their southern neighbours, and to be
only a degree or two blacker than their eastern.
But their woolly hair is the stamp of nature, by
which she has marked them as distinct from all.
These *heteroclites* of the human race, were unknown

[1] Malmesbury, fol. 84.

to the Europeans in general; till the Portuguese, beyond the middle of the fifteenth century, pushed their navigation along the western coast of Africa, and discovered them. And yet we have a curious passage in Malmesbury's history of the crusades, which pointed them out very strongly to the eye of Britain particularly; about *two centuries and a half* before. Baldwin the second, he says, marched from Jerusalem to Ascalon, then turned up into the mountains in pursuit of the Turks, beat them out of their caves by smoke, directed his course towards Arabia, and went by *Hebron* to the *Dead Sea*. ' Evadentes ergo lacum, venerunt ad villam sane ' locupletissimam, et mellitis pomis quæ dactylos ' dicunt fæcundam—;' dates from the neighbouring palms of Jericho: ' cætera timore incolarum ' abrasa, præter aliquantos *Æthiopes* FERRUGINEA ' CAPILLORUM LANUGINE fuliginem prætendentes.' These were evidently the blacks of Guinea. Their name of Ethiopians, also, points out distinctly the channel, by which they had been derived from that distant coast. In 651 the Mahometan Arabs of Egypt ' so harrassed the king of Nubia' or Ethiopia, ' who was a Christian; that' he agreed ' to send the ' Arabs annually, by way of a tribute, *a vast num-* ' *ber of Nubian or Ethiopian slaves* into Egypt. Such ' a tribute as this at that time was *more agreeable* to ' the Khalif, *than any other*; as the Arabs *then* ' made *no small account* of *those slaves*[1].' At this

---

[1] Mod. Univ. Hist. i. 525.

time therefore, began that kind of traffick in human flesh,

<blockquote>Which spoils unhappy Guinea of its sons.</blockquote>

Compelled to furnish 'a vast number' of slaves every year, to the Arabs of Egypt; the king of Ethiopia naturally endeavoured to feed this great drain upon his subjects, from the natives of the neighbouring countries; ranged accordingly into all that vast *blank of geography* upon the map of the world, the spreading bosom of this ample continent; and even pushed through it to its farthest extremities in the West. He thus brought the blacks of Guinea for the first time, into the service and families of the East. All these slaves, whether derived from the nearer neighbourhood of Ethiopia, fetched from the Mediterranean regions of Africa, or brought from the distant shores of the Atlantick; would all be denominated *Ethiopians*, from the country by which they were conveyed to the Arabs of Egypt. The Arabs therefore appear to have trained up blacks for the uses of war, as we do a few occasionally for drummers and fifers to our regiments; and even to have thrown them into large bodies of soldiery by themselves. So early as the siege of Jerusalem by the crusaders in 1099, when the Arabs of Egypt were now in possession of the city, having recently taken it from their Mahometan brethren the Turks; there were no less than *five hundred* Ethiopians at the storm, that took refuge from it in the Tower of David, and there surrendered to the crusaders, on condition of being
allowed

allowed to march out to Afcalon¹; and, in the following year, the crufaders met with fome Ethiopians near Hebron, that are diftinguifhed from the former by their woolly heads, and were therefore the blacks of Guinea. So much earlier did the purchafe of the inhabitants for flaves commence, than has been ever imagined; even ages before the Portuguefe laid open their country, to the intercourfe of Europe. Even after they had, the inhabitants were as regularly purchafed for flaves by fome of the ftates adjoining, as they are now by the maritime Europeans. The Arabs of Egypt having reduced all the north of Africa, and carrying with them their love of black fervants, would be fure to open a ready communication for themfelves to their country. They certainly had one fo early as 1512, and before the Europeans had any, for that purpofe. They went from Barbary by a route, that was fo much practifed, as to be denominated exprefsly ' the way of ' the Camels.' Meeting together at ' the town of ' Cape Cantin,' that of Valadie near it, the commercial caravan traverfed ' the vaft deferts,' thofe of Sarra which run, like the Tropic of Cancer over them, in a long line acrofs the country; to ' a place ' of great population called Hoden,' the Waden or Hoden of our maps, and a little to the fouth-weft of Cape Blanco. From Hoden they diverted on the left, and pufhed directly into the interiours of the continent, to reach ' Tegazza,' the Tagazel or Tagaza of our maps, and lying nearly eaft of Ho-

¹ Malmefbury, p. 80.

den.

den. Here aſſuredly they did, as the caravan does certainly at this day; and added to the other wares upon their camels, a quantity of *ſalt* from thoſe mines of rock ſalt, which are extraordinary enough to be noticed as rocks in our maps. This they carried, as they ſtill carry it, to ' Tanbut,' the Tombut of the maps, and a town in the heart of the African continent. And from this town they turned on the right for the ſea-coaſt again, and reached it in ' the great kingdom of Mele,' the Melli of our maps, to the ſouth of the Gambia, and juſt at the ſpringing (as it were) of that grand arch of ſea, which curves ſo deeply into the body of the land, and conſtitutes the extenſive Gulph of Guinea. At Melli and at Tombut they received *a meaſure of gold* for *a meaſure of ſalt*. The caravan collects gold at Tombut, to the preſent time. But at Melli they purchaſed gold, and alſo *ſilver*, in *pieces as large as pebbles*. And at Hoden they had *a great mart for ſlaves*; the blacks being brought thither from the countries adjoining, and bartered away to the traders[1]. Such was the Slave Coaſt and the Gold Coaſt, of former days! The ſtaple commodity of Hoden, is only transferred now to Whidah; and diverted from the Arabs of Barbary, to the Chriſtians of Europe. And ſhould any thing ſo wildly incredible happen, as that *all* the nations of Chriſtendom, in one common paroxyſm of philanthropy, ſhould

---

[1] Peritſol, p. 122—125, and maps for Mod. Univ. Hiſt. Peritſol wrote (as I have obſerved) about 1512, in general (p. 179); but after 1534, in one particular, p. 91.

abandon

abandon this commerce in servants, which has been prosecuted in all ages and under all religions; they would only abandon it to those, who were originally possessed of it, who still penetrate into the country, and who even push up to Gago at the very head of the Slave Coast; and leave the wool-headed natives of it, to *Mahometan* masters in preference to *Christian*. Under such masters they were in Judea, at the time of the crusades. Nor had any European eye *then* seen one of *these* blacks. This is plain from what immediately follows in Malmesbury. ' Quo-
' rum cædem,' he adds, ' nostri æstimantes infra
' virtutem suam, non eos irâ, *sed risu*, dignati sunt¹.'
And an army of Europeans, finding a number of Guinea blacks left in a town, near the southern end of Judæa; seeing these blacks for the first time; and bursting out into a general fit of laughter, at the sight of them; forms one of the most curious sketches in history.

In the arrangement of the parts of this chapter, we have great confusion. In p. 75 we have an intimation of a supply sent to the first crusaders, of a second crusade, and of a third. We then have an account, of the general numbers and character of each, 75—77; the conduct of the emperours towards them, 77—80; the general history of the supply, 80; of the second crusade, 80—81; and of the third, 81—82; and of the perseverance of Europe in these crusades, 82 —83. And, after all, we come back in 83—84 to the character of St. Bernard, and his success in preaching up—a *new* crusade, to be sure. But let not the

¹ Fol. 83.

reader presume too freely on propriety, in Mr. Gibbon. The crusade, which St. Bernard is *now* preaching up, is one of the *foregoing*. It is one of those which we have already dispatched. It is not even the last of them. It is the *second*. So strangely are we moving sometime backwards and sometime forwards, in the course of the history! But there is also a grand omission in it. In p. 73 we are told, that Bohemond and ' his Norman fol-
' lowers were insufficient to withstand the *hostilities* of
' the Greeks and Turks.' But what had provoked the hostilities of the *Greeks*, whether actual or apprehended, between this Norman prince of Antioch and the Greek emperor? This Mr. Gibbon has most strangely concealed. And, for want of this necessary information, the reader is all in the dark about the meaning of the movements before him. He sees Bohemond ' embracing the magnanimous
' resolution of leaving the defence of Antioch to his
' kinsman, the faithful Tancred; of arming the
' West against the Byzantine empire; and of exe-
' cuting the design, which he inherited from the
' lessons and example of his father Guiscard.' But what the cause, real or pretended, of this resolution is; Mr. Gibbon does not tell us. We then behold Bohemond ' embarking clandestinely' for Europe, received in France with applause, married to the king's daughter, and ' returning with the bravest
' spirits of the age.' Yet still what the ground for all this is, Mr. Gibbon never tells us. And his history, for want of this intelligence, becomes a mere scene of puppet-show to us; movements without any moving principles, and operations without any impelling

pelling cause. Mr. Gibbon should have told us, that the emperour required Bohemond to hold the sovereignty of Antioch in dependence upon him; a point, to which Mr. Gibbon himself, however absurdly with his previous suppression of it, makes a direct reference in p. 74, when, on terminating the quarrel, he says ' the homage was clearly stipulated:' that Bohemond refused, even claimed Laodicea from the emperour as a part of his principality of Antioch, and even went so far as to seize it; another point to which Mr. Gibbon himself alludes, when, at the same time, he says ' the boundaries' of his principality ' were strictly defined:' and that, in consequence of this rebellion against and attack upon him, by one of the chief of the crusaders; the emperour attacked and defeated a fleet of new crusaders, coming from the West[1].' These incidents throw a full light upon the darkened narrative. We see the designs of Bohemond, and the hostilities of the Greeks, clearly elucidated. And the scene of puppet-show becomes, a picture of living manners and of human transactions[2].

' The principality of Antioch was left without a
' head, by the surprise and captivity of Bohemond;
' his ransom had oppressed him with a heavy debt[3].'
What all this means, no one shall know from Mr. Gibbon. He must refer to Malmesbury or some other author, to be his commentator upon Mr. Gib-

[1] Ant. Univ. Hist. xvii. 151.
[2] It is remarkable, that Malmesbury has equally omitted these impelling incidents.
[3] p. 73.

bon.

bon. From Malmesbury he will then learn, 'Boa-
' mundum—captum et in catenas ejectum, a quo-
' dam Danisman gentili, et in illis terris potenti;'
that 'pollicitus—Boamundus continuam gentili con-
' cordiam,' and not, as Mr. Gibbon states it, paying
a *ransom*, ' revertit Antiochiam, *argenteos compedes*
' quibus illigatus fuerat *deferens secum*[1].' This is
another instance, of Mr. Gibbon's dark mode of
writing the history, where he thinks himself obliged
to be brief. And these unite with many other instances to shew us, that this historical painter knows
not how to give us the features of the times, com-
pressed into a miniature piece; and that he can work
only upon figures nearly as big as the life.

' The sword, which had been the instrument of
' their [the crusaders] victory, was the pledge and
' title of their just independence. It does not ap-
' pear, that the emperor attempted to revive his ob-
' solete claims over the kingdom of Jerusalem;
' but the borders of Cilicia and Syria were *more*
' *recent* [he should have said *more recently*] in his
' possession.' Note. ' The kings of Jerusalem
' submitted however to a nominal dependence, and
' in the dates of their inscriptions (one is still legible
' in the church at Bethlem) they respectfully placed
' before their own, the name of the reigning empe-
' rour[2].' We here see again what we must again
call, the *natural confusedness* of Mr. Gibbon's understanding. The sword of the crusaders, we are told,
became with them ' the pledge and title of their

[1] Fol. 82 and 85.   [2] p. 73.

' just

'just independence.' Yet with this sword in their hands, and in their most powerful kingdom, we find, they actually resigned their 'just independence,' and 'submitted to a—dependence' upon the emperour. This dependence is said indeed to have been 'nominal;' but what did the emperour ask more, or what more did their sword refuse to allow him? When the dispute with the kingdom of Antioch was terminated by the emperour, as Mr. Gibbon himself tells us, 'the boundaries were strictly defined,' and 'the homage was clearly stipulated.' The homage, therefore, was all. This was a real, not a nominal, dependence. As such, it was insisted upon by the emperour; and, as such, it had been refused by Bohemond before. It was as real, as the definition of the boundaries was. The kings of Jerusalem always paid it, we *find*, though the first king of Antioch refused it; *because* there was no dispute between them and the emperour, as there was between the emperour and him. And accordingly we find also, from that most authentic of all evidences, a formal inscription set upon a church by them; that they *shewed* and *owned* their *real* dependence upon the emperour, in the most striking way in which they could own and shew it, by 'respectfully placing *before* their 'own *the name of the reigning emperour.*' Yet 'it 'does not *appear*,' we are told by Mr Gibbon, 'that 'the emperour *attempted* to revive his *obsolete* claims 'over the kingdom of Jerusalem.' It certainly *does* appear from Mr. Gibbon himself. It appears from this very inscription. He not only *attempted* to revive his claims, but actually *revived* them with-

out refiftance. Yet, becaufe Mr. Gibbon finds no refiftance, he afferts there was no revival; and the unrefifted acknowledgment of the claim, he confiders as an evidence againft it's exiftence. So ftrangely does his underftanding wreft objects, from their natural and obvious propriety! At laft however he found an apparent and a pofitive proof, of their dependence. He did not then correct what he had faid before, by what he had difcovered now. No! he was too indolent, or too prefuming, for that. He makes this new difcovery to bend and warp with his old ideas. He afferts the new-difcovered dependence, to be merely nominal; when even, if nominal, it goes *againft* his affertion, and when it is apparently real. And he finally places this new difcovery at the foot of the old affertion, muffled indeed by this diftinction of a *nominal* dependence, and yet fpeaking loudly againft the affertion.

But we have not done with this paffage. The claim of the emperour over the kingdom of Jerufalem, is faid to be 'obfolete.' This therefore is urged as an argument, *why* he did not attempt to revive his claim. Yet he revived it, as Mr. Gibbon has already fhewn us, over *Antioch*. In what year, then, was Antioch reduced by the Saracens, and in what Jerufalem? Jerufalem was reduced in 637, according to Mr Gibbon himfelf, and Antioch, according to Mr. Gibbon alfo, in—638 [1]. Yet the emperour's claim of homage from Jerufalem, was never revived *becaufe* it was obfolete; and was not too

---

[1] Vol. v. 320 and 323.

obsolete, to be revived over Antioch. So much efficacy has the difference of a *single year*, in annihilating and preserving rights! But the ' borders of
' Cilicia and Syria were more recent in his possession,'
than Jerusalem. Was not Antioch, then, on the
borders of Syria towards Cilicia? It certainly was. *All*
Syria, according to Mr. Gibbon himself, was reduced
by the Saracens in 638[1]; and, ' to the north of
' Syria, they passed mount Taurus,' in 639, says the
margin, ' and reduced to their obedience the province
' of Cilicia[2].' So *much more* ' recent' in their possession were ' the borders of Cilicia and Syria,' than
Jerusalem! They were even *one or two years*.
This, in Mr. Gibbon's forgetfulness of facts and
indistinctness of recollection, is made equivalent to
one or two ages. And, what aggravates very greatly
the contradictoriness of all this, he has said it all,
concerning the *obsoleteness* of the emperour's claim
over the kingdom of Jerusalem in the province of
Syria, concerning his not *attempting to revive* it, and
concerning the borders of Cilicia and Syria being
more recent than Jerusalem in his possession, and
therefore claimed by him; when he previously tells
us in the most explicit terms, that ' his *ancient* and
' *perpetual* claim *still* embraced the kingdoms of *Sy-*
' *ria* and *Egypt*[3].' Such a chaos of confusion, such
a mass of fighting and warring elements, does the
hand of contradiction work up, in the pages of Mr.
Gibbon's history!

[1] Vol. v. 326 [2] Vol. v. 330.
[3] P. 34.

Text. 'The *Seljukian* dynasty of Roum' had, 'after the loss of Nice' to the crusaders, 'Cogni or *Iconium* for its capital.' Note. 'See, in the learned work of M. de Guignes—, the history of the *Seljukians* of *Iconium*—, as far *as may be collected* from the Greeks, Latins, and *Arabians*. The *last* are *ignorant* or *regardless* of the affairs of *Roum*[1].' This is a very extraordinary instance of contradiction, in two *near* and *neighbouring* positions. *In proof* that 'the Seljukian dynasty of Roum' had Iconium for its capital, we are referred to a history in M. de Guignes.. *In proof* that this history is sufficient evidence, we are told it is collected from the Greeks, Latins, and Arabians. And then we are finally told, that it *cannot* be collected from the Arabians, because the Arabians are 'either ignorant or regardless' of this part of the history.——Text. 'Iconium, an *obscure* and inland town.' Note. 'Iconium is mentioned as a station by Xenophon, and by Strabo with the ambiguous title of Κωμόπολις,' or the city-village. 'Yet St. Paul found in that place a *multitude* (πληθος) of Jews and Gentiles. Under the corrupt name of Kunijah, it is described as a great city—(Abulfeda—)[2].' Thus Iconium is pronounced an *obscure* town. The evidence for this is one authority, which speaks of it as a mere *station*; two authorities, that make it *a great and populous* town; and a fourth, that *trims* between the opposed testimonies, and calls it a city and a village in one. We thus advance by regular

[1] p. 74.   [2] p. 74.

steps

steps from an obscure and stationary town, to a city-like kind of village, and to a populous and large city. And three out of the four references, contradict at once the first and the text.——Text. ' *Only* ' one man was left behind for—seven widows.' Note. ' *Penè* jam non inveniunt quem apprehendant sep-' tem mulieres unum virum [1].' The *penè* of the primary historian is made *only* in the secondary, and the text violates the truth of the note.——We saw in the last volume, that Mr. Gibbon made a grand attempt, to prove the nocturnal journey of Mahomet from Mecca to Jerusalem, and from Jerusalem to heaven, *not* intended by Mahomet for a reality, but *only* a dream. I particularly produced in proof to the contrary, that the general of Omar, the second successor of Mahomet, considered it as a reality; because he urged the surrender of Jerusalem to him, as the place, from the temple of which Mahomet ascended in one night to heaven. I might also have added, that, in the very same year, one Kais Ebn Amer, an old man who had been particularly conversant with Mahomet, being brought as a prisoner before the Roman emperour, and being interrogated by him concerning Mahomet, answered; ' that he *really* performed a night-journey to heaven, ' *actually* conversed there with God himself, and ' received several institutions *immediately* from him [2].' And, to my agreeable surprise, I find in this volume, that Mr Gibbon *now* is *entirely of my opinion.* The Mahometans at Jerusalem, he says, were allowed to

[1] P. 85. [2] Mod. Univ. Hist. i. 450.

'pray and preach in the mofch of the temple' [he fhould have faid, in the mofch *or* temple], '*from whence the prophet undertook his nocturnal journey to heaven*[1].' So little impreffion do Mr. Gibbon's *own* arguments make upon *himfelf*, even in points important to *his* caufe of Mahometanifm, and laboured with particular care by *his* pen; that he foon forgets them, relapfes back into the opinions that he had *refuted*, and fhews the triumph of nature evident over the fophiftications of art.

In the two preceding volumes, I have pointed out the frequent recurrence of Mr. Gibbon's fpirit, to ideas of lafcivioufnefs and to intimations of impurity. We have another inftance of this, in the prefent volume. This is fuch as I *can* lay before my readers, without offending their delicacy. I fhall therefore do fo. Text. 'Only one man was left behind for the *confolation* of feven *widows*.' Note. '*Penè* jam non inveniunt quem apprehendant feptem *mulieres* unum virum[2].' Here is no hint about *widows*; the paffage fpeaks only of *women*. The *confolation* alfo is adminiftered merely, by the prurient pen of Mr. Gibbon. And, to crown this fally, Mr. Gibbon adds this to the note: 'We muft be careful not to conftrue *pene* as a fubftantive.' So apt is Mr. Gibbon to take fire in his fancy, at the flighteft approach of a fenfual idea; and fo ready to twift and torture an innocent word, in order to gratify his fenfual luxuriance of tafte!

Mifquotations. 'In the CALIPH's treafure were 'found

[1] p. 113.   [2] p. 85.

...ound a *ruby* weighing seventeen Egyptian drachms —(Renaudot, p. 536)[1].' The words in Renaudot are these: ' *Rubinorum* majorum, qui drachmarum ' Egyptiacarum septemdecim pondus æquabant, ' *linea*,' a *string* of *rubies*, not a single ruby.—— ' The most numerous portion of the inhabitants was ' composed of the *Greek* and *Oriental* Christians, ' whom *experience had taught* to prefer the Maho- ' metan before the Latin yoke (Renaudot,—p. ' 545)[2].' Renaudot's words are these: ' Mox Sa- ' ladinus Hierosolyma obsedit; nec cepisset absque ' civium discordiâ et *Christianorum Melchitarum* pro- ' ditione. Nam per quendam Josephum Elbatith ' *ex eâdem sectâ*, qui negotiandi causa multoties in ' urbem receptus erat, eos ad excutiendum Fran- ' corum jugum, quos numero superabant, incitavit.' *Here* we have no intimation, whatever we may have in Mr. Gibbon, of ' experience having taught' the old and Melchite Christians of Jerusalem, to prefer the Mahometans to the Latins for masters. A fear of the siege, a feeling of its terrours, a despair of relief, and a promise of favourable terms, might each or all induce them to clamour for a capitula- tion. And Mr. Gibbon has again loaded the credit of Renaudot, by saying from him what he does not say himself.

[1] p. 88.   [2] p. 98.

Chapter THIRD,

or Sixtieth.——This represents to us the Greeks arrogating to themselves the knowledge of divinity, and the Latins despising the subtilty of the Greeks in it, 122; the differences between the eastern and western churches, concerning the procession of the Holy Ghost, 122-123; the use of leavened or un-leavened bread in the eucharist, 123; the eating of things strangled and of blood, fasting on Saturday, eating milk and cheese in the first week of Lent, and indulging the weak monks with flesh, 123; concerning the use of animal oil instead of vegetable in the unction of baptism, reserving the administration of this unction to bishops, decorating the bishops with rings, shaving the faces of priests, and baptizing infants by a single immersion, 124; and concerning the supremacy of the patriarch of Constantinople and the Pope of Rome, 124-126; the mutual hatred of the Greeks and Latins in the crusades, 126-127; many Latins, who were settled at Constantinople, massacred, 127-130; the reign of Isaac Angelus emperor of Constantinople, 130-131; the revolt of the Bulgarians and Wallachians from the empire and church of Constantinople, 131-132; Isaac deposed by his brother Alexius, 132-133; the fourth crusade preached up, 134-135; the persons engaged in it, 135-136; their application to the Venetians for ships, 136-137; the general history of Venice to this time, 137-139; the confederacy between the crusaders and Venetians, 139-141; the crusaders assembling at Venice

nice and being diverted into Dalmatia, 141-144; again diverted towards Constantinople, by Alexius son to the deposed emperor Isaac; 144-145; a part of the army, on this, leaving the rest and going for Jerusalem, 146; and the rest sailing for Constantinople, landing at it, besieging it, admitted into the town on the restoration of Isaac, again besieging the town on the second deposition of Isaac, taking, and plundering it, 146-173. All the first part of this chapter, therefore, is a string of digressions. The differences between the two churches, had either no influence at all, or a very slight one, in this attack of the Latins upon the Greek empire. They do not seem to have had any at all. Or, if they had, they were only as the dust of the scale in addition to the weight within it. And they ought not, if the slightest attention had been paid to propriety by Mr. Gibbon, to unity of design and to responsiveness of execution; to have been once thought of in a work; that is to give us *only* the ' important,' and ' the most' important, circumstances of the history. But nothing can stop Mr. Gibbon's predominant love, for theological dissertation. He bursts every band, that would tie him up from indulging it. And then he riots in the use of his liberty, like the fullfed stallion of the Iliad.

Δεσμον απορρηξας θειει πεδιοιο κροαινων
Ειωθως λꭣεσθαι ευρρειος ποταμοιο,
Κυδιοων· υψε δε καρη εχει, αμφι δε χαιται
Ωμοις αϊσσονται· ο δ' αγλαϊηφι πεποιθως,
Ριμφα ε γενα φερει μετα τ' ηθεα και νομον ιππων.

And the historian is transformed into the theologue, merely to exhibit the former in all the *confident* impertinence of digression, and to expose the latter in all the *common-place* futility of unbelief.

The Latins are said to have ' despised in their
' turn the restless and subtle levity of the Orientals,
' the authors of every heresy; and to have blessed
' their own simplicity, which was content to hold
' the tradition of the apostolic church'.' And
' yet,' as we are told in *the very next* words, ' so
' early as in the *seventh* century, the synods of *Spain*,
' and afterwards of *France, improved* or *corrupted*
' the Nicene creed, on the mysterious subject of
' the Third Person of the Trinity,' by adding that he proceeded from the *Son* as well as the Father. The second sentence is an *incomparable* proof, of the position in the first. The Latins *shewed* their contempt for ' the restless and subtle levity' of the Greeks, and *proved* their own adherence to ' the ' tradition of the church ;' by *adopting* the very *creed* of the *Greeks*, and even by *adding* to it. One could hardly think it possible for a rational being, to put two such contradictory sentences so close together. All must be attributed to a strange want of clearness and distinctness, in Mr. Gibbon's powers of discernment. We have seen so many instances of the same clashing of ideas before, as can leave us no room to doubt of this fatal defect in his understanding. Spirited, vivid, and ingenious, he is certainly very confused. His mind shoots out in vi-

' P. 122.

gorous sallies of thought occasionally, but cannot pursue clearly a steady train of operations. It is sometimes confounded, as it is here, by the very *second* operation. And, with such an unhappy disposition of understanding, it is no wonder that he is an infidel. How could *he* be expected to comprehend the grand system of Christianity, to see parts harmonizing with parts, and every complication uniting into a regular whole; who cannot arrange his own thoughts with precision, who is perpetually recoiling from the very line which he has prescribed to his own motions, and confounding himself by the contradictoriness of his own ideas? Nor let us overlook another, though slighter, instance of this contradictoriness. It is this. The text says, that, ' in the freedom of the table, the *gay* ' *petulance* of the *French* sometimes forgot the em- ' peror of the East[1].' And the note adds, *confirming* to *weaken* the position; that ' if these merry ' companions were *Venetians*, it was *the insolence of* ' *trade and a commonwealth.*' Could any thing in nature, but the derangement of an infidel understanding, generate such contrarieties as these?

False or harsh language.—P. 122. Text. ' The ' Roman pontiffs affected—moderation ; *they*,' &c. Note. ' Before the shrine of St. Peter, *he* placed,' &c. P. 127. ' The passage of these mighty armies ' *were* rare and perilous events.' P. 151. ' The ' four successive *battles* of the French were com- ' manded by,' &c. So p. 153, ' The six *battles*

[1] P. 157.

' of the French formed their encampment;' and p. 155, ' he found the six weary diminutive *battles* ' of the French, encompassed by sixty squadrons of ' the Greek cavalry.' Here the word *battle* is used in an acceptation, that is occasionally given it by our old writers. But it is an acceptation very harsh and violent. It is thus used as an abbreviation for *battle-array*, and means a division of an army arrayed for battle; just as it seems to be used for *battle-axe* in this unnoticed passage of the Psalms, ' there brake he ' the arrows of the *bow*, the *shield*, the *sword*, and ' the *battle*.' And as the use of *battle* for *battle-axe* would be very harsh in a modern writer, however countenanced by this and perhaps other passages in our old authors; so the adoption of *battle* for the division of an army, however sanctioned by a number of our old authors, is very violent. But in p. 154 we have another word derived from this ancient source. ' The numbers that defended the ' *vantage-ground*,' meaning not a real elevation of *ground*, but the height of the ramparts, ' repulsed ' and *oppressed* the adventurous Latins.' And, as *oppressed* is very improper in military language, and should be *pressed* or *overpowered*; so *vantage ground* is equally improper in itself, and in its application. Nor can we too much wonder at the injudiciousness of a writer, who could here take the momentary fancy, of sprinkling his compleatly modern language with *any* antiquated terms of history; and of selecting *such* only, as were obviously improper in their antient use, and are doubly improper now in his. We may speak, and some writers have spoken, of

the ' vantage *of* ground.' But the present modes of elegance certainly require us, to call it the ' advan-
' tage of ground.' And both elegance and use unite to interdict us, from talking of the ' vantage
' ground' with Mr. Gibbon. The words *vantage ground* and *battle*, as *here used*, are indeed such a *barbarism* in one of them, as we should never have expected in Mr. Gibbon, and such a *solecism* in the other, as we should laugh at in any writer.

Misquotation. Text. ' Pope Innocent the Third
' accuses *the pilgrims* of respecting, in their lust,
' neither age nor sex¹.' But the Pope, as quoted by Mr. Gibbon himself in the note, is by no means so comprehensive and general, as Mr. Gibbon makes him. He speaks not of *the pilgrims* at large. He notices only *some of them*. ' *Quidam* (says Inno-
' cent—) nec religioni nec ætati,' &c. And this furnishes another instance, how free or how careless Mr. Gibbon is in the application of his authorities. Nor does the Pope mean what Mr. Gibbon's words import when he speaks even of *some* not sparing either age or *sex*. He says, indeed, that *these*
' nec religioni nec ætati nec *sexui* pepercerunt.' But his meaning is sufficiently restricted, by his words immediately following; ' sed fornicationes,
' adulteria, incestus in ocul s omnium exercentes,' &c. And Mr. Gibbon himself states the fact in opposition to his language, to be that ' fornication,
' adultery, and incest were perpetrated.' Even as to *incest*, the original author means no more what

¹ p. 166.

his

his tranſlator means by *inceſt,* than he does what the other ſignifies by *ſex.* The impurities were all with *women.* But the *fornications* and *adulteries* were with *widows* and with *wives.* And the *inceſt* was with *nuns.* ' Non ſolum maritatas et viduas, ſed ' et matronas et virgines Deo—dicatas, expoſue-' runt,' &c. And, as Mr. Gibbon (I fear) meant to *inſinuate* more than he dared to *avow,* ſo he has certainly fixed the viciouſneſs upon *all,* when it apparently belonged only to *ſome.*

Chapter the FOURTH

or ſixty-firſt.—This ſhews us the nomination of an emperour by the Latins, 174—177; the diviſion of the provinces of the empire among them, 177—180; the provinces ſtill ſtanding out againſt them, 180—183; the diſcontent of the Greeks at Conſtantinople, 183—184; the conſpiracy of the Bulgarians with them, 184—185; the Greeks maſſacreing the Latins, 185; the approach of the Bulgarians, 185; the Latin emperour defeated and taken, 185—186; the Latin empire reduced to little more than the capital, 186—188; the ſecond Latin emperour, 188; his misfortunes, 189; his ſucceſſes, 189—191; his admiſſion of the Greeks into offices, 191; other parts of his conduct, 191—192; the third Latin emperour, a Frenchman, cruſhed with all his army in marching towards Conſtantinople, 192—194; the fourth Latin emperour equally a Frenchman, reaching Conſtantinople, 194; his misfortunes, 194—195; the fifth Latin emperour, 196—197; his succefs againſt the Greeks of Nice and the King of Bulgaria, who beſieged Conſtantinople, 197; the ſixth and laſt Latin emperour, 198; his misfortunes, 198—199; his mortgaging the holy relics, 200—202; the Greek empire of Nice gaining greatly upon him, 202—203; ſurprizing Conſtantinople itſelf, 204—206; the general conſequences of the cruſades upon weſtern Europe, 206—211; and ' a digreſſion on the family of Courtenay,' from which ſome of the Latin emperours were derived, 211—220. This acknowledged ' digreſſion,' ſays Mr. Gibbon, ' the ' purple of three emperours, who have reigned at ' Conſtantinople, will *authoriſe* or *excuſe*.' Mr. Gibbon has ſo vitiated his underſtanding by the habit of indulgence, that he can no longer diſcern the groſſeſt abſurdity of digreſſion. Blinded by the blaze of the ſun which has been ſo licentiouſly gazed upon, the eye is no longer able to behold an oppoſed mountain. And the addition of a genealogical eſſay to the hiſtory of this chapter, is one of the moſt wanton and whimſical effuſions of injudiciouſneſs, that even the preſent production can furniſh. I need not ſay, that the very purport of his work, and the very profeſſions of his preface, confine him to the hiſtory of the Roman empire, reſtrain him to the hiſtory of its decline and fall, and tie him down to the moſt important circumſtances of either. There is no need of a ſingle argument,

upon

upon the point. The digreſſion ſpeaks ſufficiently, for its own intruſiveneſs and effrontery. And this moſt ridiculous of all ridiculous digreſſions, this clumſily ſtitched-on *aſſumentum* to the records of hiſtory, and this awkwardly protuberant botch upon the mantle of it; could not, even in the judgment of Mr. Gibbon, enſlaved as his judgment is by the perpetual practice of digreſſions, have been deemed capable of any excuſe, much leſs of any ſanction; if another principle had not come in to delude him. The *zeal* of Mr. Gibbon betrays his *vanity*. He has ſome real or pretended connection, we doubt not, with the family which he blazons ſo ſtudiouſly. For the ſake of gratifying this petty pride, the hiſtorian *of the world* is content to ſink into the humble annaliſt *of a family*; the purblind critic takes care to ſhut his eyes entirely; and the race-horſe, that was perpetually ſtriking out of the courſe, reſolves to quit it with a bold leap at once. And all ſerves ſtrongly to impreſs a full conviction upon our minds of the weakneſs of Mr. Gibbon's judgment, when it comes to ſtruggle with his habits, and to contend with his paſſions; and of its readineſs when it is reduced into ſervitude, to eſpouſe the cauſe of its maſters, to 'excuſe' what it would heartily condemn in its free ſtate, and even to 'authoriſe' the moſt ſavage intemperances of tyranny over it.

I have already juſtified the cruſades ſufficiently, upon principles of policy and upon grounds of probity. Nor ſhall I now examine any new intimations

tions against them, in Mr. Gibbon. Only I cannot but notice the very violent zeal of Mr. Gibbon, which has incidentally charged the crusaders with *a most extraordinary crime*. This is no less an enormity, than working,—not upon Sundays—but—in Passion Week. ' Such was the pious tendency of ' the crusades,' he says at the siege of Adrianople, ' that *they employed the holy week*,' and the margin adds *March*; ' in pillaging the country for subsistence, ' and *in framing engines for the destruction of their ' fellow Christians*[1].'

' The empire, at once in a state of childhood ' and *caducity*[2].' This is worse than the worst of Johnson's *sesquipedalian* words. It is also absurd. *Caducity* forms no contrast to childhood. And *senility* should have been the latinized word.

Text. ' The—poverty of Baldwin was alle-' viated,—by the *alienation* of the marquisate of ' Namur and *the lordship of Courtenay*.' Note. ' Louis IX. disapproved and *stopped* the *alienation* ' of *Courtenay*[3].' This is very strange. But we have seen so much of the strangeness in the text and notes already, that even these most amazing of all contrarieties lose their effect upon us, and contradictoriness becomes familiar in Mr. Gibbon. In every other author, the text and the notes go on in loving fellowship together. The note indeed always plays the parasite to the text.

[1] p. 186.   [2] p. 187.   [3] p. 199.

Quicquid

Quicquid dicunt, laudo; id rurfum fi negant, laudo id quoque: Negat quis? nego; ait? aio: poftremò imperavi egomet mihi, Omnia adfentari; is quæftus nunc eft multò uberrimus.

But Mr. Gibbon repeatedly breaks in upon this parafitical humour, and deftroys this loving fellowfhip. His notes are behaving like impudent varlets to their mafters, and giving them the *lie direct*. This does, we fee, in the boldeft manner. And yet we find 'the caftle of Courtenay' actually *alienated* afterwards, becaufe it is faid to be 'profaned by a plebeian owner [1].' So, with an equally obvious though much lefs remarkable contradiction, Mr. Gibbon makes 'the *nummus aureus*—about ten fhillings fterling in value [2];' when he has previoufly made it, 'equivalent to *eight* fhillings of our fterling money [3].' Both unite with the *embofled* digreffion above, to fhew digreffions and contradictions continuing to go on together; and to mark by their union; the natural unfixednefs of Mr. Gibbon's fpirit, and the habitual unfteadinefs of Mr. Gibbon's judgment.

[1] p. 215.   [2] p. 200.   [3] vol. v. 397.

Chapter

Chapter the FIFTH,

and sixty-second—Here we see the private history of the empire of Nice, before Constantinople was recovered from the Latins, 221-222; in the conduct of the first and second emperors, 222-224; in that of the third, 224-225; in that of the guardians of the fourth, 226-231; and in that of the fifth to the taking of Constantinople, 231-232. So much of the chapter is all digressional. 'In the 'decline of the Latins,' says Mr. Gibbon, 'I have 'briefly exposed the progress of the Greeks; the 'prudent and gradual advances of a conqueror, 'who, in a reign of thirty-three years, rescued the 'provinces from national and foreign usurpers, till 'he pressed on all sides the imperial city, a leafless 'and sapless trunk which must fall at the first 'stroke of the axe. But *his* interior and peaceable 'administration is still more deserving of notice 'and praise¹.' He therefore pursues the subject. He thus digresses widely from the history of the ' decline and fall' of the Roman empire, more widely from the ' important' circumstances of either, and still more widely from ' the most important.' But his digression does not consist merely, in executing what he so digressionally proposes. The ' interior and peaceable administration,' in his am-

¹ P. 222.

plifying hands, becomes a history. And it is not the history merely, of the conquerour here alluded to: it is the history of his son, of his son's son, &c. Thus does one digression come riding upon the back of another,

Velut unda supervenit undam.

The chapter then goes on to shew us the entrance, of the guardian of the Greek emperour into Constantinople, 232-233; his conduct towards it, 233-234; his deposing and blinding the young emperour, 234; the discontents of the clergy at this, 235-237; his recovering some provinces of the empire from the Latins, 237-238; his attempting to unite the eastern and the western church, in vain, 238-242; the King of Naples and Sicily being formidable to the Greek emperour, 243; his history, 243-244; his designs against the emperour, 245; prevented by a rebellion, &c. in his own dominions, 245-248; some of the troops that had been fighting in Sicily taken into the emperour's pay, 248-250; their successes against the Turks, 250; their disorderly behaviour to the subjects of the empire, 250; their insolence to the emperour, 250-251; their defeating the troops of the empire, 251-252; their seizing Athens and Greece, 253-254; and the present state of Athens, 255-256. Here we have some very extraordinary digressions. Such is the account of attempting to unite the eastern and western churches, by reducing the faith of the eastern to the creed of the western, and by subjecting both to the supremacy

macy of the pope. It is purely a point of ecclesiastical history. It has no relation to the civil history of the empire. It has less, if possible, to the history of its decline and fall. And it has, if possible, still less to a narration of the important circumstances in them. We were told before, as an excuse for entering into a long labyrinth of theology; that ' the schism of Constantinople, by alienating
' her most useful allies, and provoking her most
' dangerous enemies, has precipitated the decline
' and fall of the Roman empire in the East¹.'
We then saw these allies and these enemies, reducing Constantinople, and giving several emperours to it. Here then, of course, terminated for the reign of the Latins, this separation of the two churches. But, it seems, this separation was not cured, even by the Latins. So little was the union an object of the Latin attempt, that it was never made though they succeeded. Accordingly we find the *Genoese* afterwards forming an alliance with the Greek emperours of Nice; against their Latin brethren of Constantinople². Even afterwards we hear, that ' the reign of the Latins *confirmed the se-*
' *paration* of the two churches³.' And we see that separation now attempted, seriously and formally, to be taken away. So utterly insignificant, even from Mr. Gibbon's *own* narration, does the union or the separation of the churches appear, as a civil incident! So utterly indefensible, even from his *own* state of facts, is Mr. Gibbon's long excursion

¹ p. 121.   ² p. 203.   ³ p. 207.

before

before into the regions of his own romantic divinity! And so wildly wanton again does his present digression appear, upon the face of his *own* history! But he closes the chapter with a digression, still more wildly wanton than this. The historian assumes the traveller. He leaps out of the orbit of history. He lights upon the ground of Athens. He thus exceeds the spirit, of concluding his last chapter with the genealogy of the house of Courtenay. And he concludes his present, with describing the state of Athens *as it is at this moment.* He has thus formed a digression, that overtops all his former, that recoils with a compleater energy from the course of his history, and wanders more gloriously astray from the path of propriety.

'The cause was decided, *according to the new jurisprudence of the Latins,* by single combat [1].' This is very injudiciously asserted. The cause was tried and the combat undertaken, not at Constantinople after the re-establishment of the empire at its antient capital, but even while it yet continued at Nice. In such a state of the empire, and in a situation of continual warfare with the Latins of Constantinople, it is absolutely impossible for the jurisprudence to be borrowed from the Latins. It was undoubtedly a part of the antient and original jurisprudence of the Greeks. Accordingly we see the *fiery ordeal* in Mr. Gibbon himself, equally used at the same time and in the same place by the Greeks [2]. And we even see both in another page

[1] p. 225.   [2] p. 226—227.

of Mr. Gibbon, abolished by the same Greeks at the same place, and still *before* the recovery of the old capital from the Latins[1]. Both resulted assuredly from the judiciary proceedings of the earliest ages. The *waters of jealousy* among the Jews, carry the principle to a very remote antiquity. The custom of the Germans upon the Rhine, even so late as the days of Julian, in trying the chastity of their wives by throwing their children into the river; has a near affinity with the Jewish mode of purgation, and a still nearer with the water-ordeal of our own country. These serve sufficiently to shew at once, the antiquity and the extensiveness of these judiciary kinds of divination. The Greeks would be sure to have them, as well as the Jews. And the two incidents here noticed by Mr. Gibbon, shew evidently that they had them.

'By the *Latins* the lord of Thebes was styled *by* 'corruption Megas Kurios or *Grand Sire*[2].' This is a perfect riddle. In what country would the *Latins* call the Latin lord of Thebes, by a *Greek* title? Or, if they did, in what country may we pronounce this a *corruption*? And in what country will *grandsire* stand, for a translation of μεγας κυριος?

Dic quibus in terris, et eris mihi magnus Apollo.

'It would not be easy,' he says concerning the *present* Athens, 'in the country of Plato and De-'mosthenes, to find a reader, or a copy, of their 'works[3].' This is satire overcharged. The pre-

[1] p. 229.   [2] p. 253.   [3] p. 256.

sent Athenians are *not* so inattentive to the writings of their forefathers. The late Mr. Wood tells us in his Essay on Homer, as we remember, that he read Homer with a Greek schoolmaster at Athens.

' The factious nobles were reduced or oppressed
' by the *ascendant* of his genius'.' For *ascendant* read nostro periculo *ascendancy*.

Chapter the SIXTH,

or sixty-third.——This contains the disputes of the emperour with the patriarch, 257-259, certainly *no* circumstance of the decline and fall of the empire; the character of John Cantacuzenus as an historian, 259-260, a point improper in the text of *any* history, and peculiarly so in the text of this; disputes of the emperour with his grandson, 260-262; the grandson breaking out into rebellion, 262-263; forcing the emperour to abdicate, 264-265; his own reign, 265-267; his young son's guardian, 267-268; the guardian ill-treated, 268-270; breaking out into rebellion, but defeated, 270-271; still maintaining the rebellion, 272; at last victorious, 272-275; the young emperour soon taking up arms against him, 275-276; the guardian again victorious and now seizing the throne, 277; driven from it by a revolt in favour of the young emperour, 277-278; an account of the divine light of Mount Thabor, 278-280, an amazing digression, being a dissertation on some wild notion of the Quietists, and introduced merely from the dethroned guardian

' P. 229.

writing a book concerning it; the state of the Genoese settled close to Constantinople, 280-283; their breaking out into successful rebellion, 283-285; the Venetian fleet called in to the aid of the empire, 285; and the Genoese beating the fleets of both, 286-287. In this chapter, allowing all the other articles to be circumstances in the history of the decline and fail of the empire, important circumstances, and very important too; yet we have no less than three apparently digressional. The last of these indeed is so grossly digressional, that it serves with others preceding, to shew the author totally void even of all critical decency. Nor can I too much expose this bold immodesty of writing, because it is little noticed by the herd of critics; because it is destructive of all regularity in composition and forms a kind of Gothic edifice, a mass of parts, but no whole. And the author was seduced into the last digression, by the un-resisting feebleness of a judgment that has so long given way; and by a strange fondness in his spirit, for prancing over the fields of theology, shewing the lightness of his heels in the giddiness of his motions, and betraying the ignorance of his inexperience in the wanton mettle of his blood.

' Nor were the flames of hell *less* dreadful to his
' fancy, than those of a Catalan or Turkish war'.'
When I first read this sentence, I supposed the printer had substituted *less* by mistake for *more*. So must any man have written, who believed the

' P. 257.

existence of hell. But Mr. Gibbon, we fear for *his* sake, does not. This passage shews too plainly, he does not. And thus, with a bold defiance of the common sense and common feelings of mankind, he makes the terrors of eternity, of which every good and every wise man must think with the deepest awe; to be *less* formidable in themselves, than—a host of Catalans or an army of Turks.

Note. ' The ingenious comparison with Moses ' and Cæsar, is *fancied* by his French translator [1].' What this means we *guess* as we read it. But we soon find that we guessed wrong. ' It is observed' of Cantacuzenus, says Mr. Gibbon a few lines lower in the text, than the place referred to in the note; ' that, like Moses and Cæsar, he was the principal ' actor in the scenes which he describes.' And we now see, that when Mr. Gibbon says this comparison was *fancied*, he means it was *suggested by the fancy*.——' The *vast* silence of the palace [2].' We thus find that *boyism*, which Mr. Gibbon has borrowed from Tacitus, affronting our taste again.——
' She was *regenerated* and crowned in St. Sophia [3].' He means *re-baptised*.——' His vigorous govern-
' ment *contained* the Genoese of Galata within those
' limits [4].' Here the use of the word *contained*, is more Latin than English.

Chapter SEVENTH

and sixty-fourth.——The contents of this are, the general conquests of the Mogul Tartars under Zin-

[1] p. 259.   [2] p. 264.   [3] p. 267.   [4] p. 281.

gis, 289-290; his code of laws, 290-292; his particular conquests in China, 292-294; in Carizme, Transoxiana, Persia, and some independent parts of Tartary, 294-296; the conquests of his four first successors in China, 297-299; in the countries adjoining to China, 299; in Persia, 299-300; in Armenia, Anatolia, &c. 300-301; in Kipzak, Russia, Poland, Hungary, &c. 301-304; and in Siberia, 304-305; the change of manners in the Tartar emperours upon this success, 305-306; the Tartars in China adopting the manners of the Chinese, 306-307; yet expelled by the Chinese, 307; the other conquests becoming independent of the emperours, 307; many becoming Mahometans, 307-308; *the escape of the Roman empire from their arms*, 308-310; and the decline of their power, 310. All this is evidently a chain of continued digressions. There is only one article out of seventeen, that has any connection even with the *full* history of the empire. The history of the *decline* and *fall* of the empire, has no more connection with it, than a history of the revolutions in the moon, or of the physical convulsions in our globe. Mr. Gibbon himself acknowledges, that it has not; in the noticed *escape* of the Roman empire from the Tartar arms. *This* therefore is the only point of the long narrative, that ought, in justice to his plan and his promises, to have been noticed at all. Yet under his conduct the Tartars, like Cato, enter the theatre, and *then*—go out again. He brings them upon the stage, as Homer brings half his heroes, merely to be knocked upon the head. And at the close of the

the whole we are told, after the Tartars had proved totally *innoxious* to the Roman empire; that ' the ' *decline* of the *Moguls* gave a free fcope to the *rife* ' and *progrefs* of the *Ottoman empire.*' He thus erects the empire of the Tartars, to fweep it away with a brufh of his hand, and to raife the empire of the Ottomans upon the ground; and two-and-twenty pages are employed, when two would have been too many. The chapter then goes on to the origin of the Ottoman Turks, 310-311; the fucceffes of their founder Othman againft the empire, 311-312; the fucceffes of his fon Orchan againft it, 312-315; the firft paffage of the Turks into Europe, 315-316; Orchan's marriage with a daughter of the Roman emperour, 316-317; the eftablifhment of the Ottomans in Europe, 318-319; their making Adrianople their capital there, 319; their reduction of Bulgaria, &c. 319-320; their appointment of the Janizaries, 320-321; their reduction of Macedonia, Theffaly, and Greece, 322; the character of the conqueror, 322-323; his invafion of Hungary, 323; his defeat of the Hungarians and French, 323-325; his conduct of his French captives, 325-327; the diffentions among the Greeks, 327-329; the diftrefs of the empire, 329; Conftantinople befieged by the Turks, 329; relieved by a fleet of French, 329-330; again befieged by the Turks, and again relieved accidentally by Tamerlane, 330. Thus, more than half of the whole chapter, is entirely foreign to it. Yet, in this very chapter, Mr. Gibbon can fpeak of the hiftory of Chalcondyles, as one ' whofe proper fubject is ' drowned

'drowned in a sea of episode.' So keen is Mr. Gibbon to discern the faults of another, and so blind to the view of his own, even when he is just come from the particular commission of them. We are not acquainted with the history of Chalcondyles. But no words can more appositely picture forth Mr. Gibbon's. *His* ' proper subject is' actually ' drowned in a sea of episode.' And he has dashed off his own character very happily, in that of the other. ' I have long since asserted my claim,' he says on preparing to wander away with the Tartars above, ' to introduce the nations, the immediate ' or remote authors of the fall of the Roman em- ' pire; nor can I refuse myself to those events,' the conquests of the Tartars, ' which, from their ' uncommon magnitude, will interest a philosophic ' mind in the history of blood[1].' This is Mr. Gibbon's apology, for rambling over half the globe with the Tartars. He suspected he was going to be devious, and thought to deceive himself and his reader by an apology. The eye of the mole can just discern light enough, to know he is exposing himself to the danger of being seen. But he instantly dives, to avoid his danger. And Mr. Gibbon sees, excuses, and runs into it. He has long ' asserted his claim to introduce the nations, the im- ' mediate or the remote authors of the fall of the ' Roman empire.' He *therefore* ' introduces a na- ' tion,' that, *by his own account*, was not ' the *imme-* ' *diate*,' was not even ' the *remote*, author of the

[1] p. 288.

' *fall.*'

'*fall.*' This is a glaring proof of Mr. Gibbon's powers of reasoning. '*Nor can I refuse myself*,' he adds, 'to those events,' not as in the chain of thought and of propriety he *ought* to have said, which relate to some special 'authors of the fall;' but ' which, *from their uncommon magnitude*, will *interest a philosophic mind* in the history of blood.' Mr. Gibbon evidently saw the absurdity of his digression, but ' could not refuse himself' to it. The paroxysm of rambling was upon him, and he could not resist it. His mind is ever ready to catch at any 'events of uncommon magnitude,' however foreign they may be to his plan, and however contrary to his promise. It was so, at his outset in the history. It is now a thousand times more so, from his long habits of digression. And, from both, unable to withstand the temptation, yet sensible it was a temptation, he throws the dust of an apology in his own eyes and the reader's; but wilfully turns off in it from his natural course of ideas, which would have led the reader and him to detect the *falseness* of the apology. Instead of representing the Tartars, as ' authors' *in any degree* ' of the fall of the Roman empire;' he represents their transactions as events, that ' will interest a philosophic mind in the history of blood.' He thus acknowledges, very plainly, the *episodical* nature of his Tartar history here; by deserting the ground of justification, which he had taken first, and on which alone it could be justified; and turning off to a ground, upon which he might justify the history of *any* active nation, or the account of *any* turbulent empire, upon the face of the earth.

Contradictions. Text. 'The Khan of the Ke-
raites, who, under the name of Prester John, *had
corresponded* with the Roman pontiff and the princes
of Europe,' &c. Note. 'The Khans of the Ke-
raites were most probably *incapable* of *reading* the
pompous epistles *composed* in *their* name by *the
Nestorian missionaries*¹.'——Text. 'In the attack and defence of places' by the Chinese and
Tartars, '—the use of *gunpowder* in *cannon* and *bombs*
appears as *a familiar practice*².' Note. 'I depend
on the knowledge and fidelity of the Pere Gaubil, who translates the *Chinese text* of the *annals*
of the Moguls or Yuen (p. 71, 93, 153).' So
far the note goes hand in hand with the text. *Then*
a slight doubt concerning the *veracity* of the text,
intrudes upon us: 'but I am ignorant, *at what
time* these annals were *composed* and *published*.'
Yet, upon the credit of these very annals, Mr.
Gibbon has asserted the use of gunpowder, to have
been 'a familiar practice' at *that* particular time.
He then advances into higher than doubts. He
brings a strong argument of presumption, *against*
both *their* veracity and *his own.* 'The two uncles
of Marco Polo, who served as engineers at the
siege of Siengyangfou (l. ii. c. 61. in Ramusio,
tom. ii. See Gaubil, p. 155-157), *must* have *felt*
and *related* the *effects* of *this destructive powder*;
and their *silence* is a *weighty*, and almost *decisive*,
objection.' Mr. Gibbon has thus brought an objection 'weighty, and almost decisive,' against the

¹ p. 285—290. ² p. 298.

truth

truth of *his own* assertion. And he arraigns *himself* and his *text* of *falshood*, at the bar of his notes.

Chapter Eighth

or sixty-fifth.——This contains the private history of Tamerlane to his gaining the royalty of Transoxiana, 331-335, all digressional; his conquests in Persia, 335-336, equally digressional; his reduction of Ormuz, Bagdad, Edessa, and Georgia, 336-337, equally digressional; his successes in Turkestan, Kipzak, and Russia, 338-339, equally digressional; his reduction of Azoph, Serai, and Astrachan, 338-339, equally digressional; his conquests in India, 339-341, equally digressional; angry letters between him and the Turkish emperour, 342-345, equally digressional; his invasion of Syria, now possessed by the Mamalukes of Egypt, 345-347, equally digressional; his march into the Turkish dominions, 348-349; his defeat of the Turks, 349-351; his reduction of all their dominions in Asia, 351-352; his reception of the Turkish emperour, 352-353, again digressional; the story of his putting him in an iron cage examined, 353-356, equally digressional; his making the Roman emperour swear to pay him the same tribute, which had been paid to the Turks, 357; his successes against other powers, 359, again digressional; his triumph and festivity after all, 359-360, equally digressional; his preparations for invading China, 360, equally digressional; his death baffling his designs, 360-361, equally digressional; his character examined and his merits ascertained, 361-364, equally digressional;

fional; the hiftory of the Turks after Bajazet's defeat, 364-367, equally digreffional; the Genoefe affifting the Turks of Afia to reduce the Turks of Europe, 367-368, equally digreffional; the ftate of the Roman empire, 369; the emperour offending both the rival kings of the Turks, 370-371; Conftantinople befieged by the victorious rival, but beating him off, 371; the emperour fubmitting to pay a tribute as before, and to relinquifh almoft all the country without the fuburbs of the city, 371; the hereditary fucceffion of the royalty among the Turks, 372-373, again digreffional; the education and difcipline of the Turks, 373-375, equally digreffional; and an effay on the invention and ufe of gunpowder, as practifed in the late fiege of Conftantinople, 375-377. Thus, out of twenty-feven articles, no lefs than nineteen are merely digreffional; having only a *general* connexion with the *full* hiftory of the empire, having none at all with the hiftory of its *decline* and *fall*, and having lefs than none (if poffible) with the *important* circumftances of either. But Mr. Gibbon catches at the flighteft thread that is floating in the air, in order to waft himfelf along in queft of his prey. If the Turks be *foes* to the empire, he will give us circumftantial accounts of the Turks. If the Tartars of Tamerlane be *foes* to the *foes* of the empire, he will be equally circumftantial concerning the Tartars. And inftead of a really *general* account, that fhall juft *fketch* out their hiftory to the period of their

connection

connection with the empire, and then dwell upon it particularly; he gives us *his* general history, replete with *particular* anecdotes, and spreading through a *variety* of pages; and is as circumstantial *before* the connection, as *after* it. We have seen this, in the history of Zingis and his Tartars before; though their transactions had only a *negative* connection with the empire, and the account of them concludes with their *not* affecting the empire at all. We here see it again, in the history of Tamerlane and his Tartars: where the only *spiders thread* of connection is, that they advanced to the Hellespont, after having reduced the Turks in Asia; and made the emperour vow the homage, and promise the tribute, which he had paid to the Turks before. Yet *that* is twenty pages in quarto, and *this* sixteen. Thus, because the dread of Zingis prevented the *Swedes* and *Frizelanders*, from going to the herring-fishery of England; and the *English*, having all the fishery to themselves, lowered the price considerably in all the markets of England: from this almost invisible filament of air, if he was writing the history of England, he would think himself justified, in giving us his circumstantial abstract of the transactions of Zingis, even in such a history. No fence can serve to keep in this skipping deer. And his whole history strongly reminds us of the island at Rome, which has two bridges to it, and a church and a monastery upon it; and yet was formed originally, of Tarquin's *sheaves of corn*. The history of the decline and fall of the Roman empire, is thus formed by accretions and deterrations, from the full history of the empire, and from almost every other history in the world. Nor has the author the discretion in digressing, to keep off all subordinate and accessary digressions. He indulges himself in the full and free licence of digressions *upon* digressions. When he has led Tamerlane by the hand, to the defeat of the Turks; he must superadd to his general digression, a particular one by the way, in a dissertation about the iron cage of Bajazet. Nor has he even the prudence, when he has brought down this *side-history* to that point of his own, *for which* he wrote it; there to terminate all his digressions, to leave the bye-road by which he had been rounding about to the main one, and now to pursue the main road steadily for a while. No! He strikes directly across the main road again, and diverges from it on the other side. And when he has made Tamerlane, after all his conquests, to reduce the empire into the same submission and tribute, which it had paid the Turks; he does not then close his divarications with Tamerlane, as we expect even the most impertinent of digressors to do, because he has reached the grand goal of all his digressions. He goes on in his excursions, to give us Tamerlane's successes against other powers, to paint his triumph and festivity after all, nay to tell us his preparations for invading China, to baffle them by his death, even then to examine his character formally, and to ascertain his merits precisely. Mr. Gibbon must thus

thus appear, with every allowance that can be made him, and with every sobriety that can be used in considering his conduct; the most astonishing digressor that ever pretended to write history, even when he has some little semblance of connection, between his history and his digressions.

Mr. Gibbon has *gravely* adopted a wild stroke of Oriental bombast, *as his own:* ' whole forests were ' cut down to supply fuel for his kitchens¹,' at a *particular* feast.

Contradictions. Text. ' It is *believed* in the em-
' pire and *family* of Timour, that the *monarch* him-
' self *composed*—the *institutions* of his government².'
Note. ' Shaw Allum, the present mogul, *reads,*
' *values,* but *cannot imitate,* the *institutions* of his
' *great ancestor.*' The text asserts the existence of Tamerlane's *institutions,* only as an object of *belief.* The note indirectly contradicts the text, by mounting much higher in the scale of assurance, and turning belief into *certainty.* Shaw Allum actually ' reads,' actually ' values,' this work ' of his ' great ancestor' Tamerlane. Yet we have still doubts thrown out immediately, as if Shaw Allum was not so good a judge as Mr. Gibbon, what is really the composition ' of his great ancestor.' ' The
' English translator,' as the note adds, ' *relies on*
' *their internal evidence;* but, *if any suspicions should*
' *arise of fraud and fiction,* they will *not be dispelled*
' by Major Davy's letter. *The Orientals have never*

¹ P. 359.   ² p. 332.

' *cultivated*

'*cultivated the art of criticism.*' Thus, what is noticed in the text as only *believed*, is then asserted in the beginning of the note to be *certain*, and is left at last *doubtful*. And, after all, Mr. Gibbon repeatedly refers to the work as *not* doubtful, as *more* than believed, as certain *again*. The judgement of a sceptick, may become so vitiated and debilitated by the exercise of scepticism, I suppose; as not to settle peremptorily upon any point, to fluctuate between certainty and doubt on the plainest, and to be sometimes doubtful, sometimes certain, and yet doubtful still. Scepticism is thus to the mind, what opium is to the body; an enlivener of the spirits, and an illuminator of the understanding, in a very moderate degree; but dangerous in the use, and fatal in the excess; enfeebling the nerves of the soul, destroying the tone of the thoughts, and reducing the unhappy man into a drunken paralytick in intellect.

Text. ' Timour stood firm as a rock[1].' Note says, that Arabshah makes Timour *run away*: and adds concerning the very author, from whom he has asserted Timour to stand firm as a rock; ' perhaps Sherefeddin (l. iii. c. 25) has *magnified* ' his *courage*.' He therefore, *perhaps*, did *not* ' stand ' firm as a rock,' though the text asserts positively that he *did*. Text. ' The Mogul soldiers were en- ' riched with an immense spoil of precious furs, *of* ' *the linen of Antioch*, and *of ingots of gold and sil-*

[1] p. 336.

'ver¹.' Note. 'The *furs* of Ruſſia are *more* cre-
'dible than the *ingots*;' when both are repreſented
above to be *certain*. 'But *the linen of Antioch* has
'*never* been famous; and *Antioch was in ruins*.'
The *text* therefore *ſpeaks falſely*. 'I ſuſpect,' he
adds, 'that it was ſome manufacture of Europe,
'which the Hanſe merchants had imported by the
'way of Novogorod.' Yet he expreſsly calls it
the linen of *Antioch*. And what muſt be the in-
toxication and palſy of a mind, from the opium of
ſcepticiſm; that can thus give *itſelf* the lie, in one
breath aver a point boldly and confidently, and in
the very next find ſufficient reaſon to reprobate its
own averment?

Chapter the NINTH,

or ſixty-ſixth.——We have here a detail of the
Greek emperours, applying for relief to the Weſt,
and offering to unite the eaſtern and weſtern
churches; 378-384; the perſonal viſit of one of
them, for the ſame relief and with the ſame offer,
385-387; that of another for relief only, 387-390;
the deſcriptions of Germany, France, and England,
as given by the attendants of theſe emperours, 390-
393; application again for relief with the old
offer, 394-395; the ſtate of the imperial family,
395-397; the corruptions of the Latin church,
397-398; the ſchiſm in the Weſt from the co-

¹ p. 338—339.

existence of two popes, 398; the councils of Pisa and Constance, 398; the council of Basil, 399-400; this council inviting the emperour and his patriarch to come to it, 400; his embassadours received honourably by it, 400; the council and pope being at variance, the place of meeting fixed by the pope's management to be at Ferrara, 400-401; both fitting out gallies for fetching the emperour, but the pope's taking him on board, 400-402; the emperour's train, 402-404; his arrival at Venice, 404-405; his arrival at Ferrara, 405; the form of the council there, 405-406; the council adjourned, 406; the emperour staying in Italy, 406-407; the council re-assembled at Florence, 407; the debates in it on the points of union between the churches, 407-410; the points settled, 410-414; the state of the Greek language at Constantinople, 414-416; the Greeks and Latins compared in learning, 416-417; the Greek learning revived in Italy, 417-418; the studies of Barlaam there, 418-419; those of Petrarch, 419-420; those of Boccace, 421-422; the knowledge of the Greek language settled in Italy, 423-424; a succession of Grecians teaching Greek there, 425-426; their faults and their merits, 426-427; the study of the Platonic philosophy, 427-428; the emulation and progress of the Latins, 429-431; and the use and abuse of antient learning, 431-433. We have thus a strange set of articles, forming the substance of this chapter. The applications of the emperours for relief, and their endeavours to back their applications by offers of uniting the churches, might perhaps be properly noticed; as evidences of the felt and acknowledged debility, to which the eastern empire was now reduced. But, as they terminated in no relief, they should have been noticed only in a flight manner. Two or three pages would have been sufficient, when *six-and-thirty* are employed. But Mr. Gibbon has such a *loquaciousness* in writing, that he must talk on when he has got upon a subject. Nothing can stop the torrent of indiscretion.

Labitur, et labetur, in omne volubilis ævum.

Beginning thus with the application enforced by the offer, he turns aside with the offer, goes on to the corruptions of the Latin church, the anti-popes in it, the councils, &c. &c. &c. And he dwells upon all these digressional points, with the same amplitude of description and the same circumstantiality of incident, as if the whole formed a very important part in the decline and fall of the empire. He is as much at home in every the most distant digression, as he is in the regular line of his subject; and

Then he will talk, good gods! how he will talk!

equally upon a point that has only the slightest relation to his history, or even upon one that has none at all, as upon one that has the closest connection with it. In the *least* excursive of his digressions, he will make a slight and almost imperceptible point, the central pin of a large formation; just as a single grain of sand becomes the *nucleus* to an ample stone, in the human body. We see this in the long detail of the present chapter, concerning the union of the churches. But, in others of his excursions, he scorns even this ' discretion in ' running mad.' He asks for no central pin. He rolls round no *nucleus*. But he *pastes on* his matter at once. We have seen this exemplified several times before. And here we see it again, in the description of Germany, France, and England, given by the attendants of the emperours. ' It ' may be *amusing* enough,' we are told ' *perhaps* ' instructive, to contemplate the rude pictures of ' Germany, France, and England, whose ancient ' and modern state are so familiar to our minds¹.' We are thus to be *amused*, at the expence of every propriety. We are ' perhaps' to be ' instructed,' by the violation of every decency. And, after all, this episode is nearly as petty as it is impertinent. But Mr. Gibbon, in modelling his history, is like an engineer constructing one of our navigable canals. He endeavours to draw every lively brook in the neighbourhood, into his own capacious reservoir. Like a wild one therefore, he turns, and twists, and doubles the line of his canal, in quest of it. And in some point of his course, where he sees a fine quantity of water, he commits every violence upon nature, in raising vallies, in sinking mountains, and in tossing up a whole river by the

¹ p. 391.

aid of machinery, that he may have the use of it. Mr. Gibbon having finished his *ecclesiastical* history, goes on to what is equally impertinent with his *Grecian* description of England, France, and Germany; to the revival of the antient learning of the Greeks, in the west of Europe. This he pursues, through a train of eighteen or nineteen quarto pages; and in little dissertations, on the state of the Greek language at Constantinople, on the Greeks and Latins compared for learning, on the revival of the Greek literature in Italy, on the studies of Barlaam, Petrarch, and Boccace there, &c. &c. &c. Such digressions as these stare so full in the face of criticism, that I hardly know at which I should wonder most, the astonishing *monstrosity* of them, or the easy acquiescence of the publick under them. There never was, I believe, a history written since the creation of the world, so monstrously digressional as this. And I cannot refrain from declaring, that nothing, but some wild extravagance of understanding in Mr. Gibbon, could have generated so many monsters of digressions as these.

Chapter TENTH

or sixty-seventh.———This gives us a general account of Constantinople at this period, 434—437; the opposition in the Greek church to the union settled with the Latin, 437—440; the reign of Amurath the Second emperor of the Turks, 440—443; the Poles and Hungarians engaging in war against the Turks, 443 —445; their successes, 445—447; their swearing to a peace, a peace, breaking their oath, and renewing the war, 447—448; their defeat, 448—451; the family, life, and death of him who perfuaded the perjury, 451—452; the family of him who commanded the army, his life to his defeat, his life afterwards, and his fon's, 452—454; the birth and education of Scanderbeg, 454—456; his revolt from the Turks, 456—457; his valour, 457—458; his death, 458 —459; the acceffion of Conftantine, the laft of the emperours, to the throne of the empire, 459—460; the embaffies of Phranza for him, 460—462; and the ftate of the Byzantine court, 462—463. This fhort chapter of not more than thirty pages, is full of digreffions. Mr. Gibbon is fo much in the habit of digreffing, that he cannot refift the temptation. And the naturally flender fhape of his hiftory, requires to be ftuffed out with wadding and wool to the bulk wanted. The account of the oppofition to the union in the Greeks, is juft as digreffional; as the narrative of the union before. It has no relation to the hiftory. It haftened not the fall, before it was accomplifhed. It delayed not the fall, afterwards. It has no influence upon the civil hiftory at all. Not a pin or a wheel in the political machine, is affected by it. But Mr. Gibbon proceeds to ftill worfer digreffions. He gives us the hiftory of the Poles and Hungarians, in their wars with the Turks. He adds the hiftory of Scanderbeg, in his revolt from the Turks, and in his wars with them. He dwells upon both, with all the circumftantiality of particular hiftory. And he fuperadds to the former, an account of the family, life, and

and death of him, who perfuaded the Poles and Hungarians to renew the war; of the family of him, who commanded their army in the prefent and the former war; of his life to his defeat, even of his life afterwards, and even of his fon's too. Yet, in both thefe wars, how is the decline and fall of the empire concerned? The Polifh and Hungarian wars, we are exprefsly told, the emperour 'feems to have 'promoted by his wifhes, and injured by his fears[1].' *During* thefe, he 'engaged to guard the Bofphorus[2];' but, 'according to fome writers,—had been awed 'or feduced to grant the paffage[3].' This was all his concern in the bufinefs. If this could make it proper to fhew the debility of the empire, in its being 'awed or feduced' to break its own ftipulation in the alliance; then the war fhould have been noticed flightly, in proportion to the flight concern of the empire in it. But indeed it fhould *not* have been noticed at all. It was *not* one of the 'im-'portant' circumftances, in the decline and fall of the empire. It was ftill lefs one of 'the *moft* im-'portant.' And none *but thefe* were to be noticed. Mr. Gibbon however advances an argument, for mentioning the wars of Scanderbeg, and of the Poles and Hungarians united; that 'they are both 'entitled to our notice, *fince* their occupation of the 'Ottoman arms *delayed* the ruin of the Greek em-'pire[4].' 'Entitled to our *notice*' they may be. But are they to a particular and circumftantial

[1] P. 445.
[2] P. 445.
[3] P. 449.
[4] P. 454.

defcription?

description? *This* he *gives,* though he *talks* only of *that.* Yet these wars, it is alleged, diverted the arms of the Turks and delayed the ruin of the empire. On the *same* principle however, he might notice, and even describe, *every* war in which the Turks were engaged, *every* negociation in which they were concerned, *every* commotion among their people, and even *every* fever, or *every* pleasure, which detained their sovereign from war. And accordingly Mr. Gibbon describes to us in this very chapter, the reign of Amurath the Second emperour of the Turks, *because* he did *not* attack Constantinople, during the absence of the emperour in the West; when this very point had been noticed in p. 402 before, when it is merely *negative,* and when he might *as* justly have given us the history of *all* the surrounding nations. But digressions produce digressions. Resigning himself up to the inviting histories of Scanderbeg's and the Hungarian wars, he feels himself allured still farther. The more he descends from the natural road, at the top of the precipice; he feels it the more difficult to restrain his course, and goes on with the more headlong violence. *He could not but describe* the birth and character of Scanderbeg, *previous* to his wars with the Turks. *He could not but describe* the family and life of him, who *occasioned* the second war of the Hungarians and Poles with the Turks. *He could not but describe* the family of him, who *conducted* the Poles and Hungarians in both these wars; his life before the defeat; even his life *after* it; and even his very *son*'s too. And he has thus clapped a large and

and coloured *badge* upon the patched mantle of his history, that serves to mark *its* poverty, and *his* distress, to every eye. There are therefore only four articles out of sixteen in this chapter, that have any just connection with it; the first, concerning Constantinople; and the three last, concerning the accession of Constantine to the throne, the embassies which he sent, and the state of his court. Three even of these are hardly to be reckoned, among the ' most important circumstances' of the decline and fall of the empire. But the intermediate points, are entirely the very wantonness and whimsicalness of digression.

' Voltaire—admires le philosophe Turc; would
' he have bestowed the same praise on a Christian
' prince, for retiring to a monastery? In his way,
' Voltaire was a bigot, an intolerant bigot¹.' We have produced this passage, in order to honour the fairness of it. It is indeed an astonishing proof of fairness, in Mr Gibbon. It is a vivid flash of ingenuousness, breaking through the deep gloom of his anti-christian prejudices. And we therefore behold it with wonder, and mark it with applause. But it is the more astonishing, when we consider the character to be equally adapted to Mr. Gibbon himself, as to Voltaire. The keen atmosphere of severity, which continually wraps Mr. Gibbon round when he speaks of Judaism and of Christianity; shews clearly the inclement rigour of his spirit towards them. The saucy strain of authority too, with

¹ P. 442.

which

which he presumes to dictate upon points of divinity; to penetrate with a glance, through all the folds of the most complicated doctrines; and to decide in an instant upon mysteries, that he has never familiarised to his mind; marks plainly that high conceit and overweening confidence of opinion, which always forms the stuff and substance of a persecutor. And the imperious tone of insolence with which he speaks of divines, even in their own province; men likely to have as good talents from nature, as any infidel in the kingdom; men, sure to improve them in the business of their own profession, by the general habits of a scholastick education, and by their particular attention to their professional studies; and men, actually shining in every department of science, and peculiarly eminent in their own, as all the world can witness: is not merely to insult the common-sense of mankind, but to betray the violence of the inquisitor under the moderation of the philosopher; beneath the gown and furs of religious apathy, to disclose the flame-coloured vest of persecution; and to prove Mr. Gibbon ‘ in *his* ‘ way,’ to be equally with Voltaire in *his*, ‘ a bigot, ‘ an intolerant bigot.’

Chapter ELEVENTH

or sixty-eighth.———In this are the character of Mahomet II. emperour of the Turks, 464—466; his reign, 466—468; his unfriendliness towards the Roman empire, 468—469; his avowal of intended hostilities,

hostilities, 469—470; the hesitating conduct of the empire, 470—471; the provoking and hostile behaviour of the Turks, 471—473; the preparations of the Turks for the siege of Constantinople, 473—475; the great cannon, 475—477; the preparations of the Greeks for the defence of Constantinople, 477—478; Mahomet advancing and beginning the siege, 478; the forces of the Turks, 478—479; those of the Greeks 479—480; the emperour having previously sought for aid from the West, by an offered union of the churches, 480—481; a Latin priest that officiated at St. Sophia's, having raised a great ferment among the Greeks, 481—483; the behaviour of the Greeks in the first part of the siege, 484; that of the Turks, 484—485; the effect of the Turkish batteries, 485; the advance of the Turks to the ditch, 485—486; their attempt to fill the ditch baffled, 486; the Turks attempting mines, but again baffled, 486; other expedients tried by them, 486—487; a breach made, but the Turks beat off for the day, 487; at night the breach built up again, 487; some vessels breaking through the whole Turkish fleet, and bringing succours, 487—490; Mahomet inclining to discontinue the siege, but resolving upon another effort, 490; transporting his navy over land into the harbour, 491; attacking the wall of the city there, 492; the city reduced to distress, 492; being in dissensions, 493; the Turks preparing to give the assault, 493—495; the Greeks preparing for the expected assault of the morning, 495—496; the assault given, 496—498; the Turks gaining the walls, 498—499;

—499; the emperour slain, 499—500; the Turks entering the city, 500; the confusion of the inhabitants, 500—501; the Greeks made captives, 502; their treatment, 502—503; the pillage of the city, 504—505; Mahomet entering into it, 505—507; his behaviour 507—508; his repeopling and adorning the city, 508—510; the future history of the Imperial family to its extinction, 511—514; a resolution made in the West for a crusade against the Turks, but ending in nothing, 514—516; even though Mahomet invades Italy, 516—517. In this interesting chapter, we meet with little of that everlasting disgrace of Mr. Gibbon's chapters, the impertinence and absurdity of digressions. There is so little, that I shall not notice it. And I am happy to close the *actual* narrative of the eastern empire, in a chapter so justly connected with the history, and forming such a regular conclusion to it.

False language. ' I *regret* the map or plan' [he should have said, ' I regret the *want of* the map or ' plan'] ' which Tournefort sent to the French mi' nister of the marine'.' ' To *approve*' [he should have said, ' to *make proof of*'] ' their patience and ' long-suffering[2].' ' That Constantinople would ' be the *term* of the Turkish conquests[3].' I could ' wish—to prolong the *term* of one night[4].' ' The ' Greeks, now driven from the *vantage ground*,' meaning the top of the walls[5]. ' The *term* of the ' historic labours of John Sagredo[6].'

[1] p. 469. [2] p. 470. [3] p. 490.
[4] p. 491. [5] p. 499. [6] p. 517.

I have

I have noticed before the mean and vulgar spite of Mr. Gibbon, against the Jews. It breaks out remarkably again, in this chapter. ' What use or ' merit,' he says concerning a Turkish emperor, who was learning *Chaldaic* with some other languages; ' could recommend to the statesman or ' scholar, *the uncouth dialect of his Hebrew slaves*[1]?' The spite of Mr. Gibbon here is pure frenzy. But let me now ask at the close, What is the cause of this marked resentment against the Jews, that runs through his whole history? I naturally attributed it at first, to that union of character and of interest, which Judaism has the honour to share with Christianity. Yet, on revising the whole, I see the resentment is too violent, to be merely the result of such a *collateral* connection. Something more operative than *any* principle of unbelief, must have occasioned it. I therefore believe it to be this. Mr. Gibbon, I have other reasons for thinking, has been sufficiently acquainted with the *usurious* part of the modern Israelites, *to have suffered some of their usual deeds of oppression in his own person.* The feeling of this is constantly floating upon his mind, I suppose, and is constantly giving a pungency to his speculations of dislike. And this has united with his principles in the *present* instance, I believe, to work him up into a frenzy of illiterate fanaticism, against the whole race.

Yet we see in this chapter a stroke of ingenuousness, that ought to be ranked with the remarkable

[1] p. 465.

one before. 'These annals,' he says concerning the Turkish annals of Cantemir, '*unless we are*
'*swayed by antichristian prejudices, are far less va-*
' *luable than the Greek* [1].' This is another flash of ingenuousness, not so strong and vivid as the former, but very similar to it. The stroke of *this* lightning too, I believe, is equally with the force of *that* directed at the head of Voltaire. Mr. Gibbon appears to have conceived a most *un-brotherly* hatred, for an historian who is very like himself, lively, absurd, a falsifier, and an infidel. He is not such an impertinent digressor as Mr. Gibbon, I apprehend; and Mr. Gibbon, I presume, is not such a superficialist in history as he. Mr. Gibbon therefore had *once*, I know, a very natural sympathy for the historical character of Voltaire. Yet he has *now* a pointed aversion to him. ' See Voltaire———,' he says in this very chapter: ' *he was ambitious of uni-*
' *versal monarchy;* and *the poet* frequently aspires to
' the *name* and *style* of an *astronomer*, a *chymist*, &c [2].'
In another page he adds, that ' the *pious* zeal of
' Voltaire is *excessive*, and even *ridiculous* [3].' But how nicely does Mr. Gibbon again dash out the very portrait of himself, in this second character of Voltaire!
' He' too is ' ambitious of universal monarchy;
' and *the digressor* frequently aspires to the name
' and style of an astronomer, a chymist, &c.;' and, very frequently too, ' the *pious* zeal of *Mr. Gibbon*
' is excessive, and even ridiculous.' So justly has

[1] p. 471. [2] p. 476.
[3] p. 495.

Mr. Gibbon given us his own face, in his angry attempts to draw the deformed one of Voltaire! This vain old man of Ferney, the perpetual prater of infidelity to his numerous visitants, had shewn some disrespect to Mr. Gibbon (I suppose) during his *last* retreat into Switzerland, had stung his pride, and had provoked his choler. And Mr Gibbon himself becomes half a Christian at times, we see, in mere opposition to Voltaire. Such are the principles and practices, of these *mock-doctors* in philosophy! But let it also be observed, that Mr. Gibbon's animosity is as *prudent*, as it is strong. He attacks not Voltaire in this bold manner, till he comes near to the *conclusion* of his work. And Voltaire, as well as Dr. Johnson, was *dead*; before the hero presumed to assault him. Such is the gallantry of a writer, who would *crouch* before the living lion, and *trample upon* the dead one!

Contradictions. Text. Mahomet 'removed the 'cause of sedition, by the *death*, the *inevitable* death, 'of *his infant brothers*[1].' Note. 'Calapin, *one of* 'these royal infants, was *saved from his cruel brother*.' What was un-avoidable is actually avoided, and what was dead is raised to life again.——Mr. Gibbon very properly appeals, in opposition to the scepticism and chemistry of Voltaire, to a singular fact in Baron de Tott's Memoirs. Yet, when he has done this in the note and text, he adds finally to the note thus: 'but that adventurous traveller '*does not possess* the art of *gaining our confidence*[2].'

[1] P. 467. [2] p. 476.

And

And Mr. Gibbon thus countermines himself.——
' His son,' Mr. Gibbon tells us concerning a youth,
whom the Turkish emperour wanted to abuse un-
naturally; ' ——preferred death to infamy, and
' was stabbed by the royal lover¹.' The note *at
first* confirms this *peremptory* account. ' See Phran-
' za,' it says concerning the very father of this
youth; ' his expressions are positive.' He then
quotes them. And, after all, he says thus, ' yet
' he could only learn from report the bloody or
' impure scenes, that were acted in the dark recesses
' of the seraglio.' Like Sampson, blind in his
strength, he is tugging at the very pillars that pro-
tect himself, and going to tear down the edifice upon
his own head.

We have now pursued the history of the eastern
empire, to its final extinction in the reduction of
Constantinople by the Turks. Yet, to our surprise,
we find *Mr. Gibbon*'s history of it *not* compleated.
His tragedy is ended, but he claps an epilogue to
the tail of it. He has no less than THREE chapters
of history more. But what *can* he find to say upon
the subject, after so many digressions to the right
and left, and with such a sweeping conclusion to the
whole? This Appian way, having run many a
league, broad and lofty, the admiration of numbers,
and the theme of all; but more conspicuous than
useful, a monument more of vanity and ostentation
in the constructor, than of service and benefit to the

¹ p. 503.

world;

world; and having turned aside repeatedly in its progress, to take in towns and to traverse regions, that were *not* in its *natural* line, and are now deserted by all who pursue *that*; at last loses itself near the end of its course, by plunging into the body of a great bog. ' The final extinction,' says Mr. Gibbon, ' of the two last dynasties which have reigned in ' Constantinople, *should* terminate the decline and ' fall of the Roman empire in the East [1].' It *should*, but it *will* not. For in the *very next* paragraph he goes, to the ' grief and terror of Europe,' upon the loss of Constantinople. ' As I am now,' he *adds* in another page, ' *taking* an *everlasting farewell* of the ' Greek empire;' he subjoins a short note concerning some of his authors [2]. And, after an ' everlast- ' ing farewell' of his subject, what *can* even this universal gleaner find to collect? He finds matter, that must surprise every reader. It thoroughly astonished me, used as I was to the rambling genius of his history, when I first beheld it. Much as I have dwelt upon his strange excursions before, and much as I prepared myself for a continuance or an enlargement of them, I did not expect such a wildgoose excursion as this. Nor will the reader be less surprized, when I tell him what it is. He cannot possibly conjecture. And he must look, and stare, and wonder, when he hears. ' Nor shall I dismiss the ' present work,' says Mr. Gibbon, as he first discloses this amazing *codicil* to his long *will*; ' till I ' have *reviewed* the *state* and *revolutions* of the Ro-

---

[1] P. 511.   [2] p. 517.

' MAN

'MAN CITY,' meaning Rome, the late capital of the late empire of the West, the history of which was terminated in the reduction of the capital, at the close of the *third* volume; 'which' city of Rome 'acquiesced under the dominion of the popes, *about* '*the same time* that Constantinople was enslaved 'by the Turkish arms¹.' The poor, feeble, and petty pretence, for *tacking-on* such a history to the history preceding, is merely, we see; that the *main. point* of it is almost *coincident in time*, with the concluding point of the other. Never perhaps did digression attempt to cover its wantonness, with such thin and ragged shreds before. Yet with these does Mr. Gibbon go on, through a cumbrous epilogue of no less than *one hundred and twenty-eight* pages in quarto. I shall therefore excuse myself, from reviewing these chapters as I have reviewed the others. I shall only give my usual abstract of each, that my readers may not take my words for this enormous and exorbitant digression, but may see it themselves; and that they may not comprehend it merely in general, but mark it in all its full and affecting detail. The *contradictions*, the *ribaldry*, and the *mistakes*, I shall pass over entirely. For who can stop to count the stars, when a large meteor is streaming before his eyes?

¹ P. 519.

In Chapter the TWELFTH,

or sixty-ninth, we see the French and German emperours of Rome, 519—520; the turbulence of the Romans towards them, 520—521; the authority of the popes in Rome, 521—523; the turbulence of the Romans towards *them* also, 523—526; particular instances of this, 526—528; the general character of the Romans at this period, 528—529; a revolt at Rome, 529—532; the revolters reduced, 532—533; the old republican government revived in part, 533—535; the capitol fortified, 535—536; the coinage of money given to the senate, 536—537; the præfect of the city appointed by the senate and the people, 537—538; the number and choice of the senate, 538—539; the office of senator of Rome, 539—540; an account of one, Brancaleone, 540—541; of another, Charles of Anjou, 541—542; of another, Pope Martin IVth, 542; of another, Emperor Lewis of Bavaria, 542; the address of Rome to one of the German emperours, 542—544; another address to another emperour, 544—545; the reply of the latter, 545—546; his march to Rome in favour of the pope, 546; his besieging Rome, and being baffled, 546—547; the wars of the Romans with the neighbouring towns, 547—549; the election of the popes by the senate and people, 550; by the cardinals alone, 550—551; the institution of the conclave, 551—552; the people claiming a right to elect, 552—553;

but

but finally giving it up, 553; the absence of the popes from Rome, 553—555; their translation of the holy see to Avignon, 555—557; the institution of the jubilee, 557—560; the nobles or barons of Rome, 560—561; the family of Leo, &c. 561—562; of the Colonna, 562—565; and of the Ursini, 565—566. This chapter of near *forty pages*, is obviously upon the face of the abstract, almost as abrupt as it is digressional, and as frivolous as it is devious.

In Chapter the THIRTEENTH

or seventieth, we have an account of Petrarch, 567—570; his poetic coronation at Rome, 570—571; birth, character, and patriotic designs of one Rienzi at Rome, 572—574; his assuming the government of Rome, 574—576; his taking the title of tribune, 576; his new regulations, 576—578; the freedom and prosperity of Rome under him, 578—580; his being respected in Italy, &c. 580—581; his vices and follies, 581—583; his being knighted and crowned, 583—585; the rising envy of the people against him, 585; the nobles conspiring against him, 585—586; his seizing, condemning, pardoning, and rewarding them, 586—587; their rising in arms against him out of the city, 587; attempting to enter it, but beaten off, 588; Rienzi alienating the people more, 588—589; being excommunicated by the pope, and abdicating the government, 590; feuds again at Rome, 590—591;

again

again a revolt, 591; Rienzi's return to power, 591; his adventures after he had abdicated, 591—593; his being made senator of Rome, 593; his conduct, 593—594; his being massacred in a tumult, 594—595; Petrarch's inviting and upbraiding the emperour Charles IV. 595—596; his requesting the popes to return to Rome, 596—597; their return, 597; their leaving Rome again, and finally returning to it, 597—599; a pope and anti-pope, 599—601; a schism, 601; calamities of Rome, 601—602; negotiations for union, 603—604; the schism inflamed, 604—605; at last healed, 605—606; the coinage of money resumed by the popes, 606—607; the last revolt of Rome, 607; last coronation of a German emperour at Rome, 608; the government and laws of Rome under the popes, 608—610; a conspiracy against the popes, 610—612; but crushed, 612; last disorders of the nobles of Rome, 612—613; the popes acquiring the absolute dominion of Rome, 613—615; and the nature of the ecclesiastical government of Rome, 616—618. This chapter of more than *fifty pages*, is merely a military chest of the old Romans, a paymaster's hoard of *brass farthings*. The only parts, that can attract our attention at all, are the internal convulsions of Rome. But Rome is now so insignificant in itself, and become so from being lately so significant; that, though its dissensions are nearly on as large a scale as those, which embroiled its infant state, yet they are nothing to the mind, in this its second infancy. And after all the grand events, that have been brought into the compass of this history,

like

like the wild beasts into the pit of a Roman amphitheatre; some from the neighbouring regions, most from the distant and sequestered parts of the globe, and all to exhibit themselves in their boldest attitudes before us; the squabbles of a town in Italy, that had some ages before been the capital of the world, had then become the capital of the West, and was now merely the capital of a district, are little better to the raised conceptions of the reader, than the disputes of the *ruffs* and the *reeves* among the birds.

In Chapter the FOURTEENTH

or seventy-first, is a view of Rome from the capitol in the fourteenth century, 620 – 621; an account of the ruins two hundred years before, 622—623; one of four causes of their destruction, 623—626; another, 626—628; another, 628—632; another, 632—635; the Coliseum, 635—637; the games of Rome in it, 637—639; its injuries, 639—640; the ignorance and barbarism of the Romans, 640—643; the restoration and ornaments of the city, 643—645; and the final conclusion of the work, 645—646. This chapter of *forty-six* pages, is digression rioting in its own digressiveness, digression mounting upon the shoulders of digression, and exposing its general absurdity the more by its particular excess. And it serves with a most admirable congruity of folly, to put a finishing close to this strange digression, and to reduce it to a point of absurdity, furdity, which all shall see and all shall acknowledge.

In reviewing the whole work before, we have frequently been obliged to stop, and pause, and reflect; to interrogate ourselves what we were reading, to recur in our minds to the title and preface of the whole, and to compare the current pages with both. Had we not done so, we should have been lost, like the author, in the progressive labyrinth of facts, opinions, and remarks. So, we believe, have many of Mr. Gibbon's readers been. They have glided down the stream of the history, turned in with it to the right, then turned out to the left, doubled this point, and rounded that; without reflecting on the promised direction of their voyage, and without considering the actual tendency of their motions. They must have been startled at length however, to find themselves so wide of the line expected by themselves, and so distant from the end to which they proposed to go; still turning round new points, still running down new reaches, and still diverting from the main channel of the river. But, though startled, they have been overborne; persuaded that their conductor was rambling with them, yet not presuming to rely upon their own judgment; stifling their persuasions with their modesty, believing against assurance, and confiding against conviction. And, after all their circumnavigations; when they were arrived at the very ground, to which their views had been so long and so mortifyingly directed; and when they had even moored

fast

fast at the very wharf, to which they were going, and were now to terminate all their disappointments, by stepping upon the land; to find their captain throw off the fastening in an additional fit of wantonness, to set away with them again, and to carry them round some of the very capes, which they had *repeatedly* doubled before, merely that they might see, in what condition they were since they visited them *last*; is such an enormity of wantonness, such a *superfœtation* of impertinence, as must make even the most drunken of his admirers to stare with astonishment.

All indeed arises from Mr. Gibbon's *redundancy* of ideas. He feels them continually overflowing upon him. He feels his brooks swelling into rivers, his rivers widening into seas, and his seas expanding into an ocean. And the same organization of mind, which, unchecked by judgment, made him a wild infidel; uncontroulable from indulgence, renders him as wild a digressor. He cannot confine his thoughts within any circumscription of order; or reduce them under any discipline of propriety. He has *therefore* rambled through history, with all the excentricity of one, who

  Is of *imagination* all compact.
   * * * *
  Th' *historian's* eye, in a fine frenzy rowling,
  Has glanc'd from heav'n to earth, from earth to heav'n.
   * * * *
  Such tricks hath strong *imagination!*

But

But it concludes with one trick, that greatly exceeds all the reft. We have feen the two empires of Eaft and Weft, after a tedious illnefs and a lingering death, fucceffively buried under the earth. The weftern we have particularly buried, fome nine or ten centuries ago. Yet, to our amazement, we are now fet by Mr. Gibbon to dig into the grave of the latter, to hunt for the poor and perifhing remains of it, and to collect the little handful of its afhes from their old repofitory. The modern hiftory of Rome is placed before us, *becaufe* we have had the ancient. We are even to take Mr. Gibbon for our *Ciceroni*, and make the antiquary's tour of Rome; *becaufe* we have been reading its ancient hiftory. Juft fo, in writing the annals of a king, *becaufe* ' a man may fifh with the worm that hath
' eat of the king, and eat of the fifh that hath fed
' of that worm;' a mad Hamlet would ' fhew you,
' how the king,' after he was dead, ' went a pro-
' grefs through the guts of a beggar.' But no words can fully expofe, the aftonifhing devioufnefs of fuch a digreffion as this. Never, I believe, has any thing like it been attempted before, in the world of hiftory. It is certainly a flight beyond the moon. And it marks in the ftrongeft colours, the progrefs of imagination in the mind, and the operation of digreffion in the hiftory, of Mr. Gibbon; of imagination kindling with the motion of its own ideas, and of digreffion growing licentious from the exercife of its own liberty; both rifing gradually from a leffer folly to a greater, adding impertinence to impertinence,

nence, and accumulating abfurdity upon the head of abfurdity; till they have clofed at laft, in a full confummation of enormity and wildnefs.

CHAPTER THE FIFTH.

I HAVE thus reviewed the three laft volumes of this hiftory, with a circumftantiality, which has hardly ever been ufed upon a work before; but which the prefent, from its peculiar quality, demanded of me. And I am now to draw my conclufions, from the whole.

This is a work of a very extraordinary nature. It is not in the common rank of publications, aiming at a moderate fhare of reputation, and content to reft in a mediocrity of character. It muft either be highly cenfured or ftrongly praifed, or praifed and cenfured with an equal degree of energy. It is indeed a production, that has a thoufand beauties and a thoufand blemifhes. It fhews a large and comprehenfive range of erudition, a range amazingly comprehenfive and large. But the author is even more oftentatious of his learning, than Milton himfelf; and, even oftener than Milton, clouds and obfcures what he writes by it. His notes are fo frequent in themfelves, and fo full of foreign matter, that the reader is perpetually drawn off from the fubject of the text, and his mind is diftracted in an endless variety; being tossed backwards and forwards, between historical narrative and critical observations, the deeds of the actors on the *stage* above, and the characters of the writers in the 'cellarage' below. And all forms such a complication of incongruous parts, that the one counteracts the other in its impression upon the mind, and the clashing of both destroys half the energy of either. The language of Mr. Gibbon also, is frequently harsh from the foreign idioms, and from the affectation of vigour, in it. The harshness is that of one of Dr. Johnson's dissertations, utterly incompatible with the native ease and the familiar dignity of historical language. The meaning too is repeatedly obscure. This arises generally from the quick and short allusiveness of it. Mr. Gibbon's style thus becomes like Tacitus's, too rapid to be clear, and too fantastically infolded to be readily intelligible. Yet a much more formidable failing than these, has evidently been detected before. The self-contradictoriness of Mr. Gibbon is very wonderful. In distant, in adjoining parts of his history, it is too apparent. And the opposition of the notes to the text, and of one part of the note or of the text to the rest, are striking proofs of his confusedness of judgment. We have seen his positions fighting, like so many gladiators, before us; and destroying one another.

But we are still more disgusted in reading this work, with the length and the frequency of its digressions. Two thirds of the whole, we may fairly say,

say, are quite foreign to it. The digressions too continue to grow in length, and to rise in absurdity, to the very end. Indeed they are so absurd and so long at last, that hardly any images in nature can fully represent them, to the imagination of our readers. And one of the *satellites* of Saturn, relinquishing its master-orb, and running the round of the solar system; or the moon, deserting her duty of attendance upon our earth, and losing herself in the wilderness of space; can alone image forth the strange excursiveness of Mr. Gibbon in history. But the grand fault of the whole, I believe, is its unfaithfulness. There is no dependence to be made, I apprehend, upon any one reference, or even any one citation, in it. This I have shewn sufficiently before, I think, by some special instances. It could not be expected, that in an examination of this nature I could be more particular. Yet I have done full enough, to tempt the curiosity or to urge the zeal of others. And I doubt not, but the more Mr. Gibbon is followed closely through all his quotations and references, he will the more be found either negligently, or dishonestly, doubling in them.

These are broad spots upon this historical sun. They require no critical telescope to view them. They come forward to the naked eye. But the last, from its very nature, is fatal to the whole. And, as Mademoiselle de Keralio has very justly observed, ' on peut etre *eloquent*, on peut avoir un style ' *seduisant* et *noble*, mais *n'est pas historien.*' Mr. Gibbon's history, therefore, is only an elegant frontispiece,

piece, the production of a night; which glitters to the eye, plays upon the fancy, and captivates the judgment for a short period; but dissolves in the frailty of its fine materials, and fades away into air, as soon as the sun begins to shine upon it.

But what are these faults, to the wickedness that pervades the whole? Obscenity stains it through its very substance. This must discredit it with all, who love modesty, who cultivate a spirit of elegance in their souls and of delicacy in their language, and are not compleatly vulgarized by their animal instincts. In his preface to these volumes Mr. Gibbon very truly informs us, that he is ‘now descend-
‘ing into the vale of years;’ and the volumes themselves assure us, that he is descending with all the gross lasciviousness of unblushing youth about him. How full must be the fountain of impurity in the heart, when the stream is foaming and frothing so much through the page? Yet even this bold note of wantonness is exceeded, by the daring tone of infidelity. Mr. Gibbon comes forward with all the rancour of a renegado, against Christianity. He tramples upon it at first, with the cloven-foot of Heathenism. He dungs upon it at last, from the dirty tail of Mahometanism. And literary absurdity, however glaring, even practical profligacy, however flaming, are both lost for a moment in the sense of this volcanick eruption of antichristian impiety.

The friends of literature, then, may equally triumph and lament, at a work like this. They may triumph, when, with the usual perfunctoriness of criticism, they consider the wide range of reading in it, the splendour of the sentiments, the depth of the reflections, and the vivacity of the language. But they must lament, when they come to scrutinize it with a stricter eye, to mark the harsh and the false language, the distraction occasioned by the parade of reading, the obscurity in the meaning, the contradictoriness of the parts, the endless labyrinth of digressions, and the careless or wilful unfaithfulness in the narrative. The friends of religion also, must grieve with a juster sorrow, over the desperate profligacy of all. But let not one friend to religion be weak enough to fear. There is not a particle of formidableness in the thousand strokes, that this blasted arm of infidelity has been laying upon the shield of Christianity. That shield is the immortal ægis of wisdom. Against such a cover, if we are not scared with the glitter, we need not to dread the edge, of Mr. Gibbon's sword. Mr. Gibbon is only angry at Christianity, because Christianity frowns upon him. He has been long endeavouring to shake off the terrours, which his Christian education has impressed upon him; but he cannot do so.

'He scorns them, yet they awe him.'

He is therefore acting towards Christianity, like a bull caught in a net; making every desperate effort, to break the cords that still encompass him; and straining every nerve in an agony of exertion, to burst away into the undisquieted wilds of animal enjoyment.

enjoyment. And I think I cannot better conclude my review of his hiſtory, than by applying to him this character in Milton; as, equally in the praiſe and in the cenſure, truly deſcriptive of him.

⸻ On th' other ſide up roſe
Belial, in *act* more *graceful* and *humane:*
A *fairer* perſon loſt not heaven; he ſeem'd
For *dignity* compos'd and *high exploit*,
But all was *falſe* and *hollow*; though his *tongue*
Dropt *manna,* and could make the *worſe* appear
The *better* reaſon, to *perplex* and *daſh*
Matureſt counſels; for his *thoughts* were *low,*
To *vice* induſtrious, but to *noble* deeds
Timorous and *ſlothful*; yet he *pleaſed* the *ear,*
And with *perſuaſive accent* thus began.

FINIS.

www.ingramcontent.com/pod-product-compliance
Lightning Source LLC
Chambersburg PA
CBHW031349230426
43670CB00006B/477